Colin Ward was born in W͏͏͏͏͏͏, east London, and spent his early years in Chigwell before moving to Surrey. After leaving school he graduated from Smithfield College and ran a successful meat retail business. A committed Arsenal supporter and shareholder, he first attended Highbury with his father at the age of eight. Colin's first book, *Steaming In*, is widely regarded as one of the best ever books on football hooliganism and was shortlisted for the William Hill Sports Book of the Year prize. The sequel, *All Quiet on the Hooligan Front*, was also a bestseller and was published by Headline in 1997.

Colin is married with two children and is an international meat trader.

ARMED FOR THE MATCH

The Troubles and Trial of the Chelsea Headhunters

Colin Ward
and Stephen 'Hickey' Hickmott

HEADLINE

First published in 2000
by HEADLINE BOOK PUBLISHING

10 9 8 7 6 5 4 3 2 1

ISBN 0 7472 6292 6

Typeset by Palimpsest Book Production Limited,
Polmont, Stirlingshire

Printed and bound in Great Britain by
Caledonian International Book Manufacturing Ltd, Glasgow

HEADLINE BOOK PUBLISHING
A division of Hodder Headline
338 Euston Road
London NW1 3BH

www.headline.co.uk
www.hodderheadline.com

This book is dedicated to
Eddie Hickmott, died 1982, and Martin Hickmott,
died 1997.
RIP. Much loved and always remembered.

FOREWORD

by Colin Ward

In the annals of football hooliganism there is a select band of top boys whose escapades made them known by name by every other fan. Legends grew up around their exploits. Among this group Steve 'Hickey' Hickmott has few peers and was recognised by the other top boys as being up there with the best of them. While others were renowned for their extreme violence, Hickey was the organiser. Whether it was a huge train mob or a small coach party, Hickey made things happen. Everybody else ran with the pack, but Hickey had the aura which enabled him to control it, something he loved. I knew Steve from my England travels and we became first-name friends. I even went on some of his famous sensory-deprivation coach trips. While he was no angel, his main thought in life was to use his leadership to extract the maximum return from the fun, hilarity and violence which accompanied the following of Chelsea and England during the 1970s and '80s.

When Steve got jailed he told me he was going to write a book. Despite offers after his release it never materialised, so ten years later I caught a plane to Manila on the off-chance of getting him to let me write it. The next day we sat down in a beach bar and Steve started relating his story to me. Some of what he told me was so incredible it was hard to believe; some was easy because I knew the faces as well. We aimed to tell the truth about football hooligans. In the end I believe I have told an incredible story of the courage of one man against adversity, the battle for hearts and minds, and the real story of the football hooligan era which we all survived.

The following story is written in Steve's 'voice', as it was told to me by the man himself.

Colin Ward, July 1999

INTRODUCTION

And ye shall hear of wars and rumours of wars, see that ye be not troubled, for all these things must come to pass but the end is not yet . . . for Nation shall rise against Nation and Kingdom against Kingdom . . . then shall they deliver you up to be afflicted and shall put you to death . . . but he that shall endure unto the end, he shall be saved.

Matthew 24: 6–13

This book is not a history of violence at football, nor is it a tale of police wrongdoing. This is the true story of events that got out of control, about lads who set out to enjoy themselves somehow getting lost in other people's desire to make a name for themselves.

We live in an increasingly monitored world. There are closed circuit television cameras wherever we turn, in shopping centres, motorways, shops and offices. People are encouraged to inform on other people in TV programmes like *Crimewatch* and billboard posters scream out a message to telephone and inform on a drug dealer or a social security cheat. We are told where we can smoke and how, if we do, it will harm our health or ultimately kill us. Conform or face the consequences.

Back in the days when going to the match was a great adventure for young adolescents who suddenly discovered football and comradeship, and was open to anybody with 10 shillings in his pocket, there were no boundaries and the devil took the hindmost in the pursuit of fun. Suddenly, society saw a phenomenon that was outside the closed loop of control exercised so effectively by the ruling classes.

Small wonder that many people now want to understand what really went on at football and how our ad hoc but nevertheless well-defined culture so frightened those in higher authority that they needed all their powers to control it. In the end it was only their supreme arrogance which spared us, but when the authorities go to war there are always casualties. Nobody ever spent nights worrying after a bout of terrace skirmishing, yet some of those fans affected by the establishment actions still bear the mental scars today. Perhaps this book will help to prevent any further miscarriages of justice against football fans.

But I don't think so.

1

HEYSEL UPON US

I'd read of our heroes, and wanted the same,
To play my own part in the patriot game
                                        Irish ballad

In 1984, Liverpool played AS Roma in the final of the European Cup. The match was played in the Olympic Stadium in Rome, which also happened to be the home of AS Roma. Those Liverpool supporters who declined to be bussed in and out of the city by a force of 5,000 police were subjected to a terrifying ordeal of systematic brutal attacks by the Roman *ultra* thugs. One Liverpool fan foolish enough to walk the streets alone, thinking he was a gentle tourist, was viciously and repeatedly stabbed and lay close to death for many weeks, eventually returning home to England never to be the same person again. The Roma fans had done the same to a Gothenburg fan earlier in the tournament. A group of Swedes were ambushed and ran but one fell, and the last thing his friends saw were the repeated slashing and stabbing movements of frenzied fans. He died on the operating table.

Twelve months later, Liverpool again reached the final of the European Cup, where they faced another Italian club, Juventus. The same system that had seen an Italian club awarded a European Cup final on their home ground now deemed Brussels' Heysel Stadium fit to host this match. Heysel, when it was built, was probably a

3

modern safe stadium; now, in 1985, it had become a crumbling relic with rotten, rust-eaten fences; open cracked concrete terraces eaten away by years of frost, and rickety perimeter walls ready to fall down which anybody without a ticket could scale to gain entry. It had been that way for many years, yet nobody had bothered to check on its worthiness to host a match expected to attract a sell-out crowd, with more outside clamouring for tickets. Liverpool fans would be coming there with anger in their hearts, caused by stories of Italians attacking their mates the previous year. Stanley met Roma salami and Stanley got sliced. Aye wack, those Eyeties are all blade merchants.

Heysel was going to have 50,000 people crammed inside on a warm May evening. Tales of Stanley in the cooked meat counter spread like wildfire on the terrace bush telegraph and the ferries leaving Dover, until every fan from Liverpool knew at least one story of their mates getting bushwhacked. As the Scouse invasion converged on the centre of Brussels, the salami stories sparked into life again. Liverpool fans being attacked by groups of young Italians with knives. At Brussels North station, the paranoia was hanging in the air.

'There's bleeding mobs of Italians going round slicing anybody with a red shirt on.'

'That's rubbish, that is.'

'Yeah? Well if it ain't true, then why are people telling the stories? Those Italians really worked it to us last time with their dirty great knives. We're gonna be ready this time.'

Paranoia is paranoia, no matter how you bottle it. Hope and pray the bottle doesn't smash.

UEFA had imposed segregation with a neutral zone but before kick-off it was obvious that this was only wishful thinking. Within that neutral zone next to the Liverpool sections was a large group of Juventus *ultras*. The Liverpool fans within had moved towards the comfort zone of the dividing fence looking for a transfer into their own section but that didn't stop a small group being attacked by a larger group of Italians just before kick-off. One lad ran over to the fence pleading for help from the huge contingent of Liverpool fans.

'Come on, lads, they're doin' us!'

Fear was in his voice. The dread that they'd be left at the mercy of the vicious Italians. His pleadings went up an octave as terror and adrenaline combined.

'Help us!'

Young Stanley and the rest of those on the Liverpool side of the fence reacted with fury. Full of anger and Belgian lager after a serious seven-hour session, they were never going to walk away or call for the police to sort it out. The boys will sort this one in a drunken charge. Sort this out the way disputes should be sorted out – the English way.

'Come on! Are we gonna let them humiliate us? Are we gonna let them Eyeties do us again? Let them do fellow Liverpool fans while we stand and watch?'

Arms were waved. The harder lads, ace faces, front-line terrace punchers, surged over or were beckoned over. People looked around for faces who would be prepared to go over the fences and go in first. It took a few minutes but once the Scousers got their act together, they led a charge to help their mates. Hands against the mesh, pushing, shouting, rocking. Police whacking their hands, making them let go with pain. Soon hundreds were rocking the fence. Only six police officers stood between them and the Italians. The police were frightened.

'Take the fence down! Do the Italian shits! They're doing us again!'

The roar of the charge came up from the throats. A roar of anger, one of grinding teeth and pent-up aggression. The Italians beckoned them forward, cockily holding their hands out and gesturing with their fingers because there was a fence and a line of riot police.

'It's their main firm. Come on, let's have it! Are we gonna have it or what?'

'You bastards! You're gonna cop it, you shitbags.'

First one, then another, up close to the fence, close enough for the Italians the other side of the thin police line to smell the anger and hatred. The rusty metal groaned and bent over the concrete as it was rocked to and fro. Then a surge from behind.

'Go, go, go! Come on, come on! Do the shirtlifters!'

People pushed from the back into others simply finding themselves on the front line. There is a stage when part of the crowd is reluctant, but there comes a point where it becomes one and the charge is inevitable. The Italians stood looking tough and resolute, still hitting prostrate Liverpool fans, as the fence and the line of police guarding them seemed to be holding firm. Desperately the fans pushed at the fence until the point where, in its flimsy, rusty condition, it gave way. The Liverpool fans surged forward over the fence and between its concrete pillars. The dam had burst and like sea washing away sand, the charging fans went through the police line, which melted away in terror, to punch the Italians in a mad frenzy and exact revenge.

Reasoning had departed. Over the mesh they trampled with clenched fists, punchers wanting action. Fear and loathing in equal amounts, this was their moment: 'Avenge Rome.' Here comes Stanley and wack. Across went one Scouser and nutted a young *ultra* right between the bridge of his nose and his eye socket. Those close enough heard the crunch of nasal bone being compressed and an eye-socket shattering. Blood squirted out over his friends' designer labels. Now cool was fast being replaced by panic among the Italians. Where were their front-line boys? Those that hit the floor were kicked with real venom and then stamped on. Now it was Stanley's turn to slice salami. The Italian *ultras* on the front line weren't so tough now it was unarmed combat, eyeball to eyeball, fist on face – so they ran.

'RUN! RUN! RUN!' Panic in the Italian voices. Italian, an emotive language where panicky words come out faster than Anglo-Saxon. Now the hunters were the hunted. In their fear they pushed those in front of them out of the way as they desperately tried to escape.

Huge gaps appeared on a previously packed terrace. Some Italians were caught by the Scousers, but the surge to get away created a wave of panic.

When a terrace crowd runs, it creates a rumble sound as those fleeing utter a noise which comes from within. Guttural and instinctive, an avalanche of sound, the rumble of hell on the move. Fearful air rapidly exits lungs trying to shout for help while 30,000 feet stamp at the same time, trying to keep upright against the uneven surface beneath their feet. Arms in front pushing, shoving – move, move, move, faster, faster, head half-turned to see how close behind the pursuers are, the eyes giving a manic full-moon madman look, the mouth twisted. Who or what is in front of them becomes unimportant, everything must just be pushed out of the way as fast as possible. Behind them is the terror of the unknown. When it's a few on the move, it's easy to stop. When the terrace is packed with thousands then the collective kinetic energy propelling that crowd forward is immense. Cattle stampeding towards a barbed wire fence springs to mind. In the case of a football terrace, the edge is a brick or concrete wall. The crowd propels itself forward until the mass of bodies squashes into a smaller space at the edge of the stadium, preventing the crowd progressing any further. An unstoppable force meets an immovable object but when thousands go forward in a human wave, something has to give. Usually among the squash of flesh the crunch of bone is heard, then the panic relents and calm is restored.

In Heysel's case, frightened Italian flesh and bones met crumbling concrete, brick and mortar. Those near the edge of the terrace ran away from an unseen foe and were crushed up against a wall, which collapsed. Over and down they went, with the momentum of those behind still coming forward on top of them. In the chaos that ensued, 39 Italians were crushed to death while hundreds more were injured. The whole world watched as the event unfolded on prime time television, myself included. Back in England the watching masses recoiled in shock. Like the Vietnam war when it was broadcast into American living rooms, this was drama of a different kind.

And something or somebody had to be blamed.

Plenty of people saw it clearly. It was the English hooligans. Parliament the next day demanded retribution.

An empire had been built on the need to have someone be seen to walk down the road for a crime. At the helm of this English principle this clear May morning was Margaret Thatcher. In the *Guardian*, Eric Heffer, an MP representing Liverpool constituents, tried to shout above the parapet that the deaths had been caused by a wall collapsing and that there should not be a lynch mob as there might be reasons other than pure hooligan blood lust for the outbreak of trouble. But this voice was drowned out. This was England in full vengeful mode. From the Tolpuddle Martyrs onwards, England has never liked those who upset the established order.

Mrs Thatcher immediately set up a Cabinet committee. In England's wars the first casualty is rational thinking and with Thatcher, propaganda was truth. Authority good, hooligans bad. The TV scenes had made her blood boil, so she would speak for everybody and nobody else had a view that counted. 'Everything has to be done that needs to be done to bring football hooligans to justice.' We'd heard it all before. In the dark recesses of power, people nodded because someone would be seen to pay for this. Authority good, hooligans bad. Bad football fan equals hooligan. Get hooligan, any bloody hooligan.

In the reports that followed blame was immediately apportioned.

One British supporter said that the ground was littered with British National Front leaflets, some overprinted by the British National Party with their address. One witness spoke of passengers on the boat crossing the Channel with National Front insignia singing songs of hatred and exhibiting violence.

Mr John Smith of Liverpool Football Club spoke of how six

members of Chelsea National Front – skinheads with Cockney accents – had boasted to him of their part in provoking the violence and said that they seemed proud of their handiwork. Ex Liverpool manager Bob Paisley said that a man claiming to be a Chelsea fan had forced his way into the directors' box. People stated they saw a party they observed as Londoners leaving Brussels North station carrying Union flags and having National Front and swastika tattoos. A contingent of men displaying National Front insignia on flags were supposedly seen moving around the terrace just before the main fighting erupted.

In Britain, there had to be an Official Enquiry, chaired by a learned judge, in this instance Lord Justice Popplewell. Britain's great system of justice and order meant that the pronouncement of and apportionment of blame were seen to be fair and equitable. Now, at long last, the buck passing would stop because the Prime Minister had decided that the football hooligan gangs had gone too far. And those given the task of removing football hooliganism would be granted proper resources to get to the heart of this depravity. Priorities established, no more the operational inspector who regularly lost his men on a Saturday to some other task. No, this was right from number one, so nobody would touch this budget or cut men from this duty for something more vital. These hooligans had been cutting a swathe across the continent for years now destroying the country's reputation, but England was powerless because the police had no authority to stop them. Now the order had been megaphoned through from Number 10, the Prime Minister who had used the law and the police to break the power of the unions. Maggie had defeated the miners when everybody said it was impossible; Maggie had shown the world that she alone would make a stand against everything that was wrong and corrupt in England and the world. Trades unions, Argie dictators. So a few football hooligans held no problems for her. Off-the-record lobby briefings to the newspapers told us what the establishment was thinking: 'The tragedy at Heysel has hurt our standing in Europe. Never again do we want to see this on the TV. These people are not above the law because they are in a foreign country. These actions must be terminated. People want some action from this moment on – bodies brought before the courts.'

Very soon the initial clarion call to arms by Mrs Thatcher was translated into action. Some saw it as an intelligence matter, but the Chelsea boys were part of the Metropolitan Police jurisdiction so the Met would get first bite at the cherry. The Met Police had achieved results before, but the culture of football hooligans was new so there was no precedent.

Perhaps the briefing for the Fulham police was a formal one, or it may have had other ways of going down the chain of command. Whatever, they had picked good lads, the sort that England has always relied upon to help her through a crisis. These were good old British bobbies, the kind that Americans loved to be pictured next to as they patrolled the King's Road. Somewhere in this highly charged rhetoric and Thatcher-driven results culture, Operation Own Goal was born. Exactly what went on during this period is unclear, but the pressure was on to gain a result. The orders were coming from the highest level and they demanded it. Results will be achieved.

Young police constables would be in the terrace front line, grimy station backstreets, or wherever the main protagonists did their worst. They would be gathering evidence against people they saw flouting the law every Saturday right in front of their eyes. They didn't mind football fans having a good time, but these people were taking the piss. There was a determination to eliminate the vermin that had planned and executed the violent acts which had culminated in Heysel.

History would be the judge of who was really to blame for Heysel, but many a legend started out as an apocryphal story which gained a special life of its own as fact met fiction and intermingled in the course of time. Someone always knew of someone who'd told someone else the truth. And every football fan knows how much Scousers love a story. At the opening match of the 1985–86 season, following Heysel, the Liverpool programme featured numerous pictures of people whom the police wanted to trace, with an anonymous contact number. There was a rumour floating around that when one group of Liverpool lads were questioned by the police, they had stated firmly: 'Aye, it were Chelsea. They were the Chelsea NF boys – they caused it. I saw them getting the boys fired up in and around Brussels North station. Them Chelsea boys that are always around when it goes ballistic with England. Right tasty cases, they are, carry shooters sometimes. Plus they know all the main racist geezers on the Continent, you know, Combat number crew.'

'Combat 18.'

'Yeah, that's them. Really well organised. They were there waiting to have it with the Eyeties. Some of 'em don't drink, just organise, point here and there. They rallied the boys inside near the fence then led the charge, they did. It was that Hickey and his mob. Everybody saw them.'

2

IN THE SHED

Rejoice, O young man, in thy youth . . .
                                        Ecclesiastes

In 1993, Bruce Springsteen was playing in Oslo at the end of May. Bruce, at the time, was a big earner for me. Unfortunately, England were playing in Oslo shortly after on 2 June. No worries, I'd move a few T-shirts then probably have a beer with the Chelsea boys over for the match, and perhaps catch the game on TV before moving on to Stockholm for the next concert. After all, business comes first. I was following Bruce, not England.

Having a few beers in Oslo demands millionaire status, so Saturday evening around 6pm found me sitting quietly in my hotel room when from nowhere came an almighty crash. Wood splinters flew everywhere. I looked up to see heavily armed police falling through the door wearing bullet-proof vests, then one blue-eyed boy with a fresh complexion in black fatigues and full body armour standing over me, pointing a sub-machine gun and shouting.

'You are a very dangerous man. I will not shoot you there,' he shouted, pointing the gun at my chest. 'No, I will shoot you here to finish you,' pointing at my head. Very polite, very Norwegian, I thought.

'You've been watching too many Sly Stallone movies, mate,' I said to him. Then one of them hit me with the butt of his gun on the side of the head, knocking me to the floor. They piled in.

'Get down on the floor, you bad man!'

I remember lying face down, laughing that I hadn't got this type of beating at any matches I had attended. Now the Norwegian special forces were giving me a kicking for watching Saturday evening Norwegian TV. They got the cuffs on me and dragged me to my feet, shouting at me all the while. As we burst on to the street, a small crowd had gathered.

'Police brutality,' I shouted before they threw me in the back of the van.

The van shot through Oslo surrounded by other police cars, sirens blaring. The noise was incredible.

'Shit, these cuffs are tight.'

'Shut up or else we will make you suffer.'

Down at the station, the senior officer informed me that they had received information from the British government that I was a violent football hooligan and I was in Norway to cause violence at the World Cup qualifier. ('You are the most dangerous football hooligan in the whole world,' was how they explained it.) Behind him stood a number of clean-shaven men with crisp green shirts. They all looked like Morten Harket from A-Ha. I tried to think of one of their hit records so I could hum it to wind them up.

'You are here to cause serious trouble and disorder. What have you got to say?'

'I am not here to watch the football. I am an amiable tourist and you are holding me illegally. Get some information, you fools.'

That shocked them, so they put me in the cells naked – but being Norway, they ensured that the temperature in the cell was correct. After all, they could not have a very bad, dangerous man catching a cold while in their custody. After two days and much talking, I was told I was being deported. Around two hours later, after a doctor's examination of my wrists, I was summoned back to the desk to be informed that I was in Norway selling illegal merchandise which I was not paying Norwegian tax on. I was being deported for breaking Norwegian trading and tax laws. I told them that I wished to use the Norwegian judicial system to appeal. In the end they took me to the airport on the Tuesday afternoon and threw me out without stamping 'DEPORTED' on my passport.

Coincidentally, they decided to deport me in full view of the world's media the morning after trouble in a bar involving some England fans. Amazingly, the world's media had been tipped off about the time I was due to arrive in handcuffs at the airport. 'Vicious hooligan deported for causing trouble before an England football match' was flashed all over the world. Once I knew what flight I was travelling on I was allowed one telephone call, so I phoned Martin Lindley in Tunbridge Wells and told him to meet me at the airport with £300 in cash. At the departure gate, the world's press were waiting to see this terrible hooligan.

'I am an innocent businessman being victimised for trying to earn an honest crust. Steve Hickmott is innocent. Free Steve Hickmott,' I shouted to the perplexed Norwegian reporters. I arrived at Heathrow, took the money from Martin and purchased a flight to Stockholm. Back to work. The press back in England were horrified, even more so when they telephoned my mother to be told that I had gone back to Scandinavia.

The headlines screamed out the following day, next to a picture of me at Oslo airport in handcuffs: 'SUPERTHUG DEPORTED'. They wanted me hung, drawn and quartered. How could this man be allowed to get back on an aeroplane? Stephen Hickmott is a violent hooligan with a string of past offences, yet mocks police attempts to contain him by returning abroad immediately he is deported.

When the lads read that I'd been deported from Norway for non-payment of income tax, they called me Al Capone for the next six months.

September, 1998. From the King's Head, Fulham Road, to the bars and jet-set surroundings of the Monaco seafront. Myself, Blackie,

Sam, Mugsey and other assorted fans who'd travelled the long road with me. Only a few years ago, everybody was sitting in some grotty pub in Stoke-on-Trent where the courtyard outside the toilets had forty separate piles of dog turds. I know that for a fact because Kenny counted them all then came back into the bar with one tastefully arranged on a piece of paper to ask the landlord if he felt his dogshit was a candidate for the Turner prize. His logic was that some artist had made a wad of money from an old pile of bricks so perhaps this was art, because it certainly wasn't hygiene.

Now, as we looked out across the harbour with the hundreds of gleaming yachts, we realised that Chelsea and ourselves had come a long way in the past decade. Once it had looked like we would be playing Hartlepool at Victoria Park in front of a few thousand die-hards. Now here we were sitting on the most famous waterfront in Europe waiting to go and watch Chelsea play Real Madrid in the final of the European Super Cup. Only last May we'd seen Chelsea win the Cup-Winners' Cup in Stockholm. Now we wouldn't have to listen to the fan class of 1971 telling us they were the best. We laughed as we drank the beer, which we topped up with supermarket takeaways – damn these south of France bar prices. Sam announced loudly to the bar that he was going for a meal in La Rascasse restaurant, because he'd seen it before during the Monaco Grand Prix and he'd heard that famous people frequented it. A chant went up as fans walked past. We raised our glasses to it.

> We are the famous
> The famous Chelsea.

'Hickey! Oi, Hickey!' shouted two guys as they walked past.

'Oh, no!' exclaimed Kenny.

'Don't look up, it's Long Tall Dave and Crille,' said Sam.

Too late. Over they bounded.

'Oi, Hickey! Nice to be out and among the action, eh mate?'

enthused Dave, swaying like a pine tree in the wind, much the worse for drink.

'Guess what happened to us last season?' exclaimed Crille, like we were supposed to be excited.

'Pray tell us, Crille, but don't make the story last all day, the bars shut here at 4am,' said Sam in a bored voice.

'Well, we was in this cafe bar in Blackpool late last season after the match against Liverpool when we decided to send your pals at Fulham police station a postcard. As we were writing it, two undercovers came over and confronted us. "Don't bother to send us silly postcards from Blackpool. Hickey sends us postcards from exotic places like Ko Samui, Thailand and Peru." Top drawer, Hickey,' slurred Long Tall Dave, then they staggered off, chanting.

I sniggered to myself. The postcard game had been going on for some time now. Usually I informed them that my stocks and shares were really flying. I always send them a reminder whenever the Footsie index breaks new heights. Many of the Chelsea lads had got involved in this game. One of the lads, Chubby Chris – a survivor and financial beneficiary of the Headhunters trial – owns a bar in Pattaya Beach, Thailand, and many people who come into the bar are introduced to the game by him. He requests they send a postcard from their travels mocking the Fulham police. I realised that I hadn't sent them a card from Monaco. As I stood up to walk across the road to buy one, two men got up at the same time. Blackie immediately recognised them.

'They're from Fulham police station, I've seen them at matches hanging around the Swan. Look at that ugly, shifty bastard with the long hair, like he's a trend setter.'

As I walked across the road they did their undercover following act, pretending they were in the movies.

'Watch this, lads. See you in a few minutes.'

With that, I sprinted down a side street and up the road fifty yards and sat down outside a bar. Within thirty seconds, the two English police and four French had sprinted up the road after me. As they turned the corner, they were face to face with me.

'Hello, boys, enjoying the sea air?'

Within seconds, in hot pursuit behind them were the waiters from the bar they had been drinking at, who thought these police were fans doing a runner. It was a pure French farce as the exasperated waiters berated the French police for not paying, while they shouted back, trying to explain what had happened without blowing their cover. The bar owners had been told to expect Chelsea fans to do a runner. For their trouble, they got two nations' finest police recruits sprinting off without paying *l'addition*. That's justice for you.

'Rather undignified, don't you think?' I remarked to the other Chelsea fans who were laughing at the burlesque unfolding outside the bar. It was my turn to laugh because today I was in the ascendancy, not like Hong Kong in 1996 when the ruling British authority held me with the boat people, then deported me to Bangkok for conspiracy to start gangs. As if they didn't have enough gangs of their own without pinning that on me.

The lads joined me then wandered over to the two English police.

'What are you lot on? Didn't you learn your lesson last time? Clear off and leave us alone,' said Kenny. 'Now I suggest that you walk up the road and make yourself scarce or else you might have a nasty accident.'

They looked embarrassed and stupid, not knowing what to do. Eventually they decamped two bars up and got on their mobiles, looking for instructions. The rest of their day was spent watching me have a great time sending every Chelsea fan across the road to introduce themselves to them. Their faces reminded me of the time when a vanload of them pulled up before a Spurs v Chelsea match while we were sitting at a pavement table. The smallest policeman we'd ever seen – just exactly how did you pass the height entry requirements? – jumped out.

'You're that Hickey, aren't you? If you think you're so hard, come and have a go at me!' he shouted, holding his arms out like Tom Jones doing a cabaret act.

'Grow up,' I replied. 'I'm far too rich to be scuffling around on the pavement with the likes of you.'

The police had to slink away to a cacophony of catcalls and wolf whistles. As I left for the match, I shouted over to them: 'Go back and tell Fulham police that I'm here in my helicopter and my investments are riding high!'

As they watched us stride away towards the stadium, we tunelessly whistled and chanted the 'Colonel Bogey' theme at them. We could have been back in the Shed in 1970.

The careers teacher looked over the top of his glasses in an exasperated manner and summoned up every last bit of expression he could. So what had the careers teacher offered me? Working in a chicken factory or being a grave digger. Well, in life you sure do get offered some great choices.

'Mr Hickmott, what exactly are your aspirations aside from that of being the number one Chelsea fan?'

'What, like you mean aspiring to be somebody in Tunbridge Wells, Mr Disgusted writing to *The Times*? Or aspiring to own a three-bedroom semi, or perhaps to become a pillar of society like an estate agent and learn to lie to people so that I can sell them houses which need underpinning? Or perhaps a policeman and tell lies and get people hung for a crime they never committed?'

'Hickmott, you are a bloody fool who will never make anything of himself. English society has created judicial systems and order in almost every part of the world. The history of the English-speaking peoples is one of glory and honour. Academically, you could be a contender – you know, A levels, university and all that, but what is the point in beating myself up? Now please leave my office.'

At least he was right about one thing. My aspirations at school were never much more than seeing Chelsea win the Football League.

I was born in 1955, the year Chelsea last won the League. Now, along with the rest of the Shed, I sang that song with pride.

> *We're gonna fight, fight, fight for Chelsea*
> *Till we win the Football League*
> *To hell with Liverpool*
> *To hell with Man City*
> *We're gonna fight, fight, fight for Chelsea*
> *Till we win the Football League*

English middle- and upper-class people love to tell us that Klosters is good in winter and the Maldives or Monserrat is the summer location. We told the world that the best place to be at any time Chelsea played was our terrace.

Chelsea FC played at Stamford Bridge – even the ground was named after a famous battle when King Harold's good old English boys whupped the Vikings. Like all grounds in England, there were terraces at each end behind the goals. Empty and soulless with metal crowd barriers – lifeless grey statues in a sea of tranquility, but on a Saturday afternoon barriers in a raging typhoon of emotive energy. One end usually covered to protect people from the elements.

Someone once described Chelsea's covered end as looking like a shed and so the Chelsea Shed, especially the centre of it, became a mythical place for young Chelsea fans, like the centre of a wave for surfers. To an outsider it was just steel girders set in concrete, with an asbestos roof which didn't even cover the whole of the terrace expanse, unlike other famous terrace areas. What the heck, get there early to get under the covered area so that your chanting echoed. The loudest sound in London. Two hours before kick-off, a seething mass of swaying youth and excitement. Pushing, shoving, cheering. Nothing made you prouder than to go into school on Monday and have somebody tell you that they had been in the seats with their dad and had heard the singing and, more importantly, it was the loudest singing they had ever heard. Last night of the Proms with attitude. All those twits at the Royal Albert Hall waving Union Jacks and singing 'Land of Hope and Glory'. No pain, no gain, just singing for Britain and Empire, but with the Shed there was that hard outline of violence and the threat of working-class power in the air. The edge of the working class – the smell of sweat and toil, with the chance that there would be a confrontation at some time, something working-class boys liked. Twelve thousand geezers packed together, singing and shouting. Royalty in the Shed. We were kings for a day every Saturday afternoon we clicked through the Shed turnstile.

> *Reggae Reggae Reggae*
> *Here comes Johnny Reggae*
> *Johnny Reggae Reggae, lay it on me.*

1970 was the time of the skinhead and nowhere else expressed the skinhead better than the Shed. The Shed was skinhead land, where the boys did the Moonstomp and chanted to the Harry J Allstars' 'Liquidator'. Every time the disc jockey announced 'Liquidator' on the tannoy, the cheers went up. When they died down, he said it was for Eddie and the boys from Streatham, or Vince and the chaps from Stockwell. Ace faces in the Shed, their leading of the passionate chanting and synchronised clapping silhouetted against the backdrop of Earls Court and Knightsbridge. In this harsh arena these lads were looked on almost as royalty – ironic considering the Royal Palace of Kensington was only two miles down the road, although we might as well have been on a different planet, we were so far apart.

There were better covered ends. The Liverpool Kop had been celebrated for many years for its wit and there was the notorious Stretford End of Manchester United, but the Shed was what people talked about when they mentioned Chelsea, even if the real chaps used to congregate on the section next to the away fans under the North Stand. 'Come and have a go if you think you're hard enough,' we used to sing. Dressed to kill. Boots and braces. Then we'd sing at the North Stand.

20

North Stand, North Stand, do your job

Yeah, go do it. Get stuck into the away fans. Punch the crap out of them for daring to come and support their team down here.

Ben Sherman shirts. Levis rolled up to reveal the ubiquitous Doc Marten boots, known to the boys as DMs. Real high leg DMs with the bleached jeans. Lads talked about a new pair of DMs the same way those middle-class poofs talked about their new shiny Ford Cortina Mark 2, which had just come on to the market. And while they spent their Sunday mornings washing their cars or leaning over their garden fences talking about their latest perk or washing machine, we relived the excitement of what we'd done on Saturday afternoon. While we were in the Shed, we had real power – the power to change the way professional athletes went about their business. When 12,000 people instinctively know how to chant together at the same time without anybody waving a conductor's stick, that is real people power. Not for us waiting for the first few lines of 'Pomp and Circumstance' before we launch into 'Land of Hope and Glory' at the beck and call of an orchestra. No, we were the stars; we called the tune because we made the tunes.

The players waving at us before every match. Talking to the papers about how the Shed spurred them on, even calling us an extra man on the pitch. How proud do you think that made us? Ten feet tall. Us singing their names for 90 minutes as if we had eaten the roof of the Shed and the asbestos had lined our lungs. Our chants, our players, making them acknowledge us with their waves, getting our curtain calls and bows before the match, not afterwards, because this is football and anything can happen in the next 90 minutes. Not like the poncy theatre where every performance is the same. Football wrote a different script every minute of the game. Shakespeare, Pinter, Miller, all of them could be locked in a room for ever but they couldn't recreate that kind of drama, where dreams died in a second as one of our heroes missed an open goal or gave away a stupid penalty.

Peter Osgood, our centre-forward, a man with attitude in the way he walked, scoring a wonder goal.

Osgood Is *Good, Osgood* Is *Good*

Ronnie 'Chopper' Harris hacking players over.

Ronnie's gonna getcha
Ronnie's gonna getcha

We sang that whenever one of their players did something flash or fouled one of our better players. Then Ronnie would come charging in and crunch the player to the floor before trotting away pretending butter wouldn't melt in his mouth. Dave Webb at the back, waving at us like he's one of us. Every player had his own song, culled from old standards the codgers listened to after their Sunday chats over the fence or from the new pop music that old people didn't understand.

Not that the stadium as a whole could really fire up the players like other grounds, because Stamford Bridge was basically a soulless ground for atmosphere with the fans separated from the pitch by a greyhound track. Greyhounds, working men, Friday afternoon pay packets to be signed for, then to the pub or along to watch the dogs running around a track. A fiver on trap 5 to the flat cap bookie and plenty of verbal to the punters. Working men, dogs and football; upper classes, horses and polo. Having the working man's legacy outside the pitch meant the singing had to be louder, so everybody looked to the Shed for the noise and passion because the roof would echo our songs. Standing in the middle, full-blooded, throat open, teeth-grinding singing, it felt so loud your eardrums would burst. So us working-class boys managed to overcome the lost volume effect from the rest of the ground and cheered louder, because lads

22

together do that. It never loses the thrill for those who come to experience it, because once it's got you, you're hooked. Fashions come and go but this drug was all-powerful. Mates, DMs, two-tone suits, Fred Perry shirts, braces and cropped hair that made people frightened of us as we travelled the tube chanting for Chelsea. Later the fashions would change, donkey jackets replaced by designer labels, yet always the fans dictated the fashion because the football was the main focus.

British Rail Football Specials were the ultimate day out. Leaving early in the morning and dropping thousands of you in an alien town for next to nothing. No wonder the Tories eventually privatised the trains.

Football and trains stood hand in hand, almost as if the railways' original strategic aim had been to transport thousands of noisy football fans. Diesel locomotives gently grinding to a halt as we jumped off to start running, or hung out of the doors chanting our team allegiance, looking to see where the locals were or what their station looked like. Bouncing along grey tarmac platforms, mob-handed, thousands of geezers on the main station concourse with sound-reflecting roofs, escalators underground through echoing tunnels and walkways built by Victorian craftsmen for just this moment. Hundreds sounding like thousands. Expectant football fans, worried mothers holding their children closer in the pushing throng. A gust of wind before the underground train whooshed into the station, drowning our shouts. On the front of the train, the end destination – suburbia coming to the Smoke. Wimbledon, Upminster, Cockfosters, the last two West Ham and Arsenal country. The train drivers used to see our joyous faces and always look solemn or worried. Opening doors precipitating a manic surge. Trains packed tight, a precursor to 90 minutes in the Shed, then pulling into Fulham Broadway with people pulling the door roughly open to gain an extra second, dashing out of the doors and bounding up the steps, running because they were so excited that they had to create more pressure. Once on the streets, more worried faces as Saturday shoppers were jostled noisily out of the way by youth. Coppers grabbing us out of the group, telling us to calm down or arresting others and throwing them into vans. On the trains, youth stared at the older generation. Men who'd fought for their country telling us how to behave. Look at those old faces. No energy, their vigour sucked out. Once, some silly old bastard gave us a lecture.

'You lot wouldn't have lasted 10 minutes on the parade ground. The Regimental Sergeant-Major would have had you crying for your mum.'

I remember looking at him contemptuously and telling him: 'You stupid old git. What did you have to show for six bloody years spent slogging around Europe fighting the Krauts? Ten shillings and a demob suit. Then the man told you to get back in line like a good boy, and that's what you did. Doesn't that make you proud, eh!'

The old codger thought about it for a while then shut up and returned to his paper, because it was true. The rest of the world was old and inhabited by silly old gits, while we had discovered something that would bind us and make us famous. The rest of society was frightened of us because we had something that they couldn't comprehend. Nobody could tell us how they used to do it because this was now and we had created it. We were history in the making. Every Saturday, Britain watched in awe while we attended football matches. The Beatles and the Rolling Stones had amused the ruling classes, pretending to be the new revolution, but they could control that by giving the Beatles an MBE or asking the Stones to appear at the London Palladium on a Sunday night, while the adoring masses watched on their television screens. Then at the end they all bowed to the established order. So Mick Jagger and Keith Richards refused to get on a revolving stage and got fined a fiver for pissing on a petrol station forecourt – so bloody what? Collectively, football fans pissed and trampled over front gardens every Saturday afternoon. Make the Beatles stand in line at Buckingham Palace like good little boys to receive a pat on the head from the Queen and a shiny gong. Stand in line, wack, be a good boy and have your badge which says you are now recognised as a Member of the British Empire. We never stood in line and we got our own MBE (More Beer 'Ere) every Saturday.

Trains pulled into stations and we ran the barriers, jumping over the turnstiles. When the silly gits shut the gates, we smashed 'em down.

Chelsea, Chelsea, Chelsea

Fruit and vegetable stands were pulled over in a collective V-sign to the rest of society. It wasn't just us, it was groups of fans all over the country following their team. Their town, their allegiance. Britain had imposed itself on the rest of the world using the power of allegiance to the regiment. Agincourt, Rourke's Drift, Waterloo, history was full of it. Now we were the new infantry. *The Times* said bring back conscription. Bollocks. The *News of the World* wrote that we should be banned from football grounds. The media idea was that hooligans weren't real fans. Well, believe it or not, standing on cold, unyielding, loveless concrete in all weathers watching Chelsea go to the dogs week in, week out, marks you out for a Victoria Cross in my book. It wasn't like we had a choice. Once you went through that gate and felt the power of the terrace, you were signed up for life. Only those who'd never experienced the thrill could say they didn't understand the attraction. It reminded me of the journalist meeting the surfer and requesting he tell him about surfing.

'Do you surf?' asked the surfer.

'No,' replied the journalist.

'Can't tell you, then, you won't understand.'

Sometimes journalists came and stood and tried to empathise. The *Express* sports editor stood for 90 minutes on the North Bank at Highbury, had his lighter stolen, wrote a piece about the young fans who stood alongside him and was rewarded with the Sports Writer of the Year award for 1969. Journalistic tourists visited the zoo, watched the animals, came to touch and experience then impart their new knowledge to enhance their readers' understanding. When they'd finished telling each other about their new twin-carburettor overhead cam Cortina, they could read their newspapers then tell their friends over their new glass coffee table that they alone knew how to stop the hooligans, because they'd read about it in their Sunday paper. Meanwhile, journalists received the answer to a question then asked two more to try and understand the previous answer, which made sense to us because we knew that there were many more questions than answers – yet the ultimate answer was simplicity itself. The journalistic lemmings, out of the train and sprinting up the steps trampling all before in their rush to be the first to explain it like it really was. Leader writers preached, journalists reported, witty columnists satirised while cartoonists sketched the havoc that we wreaked, yet nobody got close to any real understanding of our psyche. The rainbow of understanding was even further away than before.

'Can you tell me about football violence?'

'Ever done it?'

'No, but I'd like to understand.'

'What's the point of talking to a journalist as dumb and worthless as you?'

Trying to write about it while remaining detached would always be a self-defeating exercise. We were untamed and violent or passionate and loyal, depending what side the coin landed and what was fashionable that week. Back they all went clutching their journalistic gold, their iron pyrites for the masses.

It got to the stage where after a goal was shown scored on *Match of the Day* the camera would pan in on the crowd to show the scenes. We were the Bayeaux Tapestry for the football drama. Thousands surged forward in one huge mass. Crowds packed so tight that when a few swayed, the whole terrace moved. People hemmed in so tight they urinated where they stood, unable to move. Stadiums packed so tight that the grey metal barrier sentries gave way under

26

the pressure. The injured being lifted over the top of the crowd while the match continued.

But this was how tough we were. Every time the police walked around the pitch we'd whistle 'Colonel Bogey' or chant the refrain together, going 'Da Da'. Then someone would go too far, so the police would surge in and we'd all push towards the police, hoping to knock off a helmet. When one inevitably took a tumble, the cheers would go up while the luckless bobby frantically retrieved it. Meanwhile, someone was dragged out kicking and struggling, more often than not to be chucked out into the street with a clip around the ear. Those poofs the other side of the river, Arsenal, thought they were hard, but we had a song about them. Max Bygraves and his 'Tiptoe through the Tulips' song.

> *Tiptoe through the North Bank*
> *With your boots on*
> *And your cut-throat razor*
> *Tiptoe through the North Bank with me*

1970, two hours to kick-off against Arsenal and the Shed is in real singing mode, taunting the Arsenal fans. Arsenal, where are you? Then the Shed shout went up.

> *Zigger Zagger Zigger Zagger Oi Oi Oi*

Micky Greenaway with the rasping voice was in the centre, starting the chant. The lads pushed towards the centre trying to get closer to hear the shout, to stand next to Micky. One thousand trying to get next to one person. Hear the Zigger close up, then go to work on Monday and say that you stood next to the Shed Zigger Man.

Then came the roar from the Arsenal: 'Do the Zigger Man.'

> *Let's all do the Chelsea*
> *Let's all do the Chelsea*

27

Hundreds of voices chanting and surging as one. Going for the centre but with malice aforethought, not the gentle pushing of crowd rearrangement which went before. The crowd parted. On a packed terrace, huge gaps appeared from nowhere.

> *Ooh, all together*
> *Ooh, all together*

Across the gaps came the Arsenal boys, punching, kicking, ripping the Ben Sherman shirts off the backs of Chelsea boys as they cowered. The Zigger Man retreated and took a pasting, arms up protecting his face from the punches and kicks. 'Arsenal done the Zigger, Arsenal done the Zigger,' they shouted gleefully. Then a celebratory knees-up. Organised like a small army, they had come and taken the Shed as easy as shelling peas. The Stockwell Mob were nowhere to be seen. Where were Eccles, Ginger Derek, Northern Alan, Preemo or Jesus and his mob or the North End Road boys? Nowhere, just Arsenal boys showing Chelsea that they were the boss cats. Led by their top men, Bootsy and Johnny Hoy, they inflicted maximum damage to our psyche of toughness.

Later came the stories which drove fear into our hearts. They had got off the train at Sloane Square, 500 strong, and marched down the King's Road, slapping anybody in their path. Taking Chelsea scarves from fans and using them to gain entry to the Shed, smashing the windows of a pub where the Chelsea fans had meekly stood there and counter-chanted at them. It was a sobering thought. Sometimes the stories were so fresh they came at you with the fear coming out between breathless gulps; sometimes the whole thing was contained in one or two words like 'shit' or 'Christ almighty'; or sometimes they were just grunts or noises indicating fear. Today, the Arsenal mob had shown the Shed what fear a small dedicated group could inflict on a huge crowd. The next season they put a horse right in the middle of the Shed to stop Arsenal charging us. That horse crapped right in the middle. Diabolical liberty, if you ask me.

Before 1971, the currency included the old penny. Two hundred and forty pence to a pound, in the days when a pound in your pocket was worth something. A shilling's worth of pennies was almost an artillery barrage. Even the old half-penny was pretty dangerous. Thrown from the terrace at the referee or players, it was a formidable weapon when it struck its target. Thrown at the opposing fans the other side of a dividing fence, it could really cut. Get one of those in the side of the face and you knew it. Minimum, it frightened you half to death, making you hyperventilate for 10 minutes afterwards, unable to watch the match or concentrate. Some clubs' fans took to sharpening the edges then throwing them indiscriminately.

At the end of the match, you'd stay where you were, waiting for the announcer to bring the full-time scores from around the country, giving everybody the chance to cheer when the local rivals or that team challenging you lost. Cheers or groans, then out into the crowded streets where everybody seemed to be going the opposite way to your group.

In 1970, Chelsea reached the final of the FA Cup where we played Leeds United, then one of the most powerful teams in Europe. In a replay after a 2–2 draw at Wembley, we beat Leeds 2–1 on a Wednesday night at Old Trafford, the ground of Manchester United, and the Osgood legend was born. He scored with a diving header in front of the Stretford End, where instead of 12,000 Manchester United fans there was only the blue of Chelsea. That night Chelsea marched along the streets from Manchester Piccadilly station as an unstoppable force. For those who were undecided, this tipped the balance and Chelsea became the number one lads' club to support. Our numbers grew over the next few years so that trains coming in from Kent were packed with chaps. Pulling in at Charing Cross it was practically like a Football Special. Chelsea were the team of the shires, our support came from outlying areas. It made us special because we were always travelling somewhere. Every day was an away day for Chelsea.

3

HAST THOU FOWTEN?

In 1970, football was becoming our preserve, the pastime of the rougher sorts. A gentlemen's game played by thugs was how the upper class described it, so why shouldn't we attach ourselves to it? The original amateur, jolly-good-show Corinthian spirit of the gentlemen of the south was expropriated by the northern working classes who started professional football just before the turn of the century. Despite the Wanderers and Oxford University being usurped by the likes of Preston and Wolves, the FA Cup final was still held at the Kennington Oval, so those honest northern folk used to come down to London and ask their opponents: 'Hast thou fowten yet?' If the answer was in the negative, they'd reply: 'Well, let's get fowten and go 'ome then.' Then the northern lads would get stuck into each other while the southern toffs looked on in horror. And on Monday morning, *The Times* leader writer admired the simple fighting spirit of these honest northern folk.

There is no other ground like Stamford Bridge or any other team like Chelsea. That sentiment might have been echoed by every other fan about his own club, but Chelsea in the early seventies really epitomised everything that was the game. Glamour followed Chelsea. Great players by day, trendy nightclubbers by night. The players married models or were in the papers with dolly birds on their arms. Everybody wanted to be a footballer. Chelsea had youth appeal. The

King's Road was swinging and Chelsea were the fashion. Arsenal had the marble halls, Tottenham had the glory, glory aura and West Ham had a rustic roughness, but Chelsea had something extra. The players even drank like us. Tommy Baldwin was called 'The Sponge' because of the amount of beer he could apparently absorb. Peter Osgood, Ian Hutchinson and Alan Hudson were often to be seen forming a Monday drinking club after a hard game on the Saturday. Changing room, Shed forecourt, a hop, skip and a jump across the Fulham Road into the Rising Sun opposite on a Monday afternoon. Pints of lager among backslapping well-wishers who enjoyed their company because footballers were only working-class boys who could kick a ball and liked a beer.

Fans always had a story about which players were spotted where, and Chelsea's surrounding areas had plenty of watering holes. Coming out of Fulham Broadway station, there were the Swan and King's Head, the walk towards the ground past Barbarellas nightclub, the barracks for the Chelsea Pensioners, the war memorial, the Britannia pub opposite the North Stand entrance. Plenty of other pubs in the immediate vicinity of the ground. The Wheatsheaf, with the out-of-work actors sitting at the bar; the Imperial, with its fading paintwork; the Lord Palmerston, where the local lads drank. Chelsea had it all in abundance, as well as a great team of young players. The main entrance to the Shed was a wide open space – on match day a throng of bodies like worker ants in a manic colony – which nowhere else in London had. And a pub opposite: on match days the Rising Sun had water on the ceilings and running down the windows as bodies packed too tight raised the temperature. The smell of stale beer and sweat lingering in the air as you walked past and the door opened, competing with that of hot dogs and fried burger, onions and freshly dropped horse dung. These aromas hung in the air yet people accepted and expected them. Eventually the pub would become renamed the Stamford Bridge Arms, but for those who were at Chelsea in the seventies it will always be the Rising Sun.

'Tickets for the match . . . Two together . . . Best seats.' The dulcet tones of the touts, always there bobbing and weaving, one eye on the punters, one eye on the police, who more often than not turned a blind eye. Outside would be the King of the Touts, Stan Flashman, who would wait for his tickets to come out from the players inside the ground. Then his men would do the rounds. Best seats to order. The buzz of expectancy, young and old mingling in together. Dads, sons, skinheads, old 'uns. Flat caps, boots and braces together. Some people standing around slouching against walls, either waiting for mates or trying to look tough, eyeing up those who entered the forecourt. Others just posing, hanging around the little firms of locals who stood around chatting because this was their patch, or manor, as they liked to call it. The North End Road boys, every one dressed in the latest fashion of the day. Proud to say that they were the first to wear boiler suits with a newspaper in the side pocket. Fans holding four or five programmes, the new trainspotters. Newspaper boards with headlines handwritten in felt tip or telling you which reporter would be covering this match. 'READ DESMOND HACKETT IN THE DAILY EXPRESS ON MONDAY.' In 1967 Hackett had stated that if Chelsea won the FA Cup that year he'd walk barefoot from Wembley back to Stamford Bridge. Plenty of lads took him up on that offer. When Chelsea reached the final, he backtracked in his paper: 'What I meant to say was that I'd walk barefoot if they won the Cup playing poor football, but this Chelsea team have the flair to do it in style.' That was my first exposure to the duplicity of the press. In the final, Chelsea lost to Spurs. It was our first taste of Wembley and we had lost to Spurs. Many Chelsea fans felt hatred towards Spurs after that day and many intense rivalries and future battles sprang from it.

The Shed's big blue gates swung open with 20 minutes to go as people swarmed home, while local urchins without the admission money sneaked in. They resembled those big factory gates of the northern shipyards which we saw in the news as men flocked through them at the sound of the end-of-day hooter. The old newsreels in black and white with Chelsea fans swarming out in striped scarves and rosettes. When Chelsea were two goals down, the numbers going home early made you wonder how so many actually got into the ground in the first place. Now the workers would enjoy their leisure.

Then there was the Bovril entrance, a small alleyway further down the Fulham Road with a few turnstiles. It seemed as if you would queue for ever and all you could see were bodies in front. Every so often someone would climb up the fence and shout that one of the turnstiles was shut. The quaint wooden boards painted royal blue without the courtesy sign on the front 'Sorry, Closed'. It was just tough, because that's how it was at football. When the match was a sell-out they'd whack a piece of wood across the entrance while a few more fought to get in.

'Get back, you lot, it's full up,' shouted the turnstile operator.

'Rubbish, I'm coming in,' and more bodies would surge over the top.

Just past the entrance, the cobbles, so it felt like it was old. Old England was all about the cobbled streets of Dickens, when boys like us would be in the factories or out on the streets as pickpockets. As you went in, you suddenly went beneath a building propped up on concrete stilts. Windows with old metal frames, painted blue many years ago, now with the rust stains in the ascendancy.

In 1966, the chairman Joe Mears made a prophetic statement about Chelsea in the match-day programme. Joe had spent his entire life trying to buy the freehold of Chelsea Football Club. Now he had achieved his life's ambition, he predicted a bright future for the club. He saw Chelsea becoming one of the giants of English football. Sadly, he never lived to see his vision. He died shortly after and his son, Brian, took the reins. He embarked on an ambitious building programme which went horribly wrong. Within a couple of years, Chelsea were in debt and the property vultures circled. Chelsea were in dire straits but it wasn't our fault.

* * *

Around this time, the Tunbridge lads became faces in and around Chelsea. Part of the attraction of going to football was becoming a face, like Ace Face in *Quadrophenia*; you'd want to be seen and known for something. Our reputation as lads that would have a row and hold the line was made the day Tottenham tried to walk down the middle of the road from Fulham Broadway. When the first full can of coke bounced off a Spurs fan's head and exploded, it was followed by a barrage of cans and shouts of '*Chelsea aggro, Chelsea aggro*'. Scattered them like ten pins at a bowling alley. On such actions reputations are made. At every away match that season, we got the looks and nods because we were seen as the chaps who would uphold the honour of Chelsea.

Later Tottenham got their revenge and waited for us at one match as we got off the train at Charing Cross. Fifty of them chased us halfway around the West End for over an hour. But even getting chased was half the fun of it because nobody could say that they didn't enjoy being close to the action. Breaking the confidence of rival fans so that they would look at the fixture list and worry for a whole week before they met us was all part of the game. Not that we were vicious, unlike some groups of fans who would be waiting for you from 9am in the morning at grotty cafes opposite the railway station. No humour, no dialogue, just full-out attack as soon as they saw the whites of your eyes or the colour of your scarves. A whole week of tension and boredom could be relieved just walking across a station concourse, having a brief confrontation where a few punches were thrown, then off to the match. People walking around telling others what you did. Nowadays, young professionals compete at the gym or organise American-style sales meetings where everybody gets a feelgood factor or jumps up and down and hollers their lungs out to celebrate because some peroxide blonde has made more sales calls or a snotty idiot in a Top Shop suit, wearing an imitation Rolex oyster, has sold more chipboard kitchens than anybody else. Compare their feelings to that of walking in front of 500 other guys who are ready to follow you into the unknown, yet even as they follow, they too have a chance to call the shots in a confrontation and make themselves top dog for a minute. Education or breeding might have made us sales or managing directors of dynamic kitchens or Luvverly Leisure Clubs; instead it gave us the football terrace and our mates.

Throughout history, leading fellow men has been a great feeling for the upper classes at places like Agincourt and Waterloo, so why should terrace lads be any different? Boys got off trains, then an hour later they had led a charge and seen thousands scatter in panic. It was their coming of age, like a ritual. You learned all about cowardice, suffering, cruelty and comradeship, and nobody was going to die – at least, they weren't at the hands of the group I was involved in. We were peacocks strutting our stuff on somebody else's turf. A giant catwalk, a fashion show and lessons in life to boot. The great feelings we experienced became something to be proud of. Graduates in the academy of Hooligansville and every time they showed it on the news or broadcast it on the front pages of newspapers, more converts to the religion were added. It was seductive, more glamorous than anything else anybody had ever thought of – and we invented it, then patented it. This was the English equivalent of rock and roll. We were Presley, Sinatra and Jim Reeves rolled into one but we didn't just sing the songs, we wrote the lyrics as well.

It was a peculiar enjoyment because it was mixed with pain. Following Chelsea meant that you'd see plenty of defeats. When the other team scored or you lost and the local riff-raff were taunting you, then it demanded you take physical retribution – punch the snivelling gits in the mouth. But to everybody who was there in the early days there was something extra, because this was something nobody had experienced so nobody could say with conviction where it was all leading. You didn't have to read how others had felt their pulse racing, heart thumping and a sudden surge of adrenaline as you sang in the biggest, noisiest choir ever assembled. Your senses became elevated above anything else previously experienced, and, unlike with drugs, you didn't need a stronger drug to recreate the feeling because each dose was just as powerful as the one before and no confrontation was ever the same. It was as addictive as anything could be. At the end of a day of running up and down roads, we'd all go home laughing. Nobody got hurt and that was funny in itself. Sometimes after a fist fight you'd touch your face just to make sure it was all there. Bruises and stories aplenty the next day. Fun. Sure it was fun, and everybody who was there from both sides agreed.

In the home counties in the early 1970s there was plenty of work, but all that stared us in the face was a free National Health Service and 49 years of work to get a pension. Football offered us the chance nothing else in England would – to become as famous as the Beatles or the Queen. Pretty soon we would be on every front page in England and the world, more famous than in our wildest dreams. So famous that people who formed opinions in the media spoke about us in hushed tones, then exclaimed that they were frightened to be in the same vicinity as us. Eventually, whole cities shut down while governments tried to work out our next move – which was ridiculous in itself because even we didn't know that.

We even had a disease named after us. Every time hooliganism erupted in Europe, it was called the English disease. It was a simple philosophy and for a short while we were unstoppable. Our aim was not to hurt anybody but just to make the other guy relinquish his space. It didn't matter if it was only for 20 seconds, the fact that he'd moved in the face of our togetherness meant that we'd made him lose face. In some societies in the Far East, losing face is so terrible that people commit suicide. All it meant to us was that we'd laugh and jeer a lot and tell stories to our mates. What we were doing was exposing the ridiculous notion of community which had made England its empire. In fact, all of our actions exposed England for what it really was. Life was made up of work on Monday to Friday to earn enough to enjoy great days out watching Chelsea play every week. So what if they got beat every other week? Only those with no spine support the team which is winning. Supporting a team is for ever. It becomes a part of you, your fabric, as necessary as food – the bread of life. Aided by British Rail, we travelled the length and breadth of England singing and chanting, seemingly invincible.

Not that all the lads were decent. Places and people could be grim. What about the Manchester Ship Canal? Like you are interested in sightseeing when some nasty mob of knife merchants are looking for a Cockney's face to slash. Getting off a train in a small group to find hundreds waiting for you. Fans could travel to places and spend the whole match worrying, then find it necessary to run from the ground back to the station, with famous landmarks disappearing into a grey blur. Towns which came stamped with a fans' X-certificate memory. Good memories and laughs relived every waking moment. Frightening times when people really did shit their pants forgotten as soon as the train left the station and gathered speed, although some never stopped shaking until they smelt the smoke of London. Not that the pain was over. Sometimes you'd get back to Kings Cross and another London firm or returning northern mob was waiting to relive hostilities and settle scores. In London, the West Ham lads took the violence far too seriously, but there again, they were from Essex. All mouth and trousers was how they described Chelsea. Never any humour or decency. One day a Manchester City fan from the home counties walked out of Upton Park tube station scarfed up and got scarred up with a cut-throat razor across the face. When *Clockwork Orange* came out, those West Ham lads started whacking people with walking sticks, like that sort of violence was fun. Well, it never seemed to be violence to me having fisticuffs with like-minded minded football fans. We were all fully grown and of sound mind and body (even if we still had acne) so what the hell.

Chelsea were the great organisers and I suppose that part of it must come down to people like me. Numbers and organisation made for a better day out, especially when you turned up in a town and practically took it over. Their local finest cowering in shop doorways, running at every juncture, before and after the match. You wanted to be known as the top dogs in London, to be recognised as number one. You always had to be organised in the other fans' lair. Stories about

Arsenal travelling to away matches with huge numbers and getting murdered abounded. That hardly ever happened to Chelsea because we'd make sure that we organised ourselves ready for the action.

At away games there were various distances between the station and the ground. The local lads would know where you'd be spread out and would ambush you at strategic points. So while others lost their organisation in the milling crowds and let panic set in, Chelsea faces held the lads back. Wait, hold it here. Then five minutes later emerge into empty streets. Just you and them. Every one of them a group of individual mobs while we were a single mob going one way – towards them. A determined marching force organised by the ace faces. Chelsea also developed the fear chant, using concentrated sound to unnerve those who were not sure: walking towards people going 'Ooh, ooh, ooh' while punching their fists forward and slapping their fists on their thighs. Ninety per cent of fans ran from this. Once they started running it was all over, the rest always joined them. Fear creates mass hysteria faster than anything else. Those that didn't got spanked as individuals.

In 1974 I travelled up to Sheffield United for a match on New Year's Day with the official Chelsea Supporters' Club. I had bumped into an Arsenal fan called Clive and Arsenal were playing such rubbish at the time that he had decided to come with me. That was the fun of it in those days. Lads from different London clubs mixed in with each other. Who wants to watch your team playing a nothing match at home to some team like Norwich when you could go for a beer-up and awayday with your mates? One was a chore while the other was an adventure. Clive was typical of people then. He didn't look like a thug, he was just another face in a crowd. He loved his mum and didn't come from a broken home, nor was he an anarchist. Only a few years previously we'd been bought *Boy's Own* annuals for Christmas, now we were boys together for real. Inside the ground the Chelsea boys scattered the Sheffield end then stood firm, with the local police putting a line up in the middle of their terrace. The Sheffield fans' response was to throw coins and pies at us. Different grounds, different mentality and metabolic response. Sheffield wouldn't react the same as Millwall, who had a real war mentality, digging deeper within themselves to extract pure nastiness, going over the top of the police lines and fences if they wanted to. You couldn't take a liberty with Millwall, who wanted to rip your heart out through your chest, in the way we did at places like Sheffield. After the match we ambled back to the coach. Someone cracked the Sheffield steel city joke that he knew someone who'd once thrown away all his knives after a defeat at Sheffield United.

Early evening in Sheffield. There is something about northern fish and chips which seems to make them taste better than London ones. Perhaps the fish is fresher or the chips really were done in beef dripping, but I always looked forward to my northern après-match chip shop delight. Then, from nowhere, a small group confronted us. Six youths, with one of the half-wits waving a knife around. They were around 18 years old but didn't look mature enough to have started shaving.

'You Cockney bastards, I'm gonna stripe you lot.'

'What's this, a six o'clock thrill? You showing us what you nicked from the factory last week?' asked Clive.

'What, all of us? All on your own?' I said to our friend, who was shaking like a leaf while cutting the surrounding air frantically. He looked to be more of a danger to himself than us and backed away. One of our group walked forward, punched the reluctant knifeman in the mouth and he went straight down in an untidy heap. With that his mates ran. A couple of the lads gave him a London bootstamp to his face, a physical reminder that he'd met Chelsea, then we sauntered off to a local pub for a drink. As we arrived back at the coach there were three policemen and two spotty youths standing around surveying the faces. As I went to get on, one of them pointed out Clive and me.

'That's him. The one who robbed us.'

A brief scuffle ensued and Clive and I were bundled into the back of a Black Maria van. Some overweight sergeant sat in the back with us all the way back to the police station.

'You're for the high jump, son. Robbery with an offensive weapon is a very serious offence.'

His mate chipped in: 'We hate you Cockney wankers coming up here causing trouble.'

Well, I sat there laughing at him because I had no worries. After refusing my chance to come clean and confess, I was charged with possession of offensive weapons and robbery. It seemed as if our friend had been found by the police and concocted a story about being beaten up and robbed. He said that the knife was one of ours. A Cockney in Sheffield with no marks on him against a poor local with a DM imprint on his face and coughing up blood was no contest. I was held for seven weeks at Thorparch remand centre at Wetherby, south Yorkshire. When I came to court I received a stern lecture plus three months and served two months at North Sea Camp. The first thing I did when I got out was attend the next Chelsea match.

In retrospect the seventies really was the golden age of football violence, when boys were boys and England stood back terrified. The police always seemed to be in the wrong place at the right time for us, leaving hordes of lads to recreate their violent fantasies across the urban canvas. Seeing hundreds of Chelsea lads charge across the scarred industrial wastelands of the north to do battle with their finest was more poignant than we realised at the time. Wherever the lads travelled in their thousands, British Rail football specials became the ultimate recipient of the urge to smash. Something had to give, so in September 1975 the much-loved football special was finally given the boot by British Rail.

In September 1976 England waited with bated breath as the Chelsea hooligans were awarded the dubious distinction of a trip to Millwall now they were in the Second Division. Whatever level of football the teams competed at, this was the first division of violence. It would be the first time Chelsea had played Millwall in 46 years. Imagine that, the last time we'd played them the Great Depression of the thirties was just under way. I suppose that gave those grim Millwall types an excuse to bite your ears off: 'Needed the sustenance, officer!'

Not that they needed an excuse for violence, as they'd had their ground shut three times, in 1934, 1947 and 1950, plus they'd smashed up the chairman's car showroom when the team had a bad run. In between they had created such an oppressive atmosphere within the ground that the Millwall team had remained undefeated for a record number of matches. When that run ended, a nutter ran on to the pitch and punched out the referee! Millwall, tough or thick, depending on which way you looked at it out of ear-biting range.

Millwall always was horrible; no wonder Jack the Ripper operated on its fringes. Now its decay was brickwork necrosis surrounded by a terminal disfiguring illness. Scruffy pubs, faded fascias, old dockers sitting in the same place they had always sat playing Colloquy. Twenty years ago they had sat waiting for the next ship to dock so they could go and earn some money. Now they sat passing time because the last ship to dock at Millwall was long since scrap metal. Colloquy or nap hands that could go on for days, remembering the days when Millwall was something and these guys were somebody in the docks. Men with deep frown-line faces from years spent concentrating on their cards. Now the work was gone they had nothing except the mental images of work and full wage packets. The docks were a memory but the toughness that Millwall dock life engendered remained, so Millwall fans were hard. They had to keep up the rough welcome especially to the young pretenders from Chelsea. Even their ground name of Cold Blow Lane was uncompromising. Millwall, where fans went with hearts in mouths making a lump so big you couldn't swallow – but don't admit it to the guy standing next to you. As the train pulled into the station the song by Johnny Wakelin about the Muhammad Ali v George Foreman boxing match in Zaïre went up. It was to be our chant.

41

Once there was a battle there
In Mill . . . In Millwall
One thousand Chelsea there
In Mill . . . In Millwall.

But no sooner had the train pulled up and the door opened, the chant of 'Mill-waaall, Mill-waaall, Mill-waaall, Mill-waaall' echoed around the platform. They extended the end of the song as if they were retarded and couldn't pronounce the word properly, almost like they'd been crossed with a wailing banshee.

Everybody is frightened of fighting nutters because pain is gain to them. People looked around. Nobody was there, perhaps the ghosts of the Victorian bricklayers were singing it. Then down the platform they marched.

'Never a copper when you need one,' someone said quietly.

'Stand!' shouted someone else.

'Sod this for a game of soldiers, I'm off,' said his mate and legged it. That was the last thing you needed, people losing it at the last moment.

'Ooh, ooh, ooh!' we chanted, then it was pure panic as the Millwall started laughing and mimicking our chanting, and kept coming.

'RUN!' People scattered as all hell broke loose. Across the railway tracks, back into the carriages and out the doors on the other side. No looking back for those who ran. Those foolish enough to stand or not fast enough to get caught were on the floor getting a kicking, if they were lucky. It wasn't pretty. *C'est la vie*, lads.

When the match kicked off at 3pm the tension inside the ground was reaching volcanic proportions, with the Chelsea lads inside the Cold Blow Lane end coming under a sustained missile attack. Before the match, after much regrouping and strategic withdrawals, the main firm, of which the Tunbridge Wells lads were a main part, had made Millwall back off. It was eyeball to eyeball and the other fellow blinked, only the mounted police had stopped us turning it into a rout of their finest chaps. Now, in the security of the ground, surrounded by rigid metal cages so strong a charging rhino wouldn't have penetrated them, we were confronted by anger incarnate as they came at the fences in waves while a mounted copper on a white horse overlooked the mayhem from his grassy knoll vantage point. Up against the fence, growling, spitting, frothing at the mouth, they were a frightening sight. Then a lone nutter came running at the fence, his face full of venom, a total screwed-up snarl of hatred. In his right hand he had a meat hook with a wooden handle attached so he could grip it with greater effect, the type they used to use in the docks to move frozen meat boxes. He used the meat hook to propel himself over the fence. Behind him the raving monster beer-bellies, which terrified everybody, followed him over.

As 'Snarler' dropped over the fence, he waved the hook at anybody and everybody, who backed off. Shouts of 'It's a nutter!' and 'The loony's got a meat hook!' filled the air. At the front by the fence was a group of CFC TA paratroopers, who stood their ground. Spurred on by their refusal to give in to fear, the Chelsea lads went forward and managed to get the hook off this lunatic. One of the paras was beating the 'Snarler' around the head with the flat side of his own hook.

'Hit him with the sharp side!' shouted his mate.

'Kill the bastard!'

Blood squirted out from his face as the metal blows landed with a sharp thud. As the Millwall bellies came over they took a bit of a whacking they didn't expect. Not that the blows made that much difference as they thudded into all that flab. They were enjoying it, like they'd not had that much fun in weeks. Four stabbed, 113 ejected from the ground.

At the end of the game it seemed as if every Millwall lunatic in the 21,004 crowd was waiting for us. Middle-aged men were pushing their sons aside and tearing into us. It must have been rent-a-Millwall-nutter on parade that day. Chelsea ran everywhere, it was pandemonium. No wonder nobody likes Millwall. Some of those TA para lads went on to fight in Rhodesia and South Africa and they still reckon that afternoon outside at Millwall was the most frightened they've ever been in a crowd.

Somebody muttered a comment as we left the ground: 'Thank God we lost 3–0, I'd hate to have seen them really upset.' The Chelsea boys laughed because win or lose, you'd have a booze. We'd be back.

Every Saturday there would be a story about some ridiculous act of bravery or heroism from the previous week. Whether or not they were all true didn't matter because they served to bind us together, made us better mates. It also made for better fun. A few months on, some pub storyteller would have stood alone and turned the tide at Millwall that September afternoon.

Nottingham Forest had a great idea: build the ground next to the River Trent. The local Forest boys used to love to chant at the away fans, 'You're going in the Trent.' Show fear at Forest and a swim was on the cards. The first time Chelsea went there, the Chelsea boys threw the Nottingham Forest boys in, to the tune of the Eton Boating song:

> *And you'll all swim together*
> *Cos you've met the CFC*

October 9th, 1984, among the early evening hubbub of Waterloo station. Worried Chelsea faces mirrored the frightened looks we got from the bowler-hatted briefcase brigade who'd spent a day in the City. Wankers who queue in orderly line to get on the Waterloo and City line. This is Millwall away in a midweek League Cup match and we're Chelsea on a mission. Go home to your *Coronation Street*, carpet slippers and cooked dinner while we go on an adventure into the unknown.

Watching and waiting, faces looking out of the window as the train rattled across old track into the darker recesses of Docklands. London Bridge to South Bermondsey. Hadn't Hitler bombed this area almost flat? He needn't have bothered, because it looked like it was decaying all of its own accord. Docklands, a relic of Victorian power when Britain ruled the world as the greatest trading nation and most of it came through London's docks. When trading wasn't enough, they sent lads to conquer and take what was needed with force.

44

Now Surrey Quays station in the cool weather sounded quaint. The boys had been drinking since early afternoon – you needed drink to go to Millwall. What are those people on down there? An average gate of around 10,000 yet more nutters per square inch than any other ground I've ever visited. Once, when Manchester United came to Necrotown, the old grannies were coming out of their houses and hurling rubbish at Man U fans, looking like they were having a rabid fit. Basically, though, they were just honest dockland folk who loved a tear-up. 'Hast thou fowten yet?' had just become 'Have you had a smack in the teeth yet, you foreign twit?' Anybody from outside Docklands who didn't have a relative who had experienced the Blitz was a 'foreigner' to them.

The next morning we would sit in the greasy spoon admiring the simple fighting spirit of those Millwall chappies. Years before, some Millwall fans had been featured on BBC1's *Panorama* with names like Harry the Dog and Crowbar Jerry, wearing surgical masks because they dished out treatment to opposing fans. Whether or not it was true, the fact that they were happy to be seen on TV as dim-witted fans enjoying a piss-up and punch-up reinforced the stereotype of Millwall. Even the locals' pronunciation of the team invites ridicule as it sounds like they skipped substantial parts of their schooling.

A match at Millwall always entailed some sort of grief. Years later one of my mates recounted a story about the time Arsenal fans tried to drink in a pub a couple of miles from the ground and found themselves attacked because Millwall had sent young spotters around the pubs looking for unfamiliar faces. Another of their tricks to Cockney fans walking to the ground looking to mind their own business was to ask them where some obscure pub was. While the northerners asked you the time to discover your accent, Millwall had their own way to find out if a fellow Londoner dressed and talking similarly was really Millwall. Basically, they didn't need to do that because while West Ham were the scowlers, Millwall were the growlers. They had crows' feet growl marks around the corners of their mouths which no other fans had.

All through the early evening Millwall had been out and about in force, positioning young spotters at strategic points to make sure no Chelsea slipped in without meeting the reception committee. Welcome to Docklands, here's a punch in the face or a boot in the balls for starters, then perhaps Crowbar Jerry will give you a fractured skull. Yes, a smack in the teeth was almost friendly. One group of lads sat in a pub went to leave only to be confronted by an angry group with baseball bats and lumps of wood with nails protruding, silly stragglers who'd left the protection of the mob. Solitary fans running for dear life along a dark alley pursued by a howling mob, with an old toothless granny hanging out of the flats shouting, 'Do the Chelsea bastard!' Some Chelsea fans were run into the ground, but the main group who'd stuck together had more than held their own.

At night Millwall's streets look even more forbidding. Small alleyways, smashed street lamps, ubiquitous railway arches disappearing into a dark abyss. Isolated streetlights reflecting the harsh yellow sodium against grimy London brick. Walkways where Chelsea fans didn't dare venture. Fear in the step as people walked towards the ground that evening. The rattle of the trains ringing out around us from the raised railway lines. Huge electric sparks from the trains, almost like an artillery barrage, crack-crack-crack, which seemed to come at you making you duck; or perhaps it was the fear inside us that made every sudden flash exacerbate our jumpiness. The bright sparks lit up the sky, silhouetting the lifeless high-rise flats with the bottom-floor windows and doors boarded up and covered in graffiti. 'MILLWALL KILLS WEST HAM. MILLWALL F TROOP.' As if we needed reminding that these lads hated those who lived the other side of the Thames. Going through the Blackwall and Rotherhithe tunnels, you might as well be going into a foreign country. Not that the fact that the Tunbridge Wells lads were natives of the south side of the Thames cut any ice. We were Chelsea.

The desolation and decline that was endemic in this part of London stared back at you. Empty foundries which once knew the bang of metal and the glare of oxyacetylene cutters. Padlocked gates, wire mesh fences protecting dilapidated buildings with rotten corrugated iron roofs which had long since given up trying to stop the rain getting in, with years of accumulated litter piled up against the fences. Old railway sleepers just discarded in yards with rotting, rusty heavy factory equipment. I imagined that this was how Dunkirk looked when Stukas dived in and the British forces abandoned their heavy equipment before escaping back across the Channel. Then the horror coming at you, with Millwall fans everywhere attacking Chelsea fans going to the ground. The promising Chelsea reserve footballer Bobby Isaacs was slashed across the back with a Stanley knife razor as he went to go in the players' entrance, giving him a wound that required over 100 stitches. He was never really the same player again after that.

The match was played in a climate of extreme hatred, Millwall fans just staring at you from behind two layers of reinforced welded metal and a solid blue mass of police officers. 'WE HATE CHELSEA, WE HATE CHELSEA.' Small consolation was the thought that they didn't hate us as much as they hated West Ham. At least they'd never killed any of us. At the end of the game the Chelsea lads walked out as one. A match crowd of 11,157, yet in the Millwall ranks at least 5,000 hand-picked nutters waiting for a tear-up.

'Peckham this way!' I shouted, and a large mob followed me. Hickey the Pied Piper of Docklands. This was the first time I realised that a crowd always gravitates towards a leader. So now I and a few others were responsible for getting everybody back to Waterloo safely. No second chances down here. You don't want to get a kicking because the Millwall go down the Accident and Emergency and give you another spank. Going through here on the train was all pleasure, now on foot it was all pain. Frightened voices. Paranoia started setting in.

Then it got really manic. Dark streets, police dogs. Your metabolism speeding until the heart beat its way through your chest. Attempting to get used to the darkness around you or the suffocating decay which hadn't lessened because of the match itself. The power of numbers lessening as the police split us up into smaller groups. Yet through it all, the chant went up, hands slapped hard on thighs.

'Keep it tight, Chelsea. Keep it tight, Chelsea.'

In the distance came the chant of Millwall, 'No One Likes Us, We Don't Care.'

A quickening descent towards the light of the road to the Elephant and Castle where the fans ran back and forward across the road, stopping the traffic to swap punches or throw whatever they could lay their hands on. Police cars screeched to a halt. It was pure pandemonium. Startled onlookers enjoyed the spectacle which unfolded in front of their eyes. One old lady asked some of the fans what was happening, as to the untrained eye it seemed as if everybody was the same. Dressed the same, shouting the same comments and acting the same.

'Just a quiet evening out watching Millwall play Chelsea,' was the sanguine reply.

Britain loves its heroes, as long as they conform. We were fast becoming the great nonconformists. Every Saturday groups of lads were upsetting the establishment applecart. We were not falling into the little categories meant for us. We were meant to be silly for a little while then grow out of it when we discovered girlfriends. I remember reading every week how the middle classes were appalled by our performance. Plenty of fans looked forward to the Sunday papers when our exploits filled hundreds of column inches. Politicians had their Saturday evenings at the theatre interrupted by an intrepid news reporter demanding a quote for the well-ordered masses. I even started a scrapbook as newspaper after newspaper ran front page and leader comments on our actions. It would come back to haunt me years later.

Sometimes I'd be at the match with my pals and the next morning I'd read something that definitely didn't happen the way I remembered it. My favourite clipping came from the *Daily Express*. Under their logo of the man with the sword and shield, the leader thundered out to middle-class England about how the courts could end all this football violence by the dishing out of a few stiff sentences. That was what had happened when the mods and rockers clashed on Brighton beach. Put a few of them behind bars for a few months and the rest of them would soon lose the stomach for a fight. Because we were all cowards who could only run in a pack. Jail the ringleaders, that will stop their terrible wrongdoing.

The truth of the matter was that confrontation at football was fun. Anybody who was involved will tell you, if they are honest, that it was unbelievably beautiful, ballet and boxing combined, alongside sex but lasting so much longer. Your senses quickened, you achieved heightened awareness incomparable to anything else you'd ever done and you had ultimate power. Of course that concoction was going to be addictive. Throughout history, many have tried to bottle less heady stuff.

Our sole purpose in life seemed to be to fill the empty pages of newspapers, almost as if they didn't have anything else to write about. Not that any journalists ever went out on a no-story operation where football hooligans were concerned. There was always something or somebody to write about. None of them trod the Millwall walk with us so truth escaped their pens, but even if a story didn't happen there was always the police briefing. Over 500 hard-core thugs will be here. Only police vigilance and planning prevented the complete breakdown of law and order. So the readers were treated to literary scraps of English life being one step from anarchy. We were disenfranchised angry youths or affluent thrill-seekers with good jobs, depending on which influential dinner party they'd attended.

One evening at Blackburn the local coppers caught a small group of us coming out of an off-licence. Their verbal attack on our parentage and Londoners in general was unusual in so much as nothing had been done by us to initiate the aggression, but Londoners travelling anywhere aroused emotion in all locals, whatever their position in society. That was the first time I realised that not only did the football team represent the aspirations of the local people, their fans' toughness also reflected on the area. Police officers took great umbrage when we came along and humiliated their local finest. Chelsea fans making their firms run and lose face reflected badly on them because any cowardice by the young locals implicated them by association.

Chelsea away at Plymouth in the '76–77 season. The journey to Plymouth is just over three hours, which is between eight and 20 cans of lager depending upon your speed of consumption. There was, and still is, a feeling among the Chelsea lads (and all London lads, in fact) that people from Plymouth are a bit slow in the brains department. Just listen to the accents alongside all those green fields and rolling hills. Being a navy town, the locals fancied themselves as a bit hard because they were used to seeing thousands of people descend on the town en masse, drink themselves into oblivion and then start fighting. Plymouth has one of the most famous streets in Britain, Union Street. A few of the lads walked up there before the match but it looked grim, definitely rough, with prostitutes abounding in the side streets.

The Chelsea lads were determined to go into the Plymouth end. As we stood outside the turnstiles there was a large policeman (PC Dumpling reporting for duty after extra suet pudding, sir), the sort that used to be everywhere. I used to love it when his type tried to chase us. Seeing their creased faces trying to get air into their lungs used to make us fall about laughing. As we went to go into the Plymouth end, the know-all copper gave us his 'sonny' lecture.

'Right, you lot. If there are any Chelsea fans trying to sneak in, just remember this. You've got me to answer to. If I find you I will personally throw you out with all the added extras of upsetting me. (*'What you gonna do, you fat bastard? Nick my packed lunch?' someone whispered*.) However, if I don't get you then you will have the local lads to deal with. They eat Cockneys for breakfast by the dozen. (*'And you've had a dozen breakfasts, lard guts,' someone shouted*.) Don't come crying to me, because you have been warned.'

He then stood back patting his belly, looking very smug, believing he had put the fear of the Plymouth almighty into us. Some of the guys looked at him and nodded with stupid faces. Then as they got through the turnstile: 'Silly old twit. Who does he think he is, Dixon of Plymouth Ho?'

About 10 minutes into the match Chelsea surged at the Plymouth lads and they scattered like the Armada in front of Drake. While the cream of Plymouth ran or took a pasting, I spotted 'Old Fearsome', as he had become nicknamed, shaking his head, unable to believe that Plymouth yobbos had retreated without upholding the honour of the town.

Soon after a terrace confrontation, a large gap used to appear. If you were the away team you used to stand on the edge goading the locals, daring them to come across the gap. The gap was like the Bering Strait, not very wide but an area which nobody dared to cross unless it was to attack. Shortly after, the police used to appear and form a line down the middle. The locals were usually squashed into a corner against a fence, shouting obscenities at us. If they showed no fight, we'd go into them again. On this day I was standing on the edge when a girl came over and said hello. It was my old girlfriend Dawn, who I'd gone out with a few years previously in Tunbridge Wells.

'What are you doing here?' I asked in shock.

'Well, I thought you might be here so I came along with my fiancé,' she said, pointing over to the Plymouth fans. Standing on the edge the other side was a guy with a bloody nose where we'd just punched him.

'What's his name?' I asked.

'Geoffrey.'

'Oi, Geoff, nice shiner!' I shouted over. 'All the sailors will like that one.' I waved at him and he smiled back, but with a look which said that he shouldn't really be smiling as his pride was hurt.

'Look, I must go back now. Look after yourself.' With that she bounced back across the gap. The terrible violence which everybody read about next day was only lads whacking each other then laughing.

Outside the ground at Plymouth is a huge park. After the match all hell broke loose as fist fights erupted everywhere. It was pure pandemonium as rival fans engaged in toe-to-toe punch-ups. Eventually the local police let dogs loose. That just made it worse as all the noise and people caused them to bark and snap at everything. The next thing I knew there was a sharp pain in my backside. A dog had sunk its teeth into the fleshy area of my bum and gripped for all its worth. I screamed in pain but the more I shouted, the tighter it bit. Eventually, Boghead had the great idea of kicking it in the jaw but he missed with his first kick because he was a still-pissed 20-can man and booted me up under the base of my spine. I fell over on to the deck in agony. As I fell on the dog it let out a yelp and jumped out of the way, taking what felt like half my bum flesh with it. I looked up to see the smiling face of 'Old Fearsome' staring down at me.

'Go on, get up before I boot you so hard you'll fly back to that stinkhole you call London.' He then kicked me right on the wound, which was bleeding. I remember the pain shot right through me.

Suddenly I was being hoisted to my feet. It was Geoffrey, Dawn's boyfriend. He helped me all the way back to the station, where I was greeted with half-hearted apologies by the lads who'd left me to my fate. Later in the train journey, when I was sitting moaning with pain and discomfort, some of the lads started sniggering. By Paddington the carriage was full of howls of laughter as the Chelsea fans sat snarling and barking as they reflected on my bad luck after Chelsea had won 3–1. To make matters worse, British Rail shut the bar all the way back and some other idiots smashed up the toilets, so I couldn't even put any cold water on the pain.

Once in a while someone would return from a trip with a story which defied description, set apart from the usual fun 'Run 'em, punched 'em' angle. Sometimes the story had such a frightening resonance of terror that the person telling it was in shock by the time he had finished. Descriptions of people who hated Londoners so much that they wanted to do more than just beat us but really damage our bodies. Headstamping by four or five people, baseball bats to skulls and knee-caps and, horror of horrors, multiple facial slash wounds. Stay organised, stay tight to stay healthy and unmarked. Newcastle, Liverpool and Manchester weren't good places to forget your group strength.

But we could return a compliment with interest and the London Underground was a great place for a revenge ambush. August 19th, 1978, has gone down in history as an attack of Little Big Horn proportions. Five hundred hand-picked skinheads on High Street Kensington station and not a policeman in sight. When a train packed with Evertonians pulled in, Christmas came early. As the doors slid open the carnage started, guys running forward launching boots into bodies packed tight on the train. Clifford had removed a fire bucket from the wall and proceeded to throw the bucket of sand straight into the faces of the eyes-wide-open, petrified Scousers, then proceeded to flail the empty bucket at everybody standing in the train. One guy on the platform was kicking the sand, shouting, 'Here you are, Scouser, I'm kicking sand in your face!' after the famous bodybuilding advert which used to feature Charles Atlas. Someone had removed a towel holder from a pub toilet and was smashing people, shouting, 'Drag some out on to the platform.' Shouts of 'Kill the bastards!' were drowned out by the smash of glass as the windows went in. Then as quickly as it began, everybody went for the escalators to get out before the police arrived. Once outside we watched the police screech up in vans and sprint down the stairs. All they could do was survey the scene of abject people holding gashed head wounds, and the devastation we had wrought, then shake their heads.

Sometimes when the really hard-core North Standers walked along the pavement, the Shed boys shied away to one side. In the park at Cardiff it was ballistic. The Taffies were lobbing half of south Wales at Chelsea until the North Stand lads ripped out the park railings and charged. Metal to skull, crunch. Down went one Taffy. The Shed boy stood gawping at the prostrate body. Along sauntered another lad, in went the boot. Crack! A sharp, harsh sound. He hadn't stepped on a twig but smashed the jaw with one kick. He turned and smiled at the Shed boy.

'That's done his jaw. He won't sing in the Welsh choir for a few months.'

As he walked away laughing, the Shed boy vomited.

4

COUNTY COACHES

As time went by, I and the Tunbridge Wells lads became well known in and around the ground on first name or nickname terms. Big Lil, Groundsey, Clifford, Dominic, Viscount (Lindley), Garb, Boghead, Julian Wedgehead, Bimbo, Smithy, Wolvey, Matchstick and Mark the maladjusted Jock. I never met any firm at football who didn't have at least one maladjusted Jock among their ranks. They were good for business – four lagers and a couple of chasers and they would fight anybody. On the way we used to meet up with the Lewisham three, Rob, Leggit and Sebasta the Rasta. Finally there were the Bromley three, Glen, Stretch and Fat Harry.

People knew who you were and you knew them. They'd ask if you were going to the next away match in a rhetorical sort of way, assuming that you'd be there. Where's the meeting point next week? There sprang up a bush telegraph of what was happening and where. Early morning cafe meets where five or six hundred would show just on word of mouth. We were mates together. Getting nicked was seen as an occupational hazard. There was no honour in it if it was someone outside of your clique. As they were being dragged away, the shouts would go up.

'Do your bird.'

'See you in six months.'

But if one of your mates was in trouble then you were there. Our *esprit de corps* was as strong as anyone's, all united in our love of Chelsea and England.

Chelsea issued a blueprint for a brave new development. A futuristic ground which would enable us to become one of the truly big teams. Within four years the costs had escalated, the builders were experiencing problems and Chelsea had gone from the team with a bright future to the team with no future. The stars were sold, Hudson, Osgood, Webb. Nobody asked us what we thought. We were just loyal fans and we were expected to support the team whatever happened. The board could sell our team and ground from underneath us, yet all they ever did was moan if we got angry when our beloved team got beat. At the start of 1974–75, the season opened with Brian Mears proclaiming the start of a new era. Thirty thousand wondered what he meant as Carlisle beat us 2–0. At the end of that season it came down to one match, Spurs away. The tension as we did the long walk from Seven Sisters tube station was palpable. Confrontations with Spurs fans every step of the way, people running across the wide road, stopping traffic, running, shouting, Spurs retreating as we marched forward to our destiny. Then a terrible ignominy inside the ground as Spurs handed us the final humiliation, running us ragged across the terraces and on to the pitch before the match, then beating us 2–0 to seal our fate.

Life in the Second Division beckoned. No decent players and no money to buy them, therefore no future. Those were the days when some Chelsea fans were so optimistic they'd believe we'd get promotion even when it was mathematically impossible. When the dumb fools were faced with that reality they'd chant, 'Next year, next year,' like a hippie chanting 'Hare Krishna'. At the other extreme were those fans so cynical they thought a giant conspiracy was at work to get Chelsea relegated or bankrupt.

Memories of that glorious team of 1970 haunted the ground. The only salvation was the FA Cup. Every year we waited for our chance of glory. In 1976, Palace came down in the fifth round and 54,000 crammed into the Bridge. Outside it was chaos as thousands battled to get in. The police tried to shut the gates, but fans refused to let the turnstile operators get the boards across and jumped the metal turnstile to get in. Palace scored an early goal and Chelsea fans in the North Stand surged forward to punch the cheering Palace supporters. Gaps appeared while fans launched themselves at each other. When Palace scored a second, the police briefly lost control and it seemed as if the whole terrace was fighting. In a match of high tension, Chelsea came back from 2–0 down only to see Palace score a late winner to beat us 3–2. When, at the final whistle, their fans had the temerity to laugh at us, even guys like Jeff who avoided the violence led the charge that day, alongside the infamous kung-fu kicking Chelsea fan. Palace were goons. Anyone from that area who was anybody supported Chelsea, so the Palace fans got punched with real venom. The papers had a field day.

Three days later Chelsea, now out of the FA Cup, played Hull City in front of 10,000 fans. In the space of three days, the North Stand changed from a surging, seething mass of youthful anger to an empty windswept concrete beach of shattered dreams. All those Chelsea fans who had attended the Cup match had now found something better to do. It is no wonder that people watching football at these extremes were liable to explode into violence when things went wrong. It would be considered a health hazard in any other profession.

In 1978 we were returning from a match at Oldham and stopped at Birch Service Station. Across the other side of the motorway was the Leeds Service Crew. We met on the covered walkway 40 feet above the motorway. In the ensuing battle 50 panes of armoured glass got smashed. Among many others, I got arrested and didn't make bail. The trial, at Middleton Crown Court, lasted two and a half weeks. The judge started summing up on the Friday. As it was obvious that there was no case against me, and Chelsea were playing at Nottingham the next day, I requested bail and the judge granted it, but with a stern proviso: 'Don't return in a Black Maria.'

The next day the Chelsea fans invaded the Trent End at Forest and, not being able to resist a laugh, I was arrested in the fighting, but once again made bail just in time to get back to Middleton to receive a not guilty, then back to Nottingham for a small fine for threatening words and behaviour.

The youthful determination to be in the Shed two hours before kick-off gave way to an older cynical resolve to have one last drink before leaving the pub. For the hardened drinkers it became two with a spirit chaser. Departure became later and later as missing the first few minutes of the match was not deemed that important against another bucket of lager. Always, at the turnstiles, a massive crowd in front of you at ten to three yet miraculously you always seemed to get in and to your position dead on three o'clock.

And people wondered why we drank. God, things were so bad at Stamford Bridge that Mormons were driven to alcohol, Jehovah's Witnesses doubted the truth of Genesis and Cliff Richard swore. You'd sit during matches so bored that getting ejected became a sort of perverse pleasure. If we were bored, then I suppose the police were as well. Tell me that they didn't get some sort of kick out of throwing people out. Looking at their faces sometimes, I think some of them might have had a bit of a hard-on. Then Chelsea got half a team together and with the success came the returning lads, plus a season in the Second Division wasn't such a bad thing. New grounds to visit, different police superintendents to deal with. Lurking in the background for the club was the crippling financial worry of debt causing managers to come and go, yet still they wanted us to behave with dignity while they behaved with crass stupidity. Eddie McCreadie got Chelsea promoted in 1977 on a shoestring then got the sack.

Our antics in the Second Division incurred Government wrath. In April 1977 Chelsea fans were banned from attending away matches by the Minister of Sport, Denis Howell, and the matches were made all-ticket. At the next away game there were hundreds of Chelsea fans at the station. One dumb reporter asked why we were travelling and was met with the classic comment: 'You can't ban a Chelsea fan.' It became our anthem and some lads wore the saying proudly on badges and T-shirts to prove it. It culminated in a match on Saturday 7 May 1977 at Wolves where 3,000 banned Chelsea fans took over the whole home end.

In 1978–79 things got worse when they appointed the old Spurs man Danny Blanchflower as manager. By the time he left Chelsea were 20th in the Second Division. Life looked grim and people wondered why we wanted to punch the lights out of any bastard who mocked our predicament.

One day in the early seventies, a BBC Radio 1 disc jockey attended a match at Chelsea against Everton. Ed Stewart, nicknamed Stewpot, was an Everton fan who happened to be a famous media face with a girlfriend about 10 years his junior. As he walked under the East Stand towards the VIP entrance, he passed a small group of Shed Boys.

'Hello, Shitpot.'

He turned to face his tormentors with his trademark beaming smile, thinking it was a bit of banter.

'Turn again, Shitpot, we give cradle snatchers a kicking down here in London.'

He scurried away to the sanctuary of the VIP lounge.

Some lads graduated from the Shed to the North Stand – not the mythical old stand which had been demolished in the name of progress but now a big open terrace. As the away fans came out of Fulham Broadway station, the lads used to mingle in. Making out they were going into a shop then walking in the flow of the crowd, ones and twos with an inbuilt confidence, the archetypal flash Cockney that northerners loved to hate. Most of the away fans were terrified, it showed in their faces, so why not take liberties? Once inside, we smiled at them then went in and hung around at the right-hand corner next to the West Stand until just before kick-off. Sometimes we'd charge them, scattering them, giving them a few hairy stories to take back home.

In 1982 Chelsea drew Liverpool at home in the fifth round of the FA Cup. Thousands of Scousers would be down for this one. Some of the lads were fired up for a revenge mission because the Scousers had given Chelsea a particularly hard time at Liverpool in previous seasons, making the journey back to Lime Street station more nerve-racking than it deserved to be, then standing around at the bus stops and in the streets near the station really flexing their muscles. When the Chelsea lads in the North Stand turned their green bomber jackets inside out displaying the orange lining, the police thought they were stewards and let them in the Liverpool enclosure. Just before kick-off, the shout of 'Chelsea' went up and a huge charge was made with the Trojan Horse orange bombers in the thick of it. The police saw it as the Liverpool fans attacking the stewards and waded in, giving them a double dose of justice. The cameras snapped ten to the dozen as the charge was made. In the pandemonium, the orange bombers slipped away quietly. The press always made Liverpool out to be good, friendly fans whose greatest weapon was their rapier wit. Well, they weren't cracking too many Jimmy Tarbuck jokes that day, I can tell you.

Seeing the comments in the newspapers made everybody laugh. Even funnier was seeing someone you knew pulled out or arrested then pictured in the paper the next day. All the lads used to look upon getting arrested and fined as an occupational hazard. When the press stated – like they knew – that fines had no effect because everybody used to have a whipround before the match, we all thought they must be talking about some mythical group of fans from Mars. It was even reported once that some terrace terrors, because that's what we were to the rest of England, had a fine fund of thousands of pounds. It was laughable because, in reality, if you got fined you paid your own way. One of the lads even had a mock Latin expression, *Majestium Cocknius Excretius*, which he used to trot out at people in the pub when they came in and moaned that the magistrate had fined them and only allowed 28 days to pay. When asked what the hell that meant, he translated it as, 'The magistrate thinks you are a London shit.' Every time he uttered it everybody gave a hyena-type whoop.

The press said that fines were a deterrent, so up went the price of getting nicked. Soon the maximum fine for threatening words and behaviour was changed from £50 to £1,000. Not that it made much difference, it just upped the ante. Once, some northern planks were asked by a magistrate the best way for him to punish them. Instead of saying conditional discharge on good behaviour, five planks said, 'Fine me, sir.' So the beak did. Cop that fine, planks.

Huge fines also gave the police more power because an extra £1,000 made for an expensive day out. The days of great stories like Ipswich away were over. Ipswich away, 1974. Straight from the train into the station buffet. After six pints, staggering out of the station and whacking this goon who called me a horrible, thick Cockney. Wear this right-hander across the bridge of your nose, you turnip-eating bumpkin, you missed out the 'drunken'! In the police station booking area, with a ruddy-faced sergeant (his face looked like an over-ripe pumpkin) telling me that the local Ipswich magistrates took a very dim view of violent Cockney football fans: 'You Cockneys are all the same. Ignorant blighters with no respect for people outside London.' The following week I was fined £40 for fighting. Travelling up with me on the train for the same hearing was Bill the skinhead. His dastardly crime was singing 'Fuck 'em all' to the tune of 'Bless 'em all'. Bill received a £35 fine. Or the time some of the lads got into a fight in a pub in Newark on the way back from a match. The pub was so badly damaged that it had to shut down at 8pm on a Saturday evening. Four of them went to court and pleaded guilty. The magistrate fined them £25 each, despite the fact that the local paper had screamed out 'Jail These Thugs'. As they came out of the court, a local guy was bemoaning the fact that he'd been fined £200 for riding someone else's bicycle down the road for a drunken prank, then been accused of stealing the bike.

I suppose I wasn't really brain of Britain. After seeing a programme on New York graffiti artists on the subway I took a spray can up to Wolverhampton, where I sprayed 'Chelsea Sycopaths' on the wall. When it was pointed out to me that I had spelt it wrongly I decided to rectify it the following year if it was still there. I returned a year later to correct the spelling mistake. After all, it only required me to put in a P and an H and it would be OK. Just as I had finished spraying the P, a police car screeched to a halt and three of them jumped out as if I was an armed robber. Despite telling the magistrate that I was only correcting a spelling mistake on impulse so as not to corrupt the morals of the youth of Wolverhampton, I received a fine for criminal damage. No sense of humour.

Tattoos are the working man's way of expressing his identity in the same way that City types use pinstripe suits. Every Saturday somebody would come into the pub with their sleeves rolled up to show their latest artwork expressing their love for Chelsea. I never realised that there were so many bad artists masquerading as tattooists until I saw some of the offerings on legs, arms and torsos. The funniest was the dyslexic tattoo artist in Wimbledon who used to write Chelsae FC under the lion badge. Or the time he wrote a rhyme on one guy's back after the Muhammad Ali chant 'Float like a butterfly, Sting like a bee.' *Fly like a butterfly, float like a bee, that's whye the tough guys support Chelsae.* The rule of thumb was never have a Chelsea tattoo on your back from the Wimbledon dyslexic.

With the police power came more of them, combined with better organisation. Gradually they began to know who we were and they started weeding us out at Fulham Broadway station. At the gates they put on local bobbies who knew us. Sergeant Hobbs used to drag us out by the collar.

'Piss off Hickey, you ain't coming in here,' he would say with a wry smile. Then he'd walk down the line calling out first names: 'Eddie, Fitz, Gavin, OUT NOW!' Aw, shucks. Don't be such a spoilsport. When some of the away fans gave some banter out as the Chelsea fans were denied entry, others used to give them a little warning. 'Better shut up and go about your spectating quietly or we just might turn a blind eye about letting a few of the chaps in to speak to you personally.'

The hassle became too much so the lads en masse migrated to the West Stand seats. Gate 13 was now the place to be for the former North Stand chaps. First, it was still close to the North Stand, so the more unstable could hurl insults at those away fans who wanted some verbal exchanges. Also, the more superstitious among us saw 13 as an omen for better things to come. Soon it became the 'in' place – the Gate 13 club, an exclusive badge of honour. The thug's Garrick Club. You were judged on where you were in the pecking order by whereabouts you sat in the stand. Later some moved down to the benches below because Terry and the boys found it easier to play cards on the benches. Plus some didn't want to be a member of a club that everybody wanted to be a member of.

Around about the time that Gate 13 came to the fore, the leaflet craze began. There was always a leaflet telling people why they should be somewhere and why somebody should cop plenty the following week. At one match a Chelsea fan who'd been away working in Newcastle came in with their version: 'Geordies have become a joke for being soft. We want to start changing that at Chelsea. We need your help. We need 3,000 Newcastle fans to join the war against Chelsea.' Another time a Leeds Service Crew leaflet was passed around the pub. It berated their own fans for showing cowardice, then told how the Service Crew were the hardest in the land. Jeff looked at it and remarked that whoever wrote it had missed a lot of schooling. *Richard III* it definitely was not. But my favourite ever leaflet was the one done by Chelsea when it was decided to go into the Stretford End: 'Chelsea v Munich United at Old Munich. Not to be missed. All-ticket at the Chelsea end so queue in an orderly fashion only at the Munich end. All the best, lads, and good luck on our most important mission ever.'

West Ham at home. Perhaps there is something about living in Essex which makes them have to be the toughest. All those unsmiling

Essex boys walking out of the station. What have they got, bromide in their tea? There was always plenty going on when Chelsea played West Ham. For the match on 15 September 1984, leaflets were distributed telling everybody to meet at the King's Head at 11.30am. While the Chelsea lads stood around Fulham Broadway station scanning the crowds as they departed the tube station, waiting for their main faces, the news came back that the unforgiven had done their party piece. Walking from Parsons Green they had gone into Gate 13 at around 2pm. Then slowly and deliberately walked along the lines of seats, making all the Chelsea fans present scatter for it. What a right crew they'd caught: George and Mildred reading their programmes. What sort of fool gets to the ground an hour before kick-off? But when you need to stand at the top of a stand like a posing peacock, it's better to do it when nobody is there to oppose you. Bill Gardner, Swallow and the rest of the West Ham faces pretending they were contestants in a Mr Universe contest.

The fools telephoned me and everybody else they knew as a Chelsea face every Friday for the next month after that and left messages on the ansaphones: 'Gate 13, Hickey. Unlucky for some. See you down Upton Park later in the season, if you can find your way there. It is across the river. That's the Thames, you lush. Don't get dizzy thinking about it. Chelsea, hard? QPR are harder than you lot. No, that's a bit rich. Crystal Palace are harder than you lot, and that might be a bit of an exaggeration. Oh, and by the way, make sure you check out who does your leaflet printing next time.' Sometimes they'd go on until the tape was full. I found it funny, even if some of the guys used to get uptight about it. I can't speak for the grimacing ones. Another time they were playing a midweek match at Fulham while Chelsea were at home to someone else, so they caught the train to Fulham Broadway and walked up the middle of the road asking different fans if they recognised them.

'Recognise me, boys? It's Swallow. That's Bill and there's Cass. Real Men. West Ham. Top Dogs. Tell your friends you met West Ham at Chelsea.' Then they'd disappeared into the night, scarlet pimpernels every one. Eventually they were asked to appear on a TV documentary about football hooligans. All of them on show in a tube train banging the windows shouting, 'Kiddies, kiddies,' at the Chelsea fans trying to get at them on the way to the match at West Ham. The two famous TV documentaries on hooliganism featured the West Ham ICF and Under-Fives gang and Millwall with their F-Troop, Halfway Liners and Treatment boys. 'Of course I love my mum,' one of them stated. Pretty pathetic, really, especially when they went away and the police now had pictures of them all so they couldn't get a drink in any pub.

Luton away. The balmy night in the seventies that Chelsea went there and smashed the centre of the town up so badly the local council thought about declaring it a disaster zone. On the train coming back, some lads set fire to the train. When a train is travelling at 70 mph the extra oxygen fuels the flames. The train screeched to a halt somewhere in North London. It was lucky that the power cables were overhead lines because people were leaping on to the track. After the fire was put out the train continued, so the lads set it alight again. As it pulled into Kings Cross, fire crews and news teams were thronging around. Vince walked along the platform. Going the other way were fire crews. A TV journalist stuck a microphone under his nose at the precise moment that five firemen sprinted past him with a hose.

'What do you think about this terrible fire?'

'What fire?' replied Vince. Precisely what fire? What problem?

For London away matches, meeting at a pre-determined point was the order of the day, with the bush telegraph the medium. Tottenham was a favourite away match, with the long walk down to White Hart Lane from Seven Sisters, the streets full of litter. Tumbleweed connection, Jeff called it. It reminded him of an American old West ghost town with extra fast-food outlets thrown in for good measure. The Spurs fans never seemed to be around before the match as supporters ambled the two miles down Seven Sisters Road. Instead they used to wait around the railway station nearer the ground. So one year the word went out for Chelsea to meet at Liverpool Street and take the overground train up there. The efficiency of word of mouth was never exhibited so forcefully. Watching 3,000 guys trying to look inconspicuous to avoid police attention so they could get on the train unnoticed then rumble the Spurs at White Hart Lane station was hilarious. Eventually the train left with more police than fans on. Terry, in his wisdom, went with a small firm of around 20 and got chased as he came off the train, while 3,000 Chelsea chased shadows around the streets with half the Metropolitan Police, along with helicopters, shadowing them.

For Charlton away the meeting point was Waterloo station's main concourse, then across the bridge to Waterloo East for the train to Charlton. One evening the train was happily trundling along when someone in the carriage announced that the train would be travelling through Millwall country and they would have a reception committee waiting for us at every station. With that, someone appeared with an axe from the goods carriage and started chopping out the side of the train. As the train pulled through various stations in south London, the sound of Chelsea was mixed with that of various bits of debris crashing on to the platforms. By the time the train pulled into Charlton there was no need to open the door of our carriage – you just had to step off through the gap where the carriage walls once were.

It didn't matter where you went, there was always some station en route where the locals were waiting with a mob ready for an ambush. Crewe was a junction station, synonymous with railway history, yet famous in London for being the place where many a Cockney had met his Scouse nemesis. Travelling north in 1973, the word went down the train that the Scousers would be out in force. As the train pulled in to Crewe, a huge mob was spotted at the far end of the station. Hundreds of Chelsea spilled off, running down the platform to shouts of 'Do The Scousers'. The mob at the far end scattered across the tracks. Once I got there, before me was the alarming sight of petrified train spotters, resplendent in anoraks and cameras, running here and there dodging punches while their notebooks flew into the air. Those who weren't punching were too busy laughing at the mayhem.

Every train carriage had its own different types of resident fan. Women pests, those guys who'd down a couple of lagers then think that they were God's gift to the opposite sex and regale us with their sexual exploits. Bullshit Billies, those who never, ever ran and were always in the thick of the action going on until someone patted them on the shoulder: 'You've been watching too much television, mate.' Card freaks, who'd lose a week's wages between Euston and Leicester. Compulsive liars, who'd done it all and seen it all. Guys who'd slip away at the first whiff of trouble. Storytellers. Hardened drinkers, vodka and orange or sherry by the gallon even at 8am. Victor Vomit merchants who'd do half a bottle of some dodgy liqueur by Kentish Town (five minutes out) then be chucking up out of the window by Watford Junction (fifteen minutes) – their mates hanging out of the window mockingly apologising to the horrified people on the platform for their mate leaving his breakfast for their perusal – then spend the rest of the journey staggering down the carriage being told to take their noxious breath somewhere else. Then the compulsory lunatics who used to sit and brood alone with their Special Brew or in small groups, because normal people knew that they had some other agenda apart from supporting Chelsea and perhaps getting in a punch-up. Perhaps they had a score to settle over something that had happened the previous season. They might have been ambushed while walking out of the station and now they were a revenge crew. Once, one guy went to Liverpool for three seasons and waited with his four mates near a fish and chip shop for the guy who had done his mate bad. Never did find the Scouser, though. 'Today's the day,' he used to say while the four of them played cards. Nobody ever found out if he eventually satisfied his vendetta. I never asked, that's for sure.

All this in a marvellous drink-induced haze. I never met anybody who didn't enjoy a match better after six cans of lager on a train rattling through England's green and pleasant land. Coming home where most people seemed to sleep and listening to the stories: 'Sure I was scared,' and 'I thought I was a goner.' However, some of the nutty boys used to get fired up and start smashing up trains, so British Rail suddenly discovered a bylaw dating from the last century which meant that they could designate trains dry. Football without alcohol, it's like cars without petrol. Some days, trains leaving London were dryer than the Sahara from 6am till 2pm. That was no good. No drink, no go. It all came to a head when Doddy told the assembled carriage that he was planning to organise a coach for the next away match. Doddy's last famous away day was a pub day trip to France when he and the local drunkard returned three days later minus the old boy's false teeth and shoes. The last coach he'd organised was to Goodwood races. The lads had gone to Goodwood then sneaked into Butlins at Bognor Regis, come second in the world's worst singing competition, then proceeded to punch it up with the Butlins bouncers and spent the night in the cells before a court appearance to be bound over for a year. 'I'm gonna bring some fun back into the travel business,' exclaimed Doddy to the carriage.

The problem with Doddy was that he couldn't organise a trip to the loo, and as I had always fancied myself as a bit of an organiser, the idea of County Coaches was born. Why travel up to London at the crack of dawn to be met by officious British Rail posters telling you that under bylaw 16 1860 the following trains will be dry (i.e. every train travelling and returning from the town Chelsea were playing in). On trains which always seemed to break down in some obscure siding where you'd wait for hours until an hour before kick-off, before arriving at the local station where they held you in a locked, caged pen and then marched you to the ground while the locals stared at you like you were from another planet. Even skipping out for a burger or a drink of cola was deemed an arrestable offence. Later, after the match, they would keep you locked in the ground, march you back to the station and get the train moving. Nine times out of ten the local idiots would brick the train about 200 yards out of the station and miraculously no police would be around. On a cold day the draught would drive you to distraction. That, plus the fact that the buffet cars were removed from the specials, meant travelling started to resemble a walking week in the Arctic with Captain Scott. Yes, even a coach organised by Doddy which was doomed never to come back until at least a day late after a night in the cells sounded good faced with that scenario.

In the early days I wasn't sure about how to get 50 guys on board. I booked the first coach on spec without getting any deposits. It was away at Wolves in the '77 season. My 45-seater turned up at Tunbridge Wells at 10.30pm on Friday evening. By the time it left Lewisham around 1.30am I had 76 paying bodies, over 40 fully paid-for beer bellies and, I estimated, over 1,000 cans of beer on board. It arrived in Wolverhampton at 6am the next morning after six kebab stops and 25 toilet stops. Seeing 70 guys peeing on a verge to a green-yellow cornfield backdrop in the cool morning air was a strange sight.

'I wonder what Monet would have made of that?' was Jeff's thought of the day. When he was asked what firm Monet ran with by a rather less worldly sort of guy, he smiled, stated the artist's mob then went back to his book.

While I was in profit, it needed better organisation to ensure that only 50 got on board. It sounded straightforward but those who said they would turn up never did, while others often turned up on spec. However, once the method of pay on order was implemented it became easy. Of course, there were regular faces on the coaches, but many of the lads liked to vary their travelling, sometimes going on the regular trains even though it was more expensive. When Persil started a scheme that gave free rail travel for one person travelling with another, the currency of exchange in and around London pubs became washing powder coupons. That was how the West Ham

Inter City Firm got started. We nicknamed them the Persil gang because all we ever saw them do was travel on the Persil.

The method of filling up a coach was to go around the pubs from 1pm at the home match and tell everybody what time next week's coach was leaving and where it was stopping. It used to set out from Tunbridge Wells and stop at Tonbridge, Bromley South, Lewisham, Elephant & Castle, Chelsea Shed entrance and finally Kilburn High Street. At that time we used to flit between the Swan and the King's Head. There were people in there who you knew on first-name terms but never their surname. So people were known by their first name and where they came from. Glen Bromley and his firm (six), so he gave you £30 then was responsible for collecting the money from his lads; Sebasta the Rasta Lewisham (eight); Freddie E & C (dozen); Kenny Shed (four), etc. Half the time I didn't know the rest but I knew these people, we all had history with them, so we allowed them to vouch for their credibility. When someone different turned up, other people within the group always asked questions about them. We knew anybody who was dodgy because they stuck out like a sore thumb. Once a tabloid journalist tried to come on one of our trips in an undercover role. He was walking around the pub asking about Hickey's or Del's coach – a dumb tourist the muggers look out for at Miami Greyhound station. We took his fiver with a smile, spent it on beer and told him to turn up next week with a 24-pack, but when he arrived looking as thuggish as he could the boys emptied a few cans of his own beer over his head, nicked the rest he had with him and threatened to tie him to a lamp post with his trousers down by his ankles if he didn't go away.

County Coaches was a small private coach company run by Robin. Most of his work was midweek contract work transporting schoolchildren, so when I approached him he was pleased to be getting some weekend work. I told him the sort of people we would be transporting and he laid out his tariff. He wouldn't allow any alcohol on the coach and he wouldn't allow any drugs. He was also appalled by the huge number of toilet stops which he was having to make. Having 50 guys standing by the side of the motorway taking a pee was a surefire way to attract police attention, so Robin installed an in-coach toilet: a mop bucket on the floor next to the door. That way people could piss while the coach sped to its destination. The first time Wedgehead, who was always immaculately dressed, travelled with us, he walked to the front of the coach.

'What time is the next toilet stop?'

'No stops today, Wedge. There's your toilet,' I said, pointing to the mop bucket. He looked at me horrified.

'I cannot slash in that bucket while we are speeding along at 60mph. I might piss on my shoes. You are looking at £80 Italian shoes there, Hickey. I am a suave and sophisticated geezer.'

'Not on this bloody coach, you ain't,' interjected Boghead, an ex-army tramp. When the bucket needed emptying in the late summer and early spring months, woe betide any soft top car with the roof down that we overtook.

Robin always had a smile for everybody and all the lads were well-behaved. He used to drop us off in the town where Chelsea were playing two hours before kick-off and arrange to pick us up at a pre-determined point about an hour after the match finished. He'd then drop us off at a pub and wait until chucking out time, then drive us back into London. While the police stopped coaches going into city centres, our coach used to sail through to find a convenient watering hole. After all, we were not horrible football fans supporting Chelsea. No, our flag proudly announced that we were the Old Roebuckonions Rugby Football Club (the Roebuck was a pub in Tunbridge Wells). Gentlemen in a thug's game, not the thugs of popular myth. A publican actually said that to me once, when we pulled into his pub car park in Northampton: 'Oh yes, you rugger buggers are great fun, you just drink bitter and throw up outside my pub whereas those Manchester United fans are a real menace. They eat three pies, swill back three pints of lager, rush outside to throw up then come back in and order more lager.'

'Fifty pints of lager please, landlord. And have you got any pies, plus a glue-bag of Evo stick for Clifford?'

The coach would get back to London on the next morning, usually a Sunday, in time for the first train of the morning for those lads on the London drop-off. For those of us who lived in Kent there was no hassle and it was all stopping points from Tunbridge Wells to Chelsea. The coach became a way of life. Everybody became a Man Without Girlfriend, an MWG. After all, who wanted someone on the coach who was always looking at their watch wondering what time they would be home?

In April 1982, Ken Bates purchased Chelsea. Legend has it that he paid £1 in cash then took on the debt. From day one he stamped his authority on the club. After a couple of home matches, one of the stewards approached Ginger Terry and said that the hierarchy wanted to speak to him. After the match he was met by Ken Bates himself.

'I've heard you and your mates organise coaches. Well, I just want to let you know that I run this club now and everything that moves here is organised by me. This club has been neglected for too long.'

It was a friendly speech. By the end of the season, Ken's problems were excerbated as the Mears family sold their shareholding to Marler Estates, whose business was property development. Stamford Bridge looked like being turned into a yuppie housing estate.

Early season 1983–84, and a Leicester away day. The coach turned up with a spare driver. Robin had assured me that his replacement was very sound. What we got was Big John, who looked like a throwback to the late 1960s with his high leg DMs, bleached jeans and black harrington jacket. Nobody had the heart to tell him that he was a little behind in the fashions. John's vocabulary suggested he had just escaped from a mental institution.

'You're the top boys, aren't you? Billy Whizzers?' he kept asking.

'Mum's the word,' whispered Wedgehead, holding his right index finger to his lip.

'Yeah, sure. I see. You can rely on me. Mum's the word. Yee-ha.' All John needed was a cowboy hat to be Clint Eastwood. As the coach sped north, he was turning around while negotiating tricky overtaking manoeuvres. 'Who's got some amyl nitrate? I need a sniff.' With one hand John held the wheel, with the other he sniffed up the amyl. It soon became obvious that he had preconceptions about what was going to happen as he got quite animated about the forthcoming day's events. 'What time will the first aggro be?' he kept asking, almost as if this event was pre-ordained.

Boghead used to sit right at the front of the coach. He theatrically announced that today's driver was John, Big Bad John, sang a couple of lines of the old song of that name, then proceeded to add high octane fuel to the massive misapprehension fire that was burning in poor John's vivid imagination, filling his head with more stories than he could cope with.

'The aggro at Watford Gap services has to be seen to be believed.'

'Really?' asked John with open eyes. 'Top dollar, lads.'

'Yeah, every Saturday. Geezers raging pitched battles across the car parks. Mental.'

This went on for two hours until John saw the exit sign for Watford Gap. 'Tally ho, Big John the emperor now,' shouted Big John and gunned the poor County Coach into the car park.

'Pull it up in the corner,' I told him. John was having none of it. He screeched to a halt right by the steps which went over the motorway. By chance, across the other side were three coach loads of fans going the other way: Wolves, the Black Country crew. I only ever saw them as dumb Brummies. Now the Black Country crew were about to get black eyes. John was up and out of the seat with a huge lump of wood in his hand, charging at the Wolves fans. I don't blame them for running because we would have all done the same if confronted with John Rambo, the highly unstable terminator. Some of the lads were laughing so much that they couldn't stand up. By the time

John returned he was red-faced with exhaustion, but he reckoned that this was the high life.

'This is really living, boys.'

Once in Leicester, we explained to John that we needed collecting in the centre of town at 6pm. Leicester was long streets of cobbles and front doors that came right to the edge of the pavements. The least number of front gardens in England was how we saw it. All those narrow roads made for a great echo when you marched and sang. Leicester were disliked by all the London fans.

> *We hate Nottingham Forest*
> *We hate Liverpool*
> *We hate Manchester United*

'*And Leicester*,' all the London fans sang. They were sneaky. Never a mob of them until 20 of you got detached in some back street with dirty net curtains and pastel-coloured front doors. Never trust anybody who lives in a house with dirty net curtains. Suddenly half of Leicester was charging after you. Do you turn left or right? Christ, every street looks the same! The echo of hundreds of feet on cobbles focuses the mind like nothing else. The greatest feeling in the world when you finally stop running and look behind and the pursuers are not there. Yogi once started running at Leicester and rumour had it that he didn't stop running till Coventry, almost running back to London. Seeing his red trousers disappear into the distance will live in my memory forever.

After the match we arrived in the town at our spot to find an almighty rumpus going on, with people running across cars and horses breaking up fighting groups. John made his theatrical entrance by driving the coach straight into a mob of Leicester fans and jumping out with the shout, 'Follow me, boys, we'll soon have this lot licked.' The police even stopped in their tracks, then grabbed John, who went for his driver's badge to identify himself. The police thought it was a knife and battered him to the ground then nicked him. As we boarded the coach a senior officer shouted and screamed.

'Get on this coach and get your driver to get it out of here immediately!'

'We can't,' I said, holding my palms open to indicate frustration. 'Why?'

'Because you've just nicked him.'

'Well, we'll see about that.'

With that, he walked across to the van where they were holding John and grabbed him out the back by the back of his collar.

'You disgusting type, get on that coach and get driving.'

John looked quite sheepish now, what with the effects of too much adrenaline and amyl nitrate taking its toll. Over he was frogmarched while the lads chanted the funeral march in quick time, giving a loud 'Ole' as John was propelled into the front seat by the fuming senior police officer.

'Get in that seat and drive this coach away and if I ever see you in Leicester again, I will personally string you up.'

John never said a word on the return journey, became Little John and never drove us again, even though the lads asked for him continuously after that. Robin did ask me what had happened to make John swear he would never drive Chelsea fans for County again, but I just shrugged my shoulders.

When video recorders came out, Robin installed one in the coach. Some of the lads thought it was a great wheeze to show porno films on the coach. The funniest part was when cars used to overtake us on the motorway then nearly crash when they looked up and saw what the screen was showing.

Going through the night meant pills for some – white ones, orange ones, green ones. Some of the boys were wizzers, speed freaks, able to stay up all weekend gibbering away; others were acid boys, drifting into a haze and letting the joys of the countryside blur into a mass of wonderful colours. Dope smokers on the back seats, the sweet smell drifting forward helping everybody to sleep. I often wondered what Jeff's industrial vision looked like through acid eyes, but drugs were never my thing.

Then you had the beer monsters supreme, usually falling asleep around 3am, dropping their cans so the drinks sloshed down the front, making sure that nobody took their shoes off to get more comfortable. Sometimes the only sound on the coach was one or two gibbering away against a backdrop of drunken snoring and cans rolling underneath the seats. Sometimes the laughter and banter was so good that you never slept all night and arrived in the morning wrecked, causing some to fall asleep during the match. Guys waking up to see dawn, cursing, then falling back to sleep again. Wicked practical jokes being played on sleeping friends, shoelaces tied together, stickers proclaiming their sexual inadequacies stuck on their backs. Mostly, though, sleep was the drink-induced kind where people woke up with stiff-necked hangovers from where they had slept at the wrong angle, foul breath, mouths tasting like they had chewed an ashtray full of dog ends in their sleep. Moving their cricked necks from side to side, vowing never to travel on such a poxy coach again, then being there at the next away game.

You had to be pathological to find glamour in Liverpool, but Jeff did. Glamour in the docks where England made its money selling black slaves to America. Leicester had dirty net curtains while Liverpool had no-curtain houses and empty houses with smashed windows. Street after street of them, gardens full of litter – even the rats had moved on. Jeff asked Robin to make a detour around Toxteth, where some of the black faces were the direct descendants of those slaves. All we saw was graffiti and desolation of the human spirit, epitomised by people waiting around shuttered derelict and burnt shops to sell or score drugs. Robin gave the coach extra revs at the lights because it looked and smelt bad. Jeff thought it educational and interesting because he saw glamour everywhere. The twit called West Ham the Bow Peninsula. Every ground reflected an industrial heritage, it was never-ending: the Docklands railway labyrinth, the

Manchester Ship Canal, railway viaducts, Brunel's railway, Crewe station. Birmingham's derelict factories were a poignant reminder of the glory days of British manufacturing. Spaghetti Junction was a marvel of organisation where he got glazed eyes when he saw the floodlight pylons of Villa Park.

'Ah, a ground built with distinctive local red clay brick.'

'Great, that is, until one of them hits you on the side of the head.'

The sudden jolt of excruciating pain, then pure terror, the blood coming down the front of your face into your eyes making you blind, or into your mouth making you choke. On your knees retching against the taste of the blood, reaching up and touching your skull to make sure it's still intact, clawing desperately in front, blubbering, not knowing whether you're going to be kicked because you're blind and grovelling, then head down in the gutter vomiting some evil pink stuff. People turning away at the sight.

'Yeah, real bloody romantic that, Jeff.'

That was the reality. You could be in the most fearsome mob, in the most protected company, yet you were only one half brick away from pure terror.

5

WALSHY & EDNA

Different pubs and changing ambience meant different lads. The Snot crew (they would clap rhythmically then shout 'Snot!') would frequent the Gunter Arms, while the Fulham crew preferred the King's Head. I liked the King's Head because the landlord would put on obscure bands covering varying types of music. When Chelsea played a midweek match, there was often a good chance to listen to some good live bands. The Swan became a popular meeting place, so people would arrange to go there first before dispersing to different pubs because the Swan got so packed out. Sometimes in the warmer late summer or spring months, people used to congregate outside on the pavement or just around the corner. When the away fans arrived at Fulham Broadway, the police used to clear the pavement. If they'd set an alarm off in the bar they couldn't have announced it any better. Coaches pulling up at the traffic lights outside, faces at the windows, jumping up at the windows, banging on the glass. In the safety of the coach, fans used to stick up two fingers. This used to raise the decibel level in the pub even higher.

The police used to target the Swan like it was the centre of operations for the more violent Chelsea tendencies, but nothing could have been further from the truth. One day, three over-weight Newcastle fans, resplendent in their colours, stood in the doorway.

'Come on, Chelsea!' shouted one fat Geordie.

'Yeah, come on! You lot think you're hard. You're nothing but a bunch of southern poofs.'

Everybody stood open-mouthed as their bellies shut out most of the doorway. A Chelsea fan standing near the door looked at them impassively. He was eating a burger. He threw a piece of the meat at him.

'Here you are, fat boy. You obviously haven't eaten for five minutes. You must be getting hungry.'

The Geordie laughed: 'Is that the best you can do? I'll tell you something, if you lot came near our pub, The Strawberry, you'd learn a lesson about what it is to be hard.'

Then they waddled off as only those asked to carry excessive midriffs do.

Micky Greenaway was a well-known face in and around Chelsea. Once upon a time he'd been our hero when he was the Zigger Man of the Shed and we were impressionable 16-year-olds. Now that we had grown a little older, Micky seemed old before his time with his stories of the late sixties. He was that old he claimed to remember the 1955 League Championship team. Micky was everybody's favourite brother who is still living at home with his mum. He was always around and good drinking company as long as you were prepared to listen to the story about how he drank the three days away in Athens in 1971 with Osgood, Hutchinson and the rest of the team between Chelsea drawing 2–2 with Real Madrid and winning the replay 2–1. It was a great story the first time. Forty times later, I felt like I'd been there with him.

The local Chelsea lads used to drink in the Rose, a small pub off the main drag near the Imperial, Wheatsheaf and Palmerston. It was their local so they became quite protective about those who drank in there. Every so often a pub became fashionable and everybody would make a beeline for it, making a pre-match drink an audition as a bit player in a *Gandhi* crowd scene. Getting to the bar became impossible. When the Rose became the 'in' haunt, the local Chelsea boys moaned a lot about poseurs and interlopers and longed for the day when the Rose dropped out of fashion.

Later, the landlord of the Black Bull started letting the lads go straight into the upstairs bar immediately after the match. Those were the days of Saturday afternoon shutting so the pub was not officially supposed to open before 5.30pm, but the side door did brisk business between the end of the match and official opening time. Also, for Sunday matches the lads used to meet in the pub around 11 o'clock on Saturday evening and stay in there till around 4am or 5am when the coach used to set off. It meant that the lads would arrive somewhere for a drink dead on 12 o'clock on Sunday. Of course, if you were Toomsy and the rest of the beer monsters, the drink wouldn't stop for English licensing hours because that's what off-licences and tins were designed for. Twelve hours was considered a good serious session by Toomsy. For other normal people it was nothing less than life-threatening.

My life was close to the edge. I had just started my courier business yet still had to keep my evening driving job going. My pal Robbie Montgomery, the comedian, had lost his licence and needed a driver for himself and two girls on the south London and Kent pub stripper circuit. Upstairs in a smoke-filled room of a dingy pub, where the paint had long since turned into the ubiquitous sickly brown nicotine colour and the comedian worked without a stage on a beer-stained floor being heckled by up to 100 wannabe comedians who thought that they were funny after ten pints of lager – eight down their throats two down their fronts. The comedian's favourite jibe was: 'I bet your dad wished he'd come all over the sheets when he saw you.' If the person dared to come back at him, he'd say: 'Sorry, mate, he did come over the sheets but the ugly milkman didn't.' Once in Orpington a dad got really angry because I think his son really was the milkman's.

There was always some drunken idiot ready to get up to take a swing, so I also acted as a minder. However, some of the places I went to gave my heart palpitations, especially the night I picked up Robbie and he informed me, matter of factly, that his gig was at Millwall Football Club. It was only a week before that I had been on the terraces battling away with the bellies. As we walked in, two well-known Millwall faces walked over to me.

'Hello, Hickey, bit out of your jurisdiction. You must be looking to get yourself a slap, big time.'

'Come on, lads, I'm working. Plus, if you give me a good hiding, the comedian and strippers go home early. No tits for all you Millwall boys tonight.'

'Another time, eh Hickey?' said one of them, then slapped me hard twice across the side of the face, with a dig in the ribs thrown in for good measure, just to let me know that they could have if they wanted to but realised that the game they were playing was just for fun, for another day, and it could wait. Not that the games that were played between Millwall and West Ham were fun. While they used to telephone me to hurl abuse, they used to phone each other for London Bridge Saturday 6am knife fights or load up a Transit van and cruise across to each other's manors and have a tear-up with coshes and baseball bats. Between Millwall and West Ham was the River Thames. It was a physical barrier which represented the two extremes.

West Ham took themselves far too seriously. My one rule with Robbie was that I wouldn't do dodgy pubs north of the river and east of the River Lee. One night I allowed him to talk me into it because the pub was in Epping and it was worth an extra tenner.

I have never felt so intimidated in my life. I sat with a cosh inside my coat all night as well as a canister of CS gas, ready to fight and run at any moment as lads half-leered, half-glared at me for the whole three hours I was there. For good measure, someone smashed the windows out of the car just before we left. Very West Ham, that.

I went downstairs at one stage and a young woman in her twenties approached me.

'You're that Hickey, aren't you?'

'No,' I replied.

'Well, I reckon you are and I'd like to go outside round the back with you.'

I thought she meant to fight but she wanted sex standing up with Chelsea's main face. I was petrified. There were Chelsea lads who probably would have taken her on, but I wasn't one of them.

Walshy was a nutter, a complete screwball. Life had made him cynical beyond the need for Battersea survival. He used to live in a block of flats where the graffiti read: 'Double Green Shield stamps for niggers stabbed on a Tuesday, triple stamps for a Thursday' (when Walshy repeated the triple part, he sniggered). Many of the lads travelling on the coach weren't old enough to remember Green Shield stamps but they knew all about that graffiti, because Walshy had told them. Whatever those West Ham or Millwall fruitcakes were planning, Walshy always wanted to be one step ahead.

'Let's get down to Stratford and rumble those West Ham goons in that Moonlights place when they get back around 7pm,' he used to enthuse after a Chelsea home match, just as everybody was settling down for a quiet early evening drink in the Black Bull. He used to go in the pub and talk about ambushes and the military strategy required to execute the perfect plan. At one time he even thought about changing his name by deed poll to 'Hannibal' Walsh, after the man he called the greatest military commander who ever lived.

'Piss off, Walshy, you'll be known as the Elephant Man,' remarked Jeff. After Jeff explained about Hannibal, elephants and the Alps, Walshy went off that idea. He had a violent thought roughly every two minutes. It usually involved someone getting their face staved in.

'What do you think about that idea, eh? Brilliant or what?' he'd shout at you, five inches from your nose.

'Great idea, Walshy, count me in next time,' you'd stutter, while wiping away the spittle he'd deposited on your face.

As far as Walshy was concerned, East Enders were among the

most vile people on earth. 'Hitler didn't drop enough bombs on that part of London,' was one of his favourite sayings. Walshy loved his mates but in reality he made you slightly nervous because of his unpredictability. Once at Newcastle, Walshy and three others had been chased into a dead end street. As the Newcastle lads advanced on him, he pulled out a flare gun and fired it right into them. The sight of the flash and sparks was incredible.

'Aargh! Aargh!' shouted the Geordies in pure terror. 'A shooter. The Cockney's got a shooter.'

'As the bastards ran, I fired one right up the Geordie's jacksy. He went up that road like an Olympic class firecracker on legs,' laughed Walshy.

Walshy had been incensed by the story about the fat Geordies in the Swan. At the next home match he walked into the pub and remonstrated with everybody.

'Why didn't somebody chin the fat bastards?'

Nobody answered except one guy. 'Why bother? All they ever do is bitch about the beer in London.'

'Why bother? Why bother, you wanker?' screamed Walshy. 'Because they're Geordies and they're game. When we go up there, they want it big time and letting them come in here without doing them will mean that they will try and take liberties when we next go up there. They reckon they're a tasty hard firm who can have it.'

The fact of the matter was that it was all over in 20 seconds and only about six people were standing by the door. The noise was so great that nobody realised what had happened. But Walshy walked around the pub with his gang asking if they were down at the door, then demanding that they agree to get their arses up to Newcastle later in the season.

Walshy wanted a big event up there and he'd really organised it. One of the lads who drove a lorry in the north east had got a pub in Sunderland to open early and the lads had travelled in to Newcastle via the Metro. On the train in small groups, no scarves.

'Yes,' mumbled Walshy on the train, 'you fat Geordie bastards, you're gonna see how much bottle we've got today. His target was the Strawberry pub.

'Right, you lot, this ain't gonna be a tea party, this is the main event. The fuckin' windows go first, then we do any bastard who dares to come out of that door. We stand there until we hear the sirens and then we move out sharpish. Does everybody understand?'

Walshy had done his speech and without waiting for any replies he led the 60-strong mob over the brow of the hill at fast walking pace. Here to do a job of work. Into sight came the Strawberry. Outside, milling around chatting and laughing stood a small group of Geordies. As they saw the lads come down the road, they instinctively knew what was approaching. A shout of 'Chelsea' saw them scatter at speed, a couple of them shooting into the pub to alert those inside to the danger. It was ten past two and not a copper in sight.

Without breaking stride, Walshy picked up a road sign then broke into a short canter to gain momentum and hurled it through the front window. Shouts of startled people inside filled the air before the bricks went through, thrown with a venom which made the glass really smash. Then the bricks went through the holes of the smashed windows, thudding into flesh and bone. People ran forward and pitched stones in with all the force they could muster. Within seconds, not a pane of whole glass remained. All that was left were the frames; some of the wood had split. Cowering up against the bar were the Newcastle fans, all wearing scarves like black-and-white decorated Maypoles.

'Come on, then! Come out and have it, you sludge!'

'You're just wankers. No work, no bottle, nothing. You've got nothing!' screamed Walshy. Another brick was lobbed. A body could be seen crashing to the floor as the brick hit him.

'Now you've got no windows in your pub, either,' chipped in someone else.

To a man they all stood there petrified while everybody stood outside. Outside in the road people were up on their toes, twitching, half dancing, moving their arms and shoulders, almost sparring. Higher than kites. No drugs, just pure excitement caused by expectation. Then sirens in the distance caused rapid dispersal, with everybody laughing at the planning and cheek of the attack on their pub.

One day Chelsea were playing away at Blackburn and Spurs were playing down at Fulham, so I thought that there might be a little bit of fun going on at Chelsea. 'Four thousand holes in Blackburn, Lancashire,' sang the Beatles. Well, if Blackburn ever fell into one they'd be doing me a great favour. When that guy wrote about England's dark satanic mills in 'Jerusalem' he was describing Blackburn. Even though the cotton mills are gone, the soot and grime have remained. I hated Blackburn, so meeting the boys for a drink seemed infinitely more appealing. I walked into the King's Head and everybody was crying. Suddenly my eyes started to water. I looked over and saw the reason why. Walshy had a line of around 20 Jif lemons lined up and was attempting to pour an ammonia-based solution into each one. Unfortunately, he was spilling most of it.

'Stop crying, you wankers. I saw this being done on a film the other evening,' he protested. Eventually Walshy managed to get the ammonia into the lemons, then explained his tactics.

'Ambush time. Tottenham are playing Fulham today and they will be bound to get off at Putney Bridge and drink up on the Fulham Road or over Putney Bridge. You know what those poseurs are like, they are bound to want to walk back across Putney Bridge so that everybody can spot them. What we do is put two geezers on the platform while we wait upstairs. As soon as the train pulls in and they spot them, they run up the stairs and we splatter them as they leave the station.'

Walshy dished out the ammonia in the lemons and everybody departed to Putney Bridge station, waiting either in the park opposite or further along at a bus stop by the bridge. No police anywhere, but after waiting for some time people got bored, threw away their lemons and retired to the pub on the corner for a drink. At around 1pm, the shout went up and around 60 seconds later the Tottenham boys emerged onto Putney Bridge Road. They were dressed in the best-looking tracksuits you've ever seen: Tacchini, Ellesse, Nike with gold chains on the outside.

'What is this, designer violence?' shouted Walshy as he confronted them. '*This* is designer violence.' He charged forward and squirted his lemon full of ammonia. It hit the front guy in the face and he went down screaming. The sound was so terrible that other Chelsea fans dropped their lemons, almost shocked at the effect. Walshy was going berserk as the Tottenham fans scattered everywhere and anywhere they could. As they ran, they were fair game to be squirted on the back by the lads who were chasing them. For most people, seeing the designer tracksuits disappearing up the road was all that was needed. The squirted guy was left on the pavement outside the station rolling around screaming, holding his hands over his eyes. Someone lumbered over and kicked him straight between the legs. He vomited, then lay there moaning and frothing.

By the time Walshy reappeared in the pub, he reckoned he'd done over £1,000 worth of ammonia stains to the Tottenham designer labels.

Not that Walshy was without his funnier moments. One time we were all on an MWG weekend as Chelsea were playing at Derby, which meant a night out in Nottingham – a city where girls outnumber blokes at the nightclubs by two to one. It helped to lessen the blow when Chelsea lost. The coach had stopped at a pub in Derby which was near the scene of a Civil War battle. Consequently the pub was full of memorabilia on the walls. Muskets, pike staffs, swords, and pistols. At around 2pm, one of the lads came bursting in the door of the pub.

'There's a huge mob of Derby coming down the road. They'll smash this pub to smithereens.' Walshy jumped up. 'Stand and deliver,' he yelled and ran over to the wall above the fire and grabbed a six-foot pike staff. 'Follow your leader,' he shouted, then charged out of the door. Others followed.

The Chelsea lads spilled out of the door like a medieval army, with Oliver Cromwell come Dick Turpin Walshy at the front, half shouting, half singing the Adam and the Ants song.

> *Stand and deliver*
> *Your money or your life.*

The Derby lads went up the road as fast as they came down. From the looks on their faces, they wouldn't come near us again. Everybody filed back into the pub, replaced the historical artefacts and carried on drinking. Even the landlord was pleased that the Chelsea lads had saved his windows and prevented a confrontation. Walshy talked about it non-stop for a month and even purchased a copy of the record and got it installed on the juke box in the Black Bull.

Derby was always a lively day out for me. Opening day, 1973. Bright sunshine, 8,000 travelling Chelsea fans wearing Fred Perry T-shirts, Levis and braces. Gary Glitter number one in the charts. 'Do You Wanna Be in my Gang?' with the immortal chant:

> *Come on, come on*
> *Come on, come on*

At the end of the match, onto the pitch to that chant. When the Derby fans did the same, fighting was inevitable. Lads, testosterone by the bucketload and sunshine. The fights were shown on *Match of the Day* and Jimmy Hill honed in on one Chelsea lad with a moustache punching the living daylights out of some hapless Derby fan and uttered the famous words: 'If that young man's father is watching them, I hope that he gets hold of him tonight and really gives him what for!'

Walshy was like a magnet for trouble in Derby. Another time, myself, Walshy and Little Tom were walking along when a huge mob appeared from nowhere. They chased us. Normally they give up after 50 yards, but this lot kept coming. Road after road of terraced houses, their shouts getting closer, the noise of their feet echoing around the narrow streets and tight terraced houses.

'What's chasing us, a herd of buffalo?' shouted Walshy.

One right turn too many, into a dead end street. The mob started walking towards us. Horrible grinning faces. Slowing down, laughing among themselves. Walshy put a front window in while I got up against a wall, grabbed a crate of milk bottles and pitched them at anyone and everybody to keep them at bay. The police arrived within minutes. It seemed like an eternity.

For our sterling defence, we were fined £100 and bound over to keep the peace, plus we made the front page of the *Daily Mirror*. It was better than the alternative. Walshy blamed the house front window on the Derby fans. For a few weeks we were referred to by the lads as the pop group 'The Bottle Tops' and I walked into the pub to the shout: 'Hickey, the fastest milkman in the West.'

The early eighties saw Arsenal have a tidy little firm. Ambush them at Earls Court after the match, was the Walshy cry. Miller and the Arsenal boys got off at West Kensington then walked back towards Earls Court to ambush *us*. We were waiting, though, and scattered them. However, the Arsenal boys came back again, despite Chelsea arming themselves with debris from a roadside skip. Suddenly Chelsea were the hunted. I remember running and running, being chased forever. Finally, I ran down a sidestreet and straight into a pub. It wasn't until I looked around that I realised that I was surrounded by leather clones, caps, trousers with zips up the arse, and black moustaches by the hundred. I had two choices. Go outside and get fucked by the Arsenal or take my chances in here with my back against the wall. I ordered half a lager and stayed in the pub, even though I felt most uncomfortable for 15 minutes.

*   *   *

Walshy loved to go down to Covent Garden. Unfortunately, so did West Ham and Millwall. It became a war zone on Saturday evenings as old rivalries spilled out on to the streets. Northern fans sticking around for a drink would be attacked by groups of London fans in between punching and glassing each other. The Punch & Judy pub left Judy at home. Standing in bars, it looked sometimes as if the whole pub was sniping at each other, awaiting the inevitable. Hostile vibes coming at you, making certain bars no-go areas, Millwall upped my own ante by waiting for me to board the train at Charing Cross, making the journey across the concourse one of trepidation, never knowing whether they would be waiting. No drunken kebabs for me. One evening Millwall pushed it beyond the pale and stabbed to death a West Ham fan. People who did this sort of thing weren't football hooligans, they were society psychopaths.

For most, the perfect home Saturday would be a Chelsea win, followed by a serious drink – albeit not in the Toomsy league – and finally a large doner kebab with lashings of chilli sauce, topped by a huge green chilli, with most of the sauce ending up on the jacket front. You'd wake in a drunken haze the next day with red stains that defied any washing powder to remove them. Walshy used to berate people for eating 'that foreign shit', but he never stopped anybody from enjoying their kebab.

Walshy loved Brighton away for the chance to abuse Swedish birds walking along the sea front, while Jeff loved it for the rusting hulk that was the West Pier. It takes all sorts, I suppose. Brighton is the town with more pubs than any other in England, so we'd make it a Friday night out along the long windswept front – only to be confronted once by a Brighton mob with petrol bombs, one of which melted my Doc Marten boots (so much for their fireproof claims). Later on, Tony Cobbeler got a 90-stitch face-slashing by a mob of Pompey fans. Such was the melting pot of vendettas that night.

The next day, Brighton's ground erupted as Chelsea fans invaded the pitch and even attacked the referee. After the match I went back to my dad's house in Hove while Walshy and the lads marched back into Brighton. In a precinct near the sea front, a jewellers' window got smashed. Straight out of a Hollywood film script, an undercover police officer jumped out flashing his warrant card and loudly proclaiming his identity, thinking it would stop the looting. Those who weren't worried about a new Rolex proceeded to give hero plod a good kicking.

'Bollocks, you clear off and do plod, I'm having a new watch.'

You do hear some strange conversations when greed crosses violent thoughts. Two weeks later, the Met's finest rushed through my door and took me to London's Rochester Row police station.

'You'll never see daylight again. We take it very seriously when one of ours ends up in hospital.'

'Well, if you'd told me that, I'd have sent him some flowers.'

After many hours of threats, my alibi proved iron-clad but it wasn't until my release that I found out others were also in the station. Nobody could be found for the assault and nobody was ever convicted of it. After a month or so, a nice line in new watches was on offer in the King's Head.

In December 1984, after a Chelsea v Manchester United match, an American barman was glassed in Henry J Bean's restaurant in the King's Road by an unknown assailant. The tabloid newspapers described him as the Chelsea Fat Man with scary eyes. The eyes description fitted Walshy, but if it was him he never stopped coming over to Chelsea, even if the newspapers all printed major descriptions of him. The same day, Kevin Whitton had come out of the ground and stood in the road outside the Britannia.

'Come on, you wankers,' he shouted at the Man U boys.

For this show of bravado, he was arrested and charged with threatening words and behaviour. As he left the police station that evening, he saw a couple of his mates hanging around the King's Road.

'There's been some trouble in Henry J Bean's and we've left our jackets in there. Nip in there and get them for us.'

So Kevin walked in there and got them. He was identified as having been in the pub by some of the other barmen and customers, then pulled in by the Fulham police. Kevin refused to give up any names to the police and they threw the book at him. Eventually, when his case came to court, Kevin's threatening behaviour was changed to riotous assembly because he was linked to the attack on the barman. On Friday 8 November 1985, Judge Michael Argyll gave Kevin life for riotous assembly and 10 years for the attack on the barman, along with another guy called Skinny Steve who got six years for the attack. Kevin's sentence was the toughest ever imposed. PC Michael McAree received a commendation, while Tory MPs praised the judge in Parliament. The police also pulled in Billy Mathews as the Fat Man some months after for the Henry J Bean's attack. Billy received four years, though he protested his innocence.

Billy Mathews was a funny guy with smelly feet – correction, Billy Mathews was a hilarious guy with stinking feet. We used to call him Rommel Socks on England trips because they could have marched across the whole of the desert, they were that ripe. His socks had a life of their own, but he never attacked that barman that evening. In court his barrister made a speech which has gone down in history. As Billy stood in the dock, the barrister waxed lyrical: 'This man is a hero. He should not be in the dock on trial. We should be applauding him, not castigating him like we are. This is the sort of man that saved our country. People like Mr Mathews are the life blood of our society. Victoria Crosses are won by men like Mr Mathews, because it is this sort of man which asks nothing but the honour to serve his country. Men like Billy Mathews made Britain great.' Billy looked around the court to see if there was someone else there who was being described. No, it was indeed Billy, and his barrister continued with this magnificent description until he ran out of superlatives. Whether or not it helped no one would ever know, but Billy saw four years as a result after what they did to Kevin.

*   *   *

Walshy was a violence machine increasing the crime statistics until his inevitable arrest. He once got banned from the Wheatsheaf by the landlord for abusing a blonde barmaid because she didn't think his remark of 'I'd love to wank over your tits' was a tasteful chat-up line (Walshy thought it was quite exquisite and said it had worked once before for him at an Essex nightclub). Five minutes later, a road sign came crashing through the bar's front window. But Walshy had a sense of humour (in his opinion) because immediately after he did that he telephoned Eric the glazier to tell him he had some extra work for him. When an Australian truck driver got arrested for driving a truck through a crowded pub in Alice Springs after getting banned, killing nine people, we all looked to see if the surname was Walsh.

If anybody was going to be hauled in during the shake-up that was about to happen then it was Walshy. A result was needed and I suppose that when somebody is called Walshy it could sound like Welshy. After all, there's only three letters in between A and E in the alphabet. A body was hauled in. For Walsh, read Welsh.

6

NICKED

Tuesday, 25 March 1986, was a completely nondescript day. I'd had to get up early to go and deliver a package down to the south coast. My courier business was going well and the coaches were making good money. Only the previous season I'd booked seven coaches up to Manchester for the big match. Chelsea, having only just got back into the top league, had gone up there and put on a show of fan power that rocked Manchester to its red socks. For 70 minutes we'd sung them into the ground. Back in the big time. The talk for the last three months of the previous season had been about putting on a proper show in Manchester. Old Trafford was the Manchester football equivalent of the London Palladium, the greatest stage of all.

Around 20 minutes before the end, a group of 250 of us massed at the back of the away end. The smell of piss was in our hair from where the Manchester fans in the stand above us had been performing their usual party trick in a cup then throwing it down below, but no smell of fear was in the air as we marched around to the Stretford End. There is something eerie about the streets surrounding a football ground while a match is going on. The noise and chants from the crowd make the echoes of the empty streets seem louder. One of the lads kicked a can as we waited at the Stretford End entrance. The big gates were open. Nobody was around. Some fans were leaving early, but they paid scant attention to our group. Fear now dogged our every step, one step after another, no hesitation. Thinking what was going to be the worst part when in reality this was it, as everybody suffered the worry time before the shouts and contact. Once we got inside the ground, the next few minutes were low energy as people got into position, apprehension high, competing with the tension inside us. The home end just before the storm. Guess. Guess again.

The terrace was crowded but one shove and a chant of 'Chelsea' cleared some space. Then a huge surge from everyone. 'CHELSEEEA, CHELSEEEA.' Where a packed crowd had stood was now a huge empty space as the whole end scattered away from our primeval chant. The Stretford End, the academy of violence as *The Observer* described it, put to flight by the appliance of Chelsea science.

> *Chelsea took the Stretford*
> *Chelsea took the Stretford*
> *La la la la*

The Chelsea fans in the enclosure at the opposite end taunted the home crowd while more piss was thrown down on them.

Back they came at us in small numbers. Across the gap, cursing, swearing, shouting. 'Cockney wankers!' Slowly they inched forward, like soldiers negotiating a minefield. Another roar from us and back they went, but not so far. Suddenly they realised that there was only a couple of hundred of us. Then the Mancs charged for real. Three or four, then more. Frantic fist fighting, high kicking, arms and legs contorting as they tried to fight with all their fury. Uncontrolled anger, knowing that we'd humiliated them on their sacred ground. Back they went as we caned their early heroes, but more advanced. Fun over for us. Time for a strategic withdrawal.

And as we ran we laughed, uncontrolled roars of laughter as we ran back down the steps, taking two or three at a time. Out into the road we burst. 'Turn and face,' someone shouted. 'Turn and face the Mancs.' To a man we turned and stood and the pursuing pack stopped in their tracks, unsure of how many of us were outside. Because we were one person while they were just hundreds of individuals, every one of them waiting for someone else to make a move. Then we just drifted away back to our own end like primary school children returning to their classroom after playtime. We'd be mocking them from the other side of the road as they came out of Fulham Broadway tube later in the season. One of the lads kissed his fingers like a chef describing the best meal he has ever cooked: 'That was smoked salmon, roast duck, champagne and crème brûlée.'

We were immortal.

That Tuesday evening, I sat and ate a meal with my girlfriend Claire. We talked about the forthcoming World Cup and how we could travel together to Acapulco and watch some of the England games, perhaps even travelling down together to Guatemala or Costa Rica, where friends of mine had been and liked the people and food. We retired to bed around midnight. I was due to get up early the next morning but because of too much wine and the realisation that I only had that one delivery to make, I stayed in bed. My door came in at 6am on the morning on Wednesday 26 March 1986.

'Go, go, go!'

Muffled shouts as heavy boots came up the stairs, shouting and hollering. For a few dreadful moments thousands of thoughts went through my mind. What the hell is going on here? Perhaps I'd upset somebody. Have I received an early morning call from the West Ham boys? I'd heard those stories.

The door burst open and three uniformed officers came into the room, shouting and breathing heavily. 'Stay still, you wanker,' one of them shouted as I sat up in bed. They ripped open the curtains and turned on the lights, then started throwing stuff around. I recognised Sergeant Hobbs, one of the police officers from Fulham.

'Are you Stephen Hickmott?' said one of them.

'Yes, that's Hickey,' said Hobbs to his colleague.

'What the hell is this all about?' I asked.

'Get up and get dressed, you're under arrest.'

'What for?'

'We have a warrant to arrest you.' They stuffed a piece of paper under my nose then quickly withdrew it. My girlfriend looked startled then got up out of bed and put her dressing gown on. She was terrified and close to tears. The police pushed her out of the way. She sat down on the bed. I touched her arm to signify that everything would be okay. The police were charging around the house like whirling dervishes, seeming to look for things but in reality just making a huge mess.

'What exactly are you looking for?' I asked.

'Weapons, clothes you usually wear, anything to do with Chelsea,' replied the most agitated of all the policemen.

'Well, there's my programme collection in the drawer over there,' I said, pointing to a cupboard by the window, 'and anything else you might as well find yourself.'

With that, I heard noises above my head and realised some PC was crashing around in his size tens in the loft. I heard a shout through the ceiling.

'Got you, you bastard!'

'We've got something really big here, Sarge,' shouted another voice from downstairs. Two of the police officers turned and ran down the stairs. I followed.

The policeman was holding a medieval double ball with spikes on a wooden stick while another was prising two flintlock pistols off the top of the fireplace, along with two Turkish daggers which were set into a display shield. I had bought those in Istanbul when I had been to see the England match. It was a souvenir from an enjoyable trip. I'd even declared it at UK customs so there would be no problems. Now the police were looking at it like it was some sort of deadly attack weapon.

'Take this to football do we, son?' asked the senior officer.

'What sort of drugs are you using?' I replied.

Then more shouts.

'This is it, this is it! It's one of them.'

A young policeman came running in with my scrapbook made up of press cuttings about football violence over the years I had been going to matches. Big deal, a scrapbook containing press cuttings. Another had a crossbow which I had in the loft.

'Big deal, that is a legal weapon sold in any sports shop.'

'We'll see about that, Hickey,' said Hobbs, smiling. Eventually, after an hour's search, I was handcuffed and led from my house. The police were busy loading up my grey overcoat, plus a pair of black DM boots still in the box which my mother had bought me for Christmas, as well as my programmes and everything else. They also had my huge Union Jack flag with Tunbridge Wells written on it. It had been pictured on TV screens at England matches all over the world.

I'd been nicked before, so I saw no problems – I'd be out by teatime. The drop-off I needed to do would just have to wait until the next morning. Sure, the customer would be seriously pissed off, but I'd told my girlfriend not to say anything about the fact that I'd been nicked – after all, it wasn't exactly an advert for business, was it? – and I would make up a story that my brother had been rushed to hospital. One thing I had learned very quickly about getting arrested was never to show them that time is your enemy. Never try and pin them down about getting out to see the rest of the match, for example, because that gives them a lever. I remember one of my mates got nicked the evening Frank Bruno first fought for the world heavyweight title. The lads were desperate to get bail by 3am in order to see the fight, so the police kept him and his mates in until the fight ended. Then just as they got to the door of the station, because they had given the police a hard time, the desk sergeant said: 'Oh, by the way, Bruno got stopped in the twelfth round.'

However, once we got to the station they were so cocky I felt a little unsure, even though deep down I knew they had nothing. Still, one man's nothing is another man's something. One of the PCs was practically creaming his pants about the scrapbooks they had found. Sure, I kept newspaper cuttings relating to football violence, but politicians kept diaries and didn't authors keep paper copies of their reviews? I saw nothing sinister in that.

'We've got you bang to rights, sonny.'

'What are you talking about, Noddy?' I replied, shaking my head.

'You're going down for a long stretch. There is a lot of co-ordinated effort gone into this and believe me, there's some serious shit about to land on your head.'

The police often said things like that then ended up bailing you three hours later. I'd have been more worried if they hadn't said things like that. The only real power the police have is to make you frightened enough to get you to make a confession. 'Go on, sonny, get it all off your chest. Confession will make you feel better.' Only later do you realise that if you'd kept your mouth shut they had nothing to charge you with.

This time it seemed different. We were taken immediately up to Fulham police station, where the enormity of what was going on suddenly struck home. I suddenly realised that this wasn't just a small number of bobbies arresting everybody after a Saturday night drunken pub brawl, this was something bigger. It was only after four or five hours, when I realised others were also being nicked and the bulletins had been shown on TV all over the world, that it became clear this was something outrageously massive and we were the catch. My weapons were displayed for all to see, giving them some form of ghoulish attraction to the police. They started talking about transferring all of us around different London prisons, like they'd arrested hundreds and we were here for the long stretch. The way they were talking was as if it was the biggest operation since Britain invaded the Falkland Islands. We even had a grinning senior officer come down to have a look at me, like he was inspecting some giant marlin catch in the Pacific. What the hell was going on?

'I want a brief, now!' I shouted.

Normally they prevaricate but they seemed so confident it unnerved me.

'And who is your brief, son?'

I said it slowly so PC Correct could write it down: 'P-E-R-R-Y bloody M-A-S-O-N, you wanker.'

'Chuck him in the cells!' the desk sergeant shouted. 'Attitude like that will get you into trouble.'

'What you gonna do, smash my fuckin' front door down again? You're gonna pay for that.'

'Yeah, yeah.'

'I want bail.'

The sergeant screwed up his face. 'Bail?' he said incredulously, almost laughing. 'We've had half the police in southern England out arresting you and you think you'll get bail?'

The worrying part was that they didn't seem in the 'You are a low-life wanker, sign a confession now or we will arrest your girlfriend' mode, just confident faces and thumbs up. It's when the police stop slagging you off that you have to start worrying. Had I upset the taxman? Perhaps the coaches I had run were considered unfit under health and safety regulations. I might have been photographed with booze on the coaches, but even that was a little drastic to have your door kicked in, surely? The officer pushed me through the open door.

'Get used to it, son, you're gonna be here for some time.'

'Gonna take it up the arse again tonight, are you?'

Then the door slammed shut. I looked at the cell with its red plastic-covered mattress with holes in the edges and the general stink and decay of the place. I looked at the door and some goon was looking through the peephole.

'Fuck off, you nonce voyeur.'

Nothing unnerves them more than you not being frightened when the door slams shut. Refuse to be intimidated and they lose half their power. The policeman outside at the peephole laughed. It was a confident laugh, not the hollow laugh they normally give. Then the footsteps retreated and I was alone in the cell. It's acceptable to get nicked when you've done something wrong, and I always accepted that getting arrested was one of the prices to pay for a lifestyle living close to the edge, but I had no idea what this was for. I lay on the bed thinking that if only I'd got up early to deliver that package then they'd have kicked my door in to find me not there. They would have caught up with me eventually, but at least I would have had the satisfaction of them charging through the door to get nothing.

The cell door clanked open: 'Questioning, Hickmott.'

I was put into a small room. There were two of them. The questions came thick and fast.

'Who do you know at Chelsea?'

I knew Ken Bates. Sergeant Hobbs.

'When did you last see them?'

Never met Bates. Meet Hobbs every other Saturday outside the Britannia and at 6am this morning in my bedroom.

'How do you know them?'

'They are both well-known faces at Chelsea.'

I answered some of their questions. By the afternoon I was getting bored, so I requested a solicitor. This is the bit where they gloat, because nine out of ten people don't know the name of a solicitor. However, I had been doing a lot of courier work for Graham & Graham who had an office in Tunbridge Wells, so I knew the number and quoted it at them.

'You think you're bloody clever, don't you, but we're gonna have you, Hickmott,' sneered the questioning officer. I laughed. Within an hour, Bob Waddell turned up. Bob bounced in with his smile and we got on immediately. Despite the seriousness of the conspiracy charge, Bob talked of bail. He agreed to sort out the cost later.

He was with me at 7pm when they charged me and informed me that they would be remanding me until the hearing in front of the magistrate the next day. I had been in custody for 12 hours. I went back to my cell. The police never asked me another question from that moment onwards.

*　　*　　*

Thursday, 27 March. The world awoke to the news in *The Times*. It didn't make the front page but was reported as a major coup against serious football thugs: 'Operation Own Goal.'

'In a series of dawn raids yesterday, seven were held in a soccer violence crackdown. Police have recovered over 20 different types of weapon.' Next to this drivel was a picture of WPC Alison Cooper holding the medieval ball and chain. I thought it was funny how they used a meek-looking WPC. I wasn't to see the relevance of that until the trial started. The *Daily Mail* frightened their readers with the caption next to the picture, 'ARMED FOR THE MATCH'. I wonder how many of their readers have souvenirs from Spain which could be construed as offensive weapons in a dawn raid?

Superintendent Mike Hedges was credited as the leader of the operation in London. He trotted out the facts of the case, which the press lapped up: 'New Scotland Yard have undertaken five months of intensive police surveillance of Chelsea fans travelling to away matches. They had amassed intelligence to suggest that football-related violence was being organised on a big scale by certain individuals.'

Then he added: 'Police believe that the arrested fans intended to visit Russia but their visa applications had been refused. The fans also had plans to travel to Mexico for World Cup in June.' Well, unless it had suddenly become a criminal offence to leave England, I saw no problem with plans to travel to Russia and Mexico, even if the lads were not intending to travel to Russia for a nothing friendly because of the aggro obtaining a visa. Finally, Ken Bates was quoted in *The Times* saying that he was pleased by the arrests.

Hedges praised the tremendous co-operation between the Metropolitan Police and provincial forces: '. . . think they have found the ringleaders . . . hopefully there will be a decrease in violence at matches.'

Despite the fact that they claimed to have been observing us for several months, they managed to extend the charges back five years. Eventually they arrested two more people, so the total in the papers was nine. The Chelsea Nine all denied conspiracy to cause affray between January 1980 and March 1986.

Terence Last, 23, Ginger Terry – solicitor's clerk
Shaun O'Farrell, 34, Shaun – builder
Peter Brown, 19, Young Peter – postman
Stephen Hickmott, 31, Hickey – Engineer
Vincent Drake, 23, Vince – decorator
Dale Green, 25, Dale – Navy cook
William Reid, 25, Willie – chef
Stephen Toombs, 24, Toomsy – admin clerk
Douglas Welsh, 23, Dougie – builder

Looking at the newspaper reports, you would have thought that undercover information had been compiled from painstaking research and police infiltrating our ranks and living among us for years, but the specific charges levelled against us were these:

Ginger Terry, Shaun and Willie: Affray at Everton, 10 December 1985

Toomsy, Terry and Young Peter: Affray at Southport, 15 March 1986

Myself, Vince, Shaun and Dougie: Affray at Wembley, 23 March 1986, after the match between Manchester City and Chelsea in the Full Members' Cup final.

We looked at the charges. Who was Welsh? When the police had brought him in, we looked at each other and thought he was a police plant.

'Keep it tight, lads. Say anything to that mug and they will wheel him into court at a later date as their star witness, saying we'd spilled our guts to him,' whispered Young Peter.

'You've been watching too many *Sweeney* episodes,' chided Toomsy.

However, Dougie's simple demeanour and absolute belief that he'd soon be out as he was the victim of a great injustice made us like him immediately.

Dougie was one of those guys who sees life as a laugh. He attended Chelsea football matches when his mates told him it would be a good time, or he went racing or on a day trip to Calais. Mates and drink made for a good laugh for Dougie. He lived in Crawley and when Chelsea reached the Full Members' Cup final, his mates had a spare ticket so he went. It was only the third match he had attended that season. Unfortunately, Dougie got carried away with too much beer and got involved in the fighting after the match. When he saw a copper arresting a young Chelsea fan, he whacked him. At the local police station he was charged with assault and bailed within three hours to appear at a later date. A few hundred pounds in fines, he thought, as he walked away from the nick. Two days later his door was kicked in and 10 police officers came through it to inform him that he was a criminal mastermind.

'Piss off, officer, I don't even watch *Mastermind* on TV,' shouted a startled Dougie from under his duvet.

His mum emerged from her bedroom bleary-eyed.

'What's going on? What have you nicked now, Douglas?' she asked. Dougie liked a beer and occasionally nicked a bit of gear. He was known to have a few laughs on Saturday evenings and liked to go racing a few times a year and get rat-faced, but a violent criminal? They must have come to the wrong house.

As Dougie sat in the van, the senior officer was informing the control room that Operation Own Goal was a success. 'You've got the wrong person, lads,' Dougie shouted as they took him away. Dougie's mum watched the police cars drive away. A few neighbours peered out of the windows at the sight of all the vans and cars. They hadn't seen so many police in Sussex since they'd raised the haunt of Buster Edwards a few miles down the road nearly

20 years ago. Dougie had no worries, because he'd done nothing to deserve this. However, he had done a bit of business with Terry, and 'Welshy' was in Terry's diary.

The police raids were accompanied by a camera crew, invited along to ensure that the early evening national news bulletins got their exclusive coverage. Dale shared a house with a mate. It was a nice, three-bed semi in Middlesex. Being working guys in the building trade, they got up early. When the police arrived outside their house, Dale looked out of his bedroom window then called his mate in. They watched the police jump out of the vans outside, wait outside the gate until the officer in charge arrived and told them to go, then walk up the drive and knock once. Dale stuck his head out of the window.

'What do you want?'

'Open up the door!' an officer shouted up to Dale.

'Hang on, lads, I'm coming down. I'll open up.'

The senior officer turned towards the policeman who had the metal door-banger in his hand. For a moment he looked disappointed at being denied his moment of destruction.

'Smash it down,' said the officer in charge. Two whacks and it was in. On the news, you could see the senior officer fall straight onto his arse in the melee to get through the door. As they charged in, they knocked Dale down in the hallway as he approached the door to open it. The camera crew caught Dale's house-sharer in his boxer shorts, looking perplexed. Later, the *Sun* printed that when the police dramatically burst into the bedroom, Dale was in bed with his mate. But the *Sun*, along with other papers, were good at printing stories culled from anonymous police sources. Years later they would tell the world that Liverpool fans robbed dead bodies at Hillsborough.

Even as we sat there in the police station, we talked about Chelsea's forthcoming match against West Ham that Saturday, how we'd be out by the weekend and what we would be doing for travel arrangements for matches over the Easter holiday, when all transport in England shut down. We talked about the forthcoming World Cup in Mexico and what England's chances would be. We were enthusiastic about football and life in general. Dale was shouting every so often: 'This is a fit-up. You can't catch Ronnie Biggs.'

As we lined up in the back of Fulham police station for our first court appearance, the press milled about outside. We were handcuffed in pairs, the nine of us plus another guy who was in for breaking in and stealing money from his electricity meter. I got handcuffed to 'Meter Man', as Vince called him. The police asked if we wanted blankets on our heads and we nodded in agreement. Our meter thief was having none of that.

'What TV crews are outside?'

'Everybody. BBC, ITV, CNN, Reuters,' said the officer on the gate.

'Right then, I want them to see me with these arch criminals. All my family and pals will see me on the news. My brother-in-law thinks I'm a lowlife loser. Well, now I've hit the big time.' As he went out he beamed at the cameras and stood for a three-second pose. I couldn't stop laughing under my blanket. In the van on the way to court, the guy kept thanking me for making him famous.

As we pulled up outside West London Magistrates Court, the cameramen were hanging from every vantage point, including some up trees. The noise of the camera shutters – amazing.

'Over here, boys. I'm famous. Thanks, lads,' shouted Meter Man.

As we walked in, sitting in the public gallery laughing and waving at us were three West Ham marsh men. Wankers, mouthed Shaun. See you Saturday or perhaps not, they mimed back. One of Dougie's mates from Crawley had travelled up with a substantial amount of money for bail. After the hearing the marsh men set on him outside and stabbed him, giving him a punctured lung. On the Saturday, following the poof stories in the *Sun*, the West Ham boys turned up at Stamford Bridge wearing CFC BEDHUNTERS T-shirts which parodied the 'Ghostbusters' theme and the Headhunters nickname. Under a picture of Terry and Dale which they had lifted from the newspapers, they had the caption.

> *Chelsea Boys*
> *In the undergrowth*
> *Who you gonna call?*
> *Bedhunters*

Yes, very droll. Very witty. Very West Ham. That weekend, Bill Gardner gave a couple of the Redhill Chelsea lads a load of abuse at the Millionaire Club where he was a bouncer and refused them entry, saying, 'This is a straight club. You need the pink poofs' club further up the road.'

The police were opposing our bail applications as fast as we made them, but as we saw it, the flimsiness of the case they had meant we had to keep applying. We were on weekly remands and soon bail was granted for Peter in April, Toomsy and Shaun in June, then Willie in July. Then one week, out of the blue, Dougie's father came up with a £20,000 surety for him and a judge in chambers granted Dougie bail. You could see the absolute horror on the faces of the police and prosecution. A smiling Dougie left the remand hearing but by Monday he was back among us in custodial mode. Dougie had gone into a Crawley camera shop with his mate and had been arrested by undercover officers on a charge of attempted robbery and assault. While he was being held at Crawley nick, a local officer told him they didn't have anything and he would be out in an hour or so. They were famous last words because within 20 minutes he was being whisked back to London. Dougie's first words were 'Bollocks, it's all bollocks,' then he went back to his *Viz*. He boycotted the trial for three days in protest at his re-arrest. We were stunned initially, then laughed at Dougie – if I'd been given bail they'd never have got me back so quick. The Crawley charges against Dougie were later dropped, but he would not get bail again.

There was no doubt that the police seemed more interested in me, Terry, Vince and Dale rather than the others. In the end, their whole case would rest upon the jury believing that a small group of police officers, portrayed as brave and dedicated, who had risked physical injury to go undercover, had overheard certain conversations and had written them down immediately. These conversations showed a conspiracy to make affray with other youths. Essentially they had no conclusive forensic evidence, no video footage or photographs showing us committing violent acts, no witnesses of us striking people, no victims except the two Newcastle fans who'd been slashed at a match we'd attended (who'd been unable to formally identify us) and the Manchester City coach driver who claimed to recognise us. The conspiracy charge was dependent on overheard conversations.

My solicitor read the police statements. I read them again and again – what else is there to do during long, mundane months on remand, locked up for 23 hours a day? Nothing focuses the mind more than a piss-stinking cell in Wormwood Scrubs, Brixton or Pentonville. I even started to pick up legal points. I couldn't see how the case would go beyond five days.

No one will take this seriously. Twelve good men and true. British justice will see me through this little spat.

7

TALKING HEADS

On remand, I heard horror stories about people being held for 11 months then going to court and the police getting up and offering no evidence, then mocking the accused as they walked out of court with the words: 'Yeah, but it kept you locked up for 11 months, didn't it?'

So it was something of a relief when we got a definite trial date. Months of scrutiny for what I saw as the obvious frailty of the case to be made evident. The statements made by the police struck me as too ridiculous for words. Even though I had received no formal legal training, I felt able to pick so many holes in the case I nicknamed it 'Operation Colander'. I envisaged myself in a movie, sailing into the sunset with a pretty girl, sticking my fingers up to the police and establishment.

First we had the onerous task of jury selection. The lads thought this was a chore but our legal team attached great importance to it. It can be crucial to both sides in a case that the members of the jury look likely to support them. The prosecuting team was given advice on who to accept for the jury. For example, one young guy who came in looked at us without showing contempt, almost as if to say, 'Good to see you, lads.' He was immediately rejected, as was anybody who looked to me remotely like a football fan. Sometimes we objected. Toomsy and Vince wanted blonde bimbos with big tits. Myself, I didn't want anybody who looked like Mary Whitehouse, the sort that goes on TV every so often and shouts that everybody who goes to football matches is a hooligan and needs five years in the army, preferably getting their balls blown off at the same time. In the subsequent Headhunters trial the defence got the lads completely clued up about jury selection – so much so that on the first day they ran out of potential jurors.

For me, the best jury would have been 12 lads who'd been to football and suffered the excesses that the establishment now dished out. Grounds with no cover against the elements, nowhere to get any decent food. Unable to go to the toilet. Locked in here, marched from pillar to post, never given any information about trains being cancelled, arrested when you complained. Once at Chelsea in a pre-season friendly with Arsenal, I'd seen a middle-aged man with his son try to leave a line of supporters because his car was parked the opposite way to Fulham Broadway tube station where the police insisted the whole crowd go. His son got grabbed by the throat.

'You horrible, ugly specimen of mankind,' screamed the officer.

The father looked horrified. Here was a man brought up on a diet of *Dixon of Dock Green*, where villains were apprehended by the long arm of the law and innocent people had no fear. In his world, policemen were kindly, tolerant individuals who said, 'Good day, sir, how can I help you?' and smiled lovingly at children attending football matches. Now Dixon had his young son round the throat, screaming: 'Bastard, who said you could get out of that line?' Was he in Chile or Indonesia? No, he was in the Fulham Road attempting to go to his car and travel back to his centrally heated home in suburbia. He placed his hand on the officer's shoulder in an attempt to restore normality.

'Calm down, officer, our car is the opposite way to the station.'

For his trouble, he was knocked to the floor by a mounted policeman.

'You're lucky I don't get this fucking horse to trample all over you.' As the man looked up through terrified eyes, I got the distinct impression he didn't see his escape from the horse's hooves as luck. Those were the people we needed on the jury.

Eventually, after a whole day, the jury was set at seven women and five men. There then followed three days of legal arguments, which seemed such a tedious process. By now we just wanted to get the trial over and done with. I had submitted two bail applications but both had been knocked back. On the first occasion, I heard the prosecution object to bail being granted then describe me like this: 'This man is a career football thug who we believe is the leader of a highly organised network of football hooligans. If bail is granted there is a high probability that further offences will be committed.' There was also the matter of skipping the country using an alias on a false passport. It occurred to me that the only thing stopping them from claiming I would interfere with witnesses was that they didn't seem to have any!

This was so funny that I actually started laughing. The judge looked over at me sitting there. President and first member of the MWG group, international silly billies first-class, PhD in alcohol consumption, VD & scar, suddenly becoming a dangerous criminal. I'd described numerous Chelsea performances I'd seen as criminal, but that was as far as it went. Criminal performance equals guilt by association. I thought the judge would laugh as well, but he looked very seriously at me then denied the application. I wanted to shout out loud: 'You silly, warped bastard. How could you believe such trash?' Later Bob Waddell tried again in front of a judge in chambers but he, too, refused the application. All in all, I tried six times to get bail and six times I got a General de Gaulle judge. Non, Nyet, Nein, whatever language you use, it still hits you hard when you lose your liberty without being convicted. The only consolation was the long chats I had with Bob Waddell about life and Chelsea Football Club.

Our trial was set for the Inner London Crown Court. I'd rather hoped for the Old Bailey because I had romantic notions of coming out of there in the glare of the media spotlights shouting that Chelsea would now win the league after this great victory for their fans. On 5 January 1987, the waiting was finally over and I came to court. Despite being unconvicted, I had been held in various cells and institutions at Her Majesty's Pleasure, some without toilets or washing facilities, for nearly 10 months. In some prisons I had been locked up for over 23 hours a day. Had I been a dog then I would have had the RSPCA fighting my corner, yet in England in 1987 nobody cared about remand prisoners, least of all football fans. I had no rights. I had missed seeing England in the 1986 World Cup and had been unable to watch England get knocked out by the cheating hand of Maradona. We all had to hope that another injustice was not about to be served on us.

8

BARRISTERS' DAY OUT

'There is nothing as good as a cheap, spicy court case.'
Rupert Murdoch

A major trial has a life of its own, separate from the everyday existence of the common man, and while everyone appears to know their place within the legal hierarchy it seems to operate on a higher plane of existence to that of the legal establishment itself. In its most simplistic form it is similar to football terrace gangs. The law might have been described as an ass but even from our disadvantaged viewpoint it was fascinating. It's only when you observe the English law in action at close quarters in a big court situation that you really see the money and power that surrounds it. Solicitors who are looking to climb into the barrister league scurry around everywhere with huge briefcases, in a frightful hurry but seemingly going nowhere, doubling back as if they have forgotten something, like those clockwork toys people give children for Christmas. Impromptu meetings are held in corridors. Other people walk in, wave their arms and shout.

'Geoffrey, can I have a word with you?'

Then they go into a room and have discussions. Meanwhile the top-dog barristers walk around in their white wigs with that self-assured strolling motion like time belongs to them alone. The more money you have then the better your access to the higher reaches of the legal brains. Money equals fairness in England. That is what I observed during our trial. No animosity, just business. You are something for them to exercise their brains on.

As we were all defending ourselves separately, we all had our own legal teams. I listened intently and was keen to get involved in every aspect of my case, as were Terry and some of the others. I remembered the words from a film: 'Don't trust your lawyers. Don't even trust your friends. Just count on yourself.' My number one barrister was called Conningsby, but his number two, who would do much of the talking, was a barrister named Nick Price. Terry Last was represented by Derek Inman. In the lighter moments, we'd tease Terry about his lawyer with the words 'He's Free' after the words uttered by a camp actor of the time, John Inman. Dougie actually asked the guy if he was related to Inman one day, but he seemed not to understand. 'I'm not your counsel, Mr Welsh,' he replied tersely, then hurried away.

Dale had a woman barrister and she seemed okay, although I got the impression that she felt she needed to try harder because she was a woman. Vince appeared indifferent to the ins and outs of the case and the only thing that bothered Toomsy was the fact that he was being deprived of valuable drinking time.

'How soon will this be over?'

Those who took the most interest looked to me to be getting a longer attention span from the barristers. Dougie was perplexed by the whole business and seemed to think that at any moment the police would come in and tell him they had made a horrible mistake.

'It's all bollocks, this legal crap. You can't convict a person who wasn't even there,' was his reasoned, common-sense argument. After Dougie's arrest, some of his friends were interviewed. All of them shook their heads and told the same story: Dougie isn't your man. However, his name appeared in statements where he was recognised, whereas none of us had met him or seen him previously at any Chelsea or England matches. Dougie had a simple philosophy that

British justice would prevail: he took the solicitor he was offered, which happened to be the duty solicitor. Right from day one Dougie shrugged his shoulders in don't care gestures, claiming never to have met the other defendants at Chelsea FC's games.

I made a decision to be smart and well-groomed for the whole trial. After all, I had seven women to impress. And I didn't want to sit next to Toomsy, in case he let one of his belches or farts go in the court and the women looked my way. Presentation is all. A couple of days and this would be all over, we reckoned, although the defence team felt we would be in for a long, hard battle. 'Bollocks, they're only saying that,' said Dougie when he heard that. 'Listen, lads, I'll come and watch the trial once they throw my case out,' he would say, and then laugh to himself.

Just before the trial started there was a change of judge. Pete Mason, our original judge, was changed and in his place was one called George Schindler. The first time I saw him, I thought he looked pretty uncompromising. The graffiti in the room downstairs summed up our thoughts about the two judges.

Penal Pete Mason – puts you away to grim places.
Schindler the Swindler – swindles you out of your best years.

For the first month of our remand we'd been held at Wormwood Scrubs. Even though you are unconvicted, the English penal system is not geared for you or the words 'innocent until proven guilty'. Terry actually stated that to a warder and got this reply.

'I'm a fuckin' screw and you're just lockdown scum. Now fuckin' move, you wanker, or face a good hiding.'

Wormwood Scrubs was dirty, I don't think I have ever seen a more filthy place. It helped to be locked up 23 hours a day. During the one-hour exercise period, most of the black prisoners used to spill into the yards and rush around playing a manic game of football, getting out as much energy as they could. Then suddenly the break was over. They couldn't let us have more than an hour's fresh air because you are there at the behest of the people who have the keys. It seemed to us that the prison system is run for the benefit of the Prison Officers' Association, and your sole purpose is to assist in their way of life. Nothing else counts. Freedom of association, regular showers, a gymnasium, fresh air, good food? Forget it. Books and a TV? You are some sort of comedian.

Bollocks, scum, stay in your cell for 23 hours a day and piss and shit in that little pot in the corner of the cell. Grey walls, black doors and horrible metal walkways designed to oppress. At night you heard door after door slam shut, then the wailing from those who couldn't hack it. Nothing chills the bone more than people losing their minds then getting a kicking for doing it and being put in a cell with the lights on 24 hours a day as punishment. Doubly worse was the thought that they might be innocent men. The warders seemed to enjoy their power, especially when someone asked for something, because then they could say no. Always a rule which prevents it happening.

Emptying the toilet bucket one day it reminded me of a trip on County Coaches. Standing in front of me was a tattooed man with a moustache. It could have been Paul Scarrott throwing a bucket of piss over the Derby or Celtic fans he hated so vehemently. Scarrott was okay, just a loud Nottingham pisshead who I'd met on England trips. Once, he'd gone on Central TV on one of those Jerry Springer-type chat shows that England attempts to imitate (but is really so crap at it should leave well alone) and Gary Newbon, the journalist who likes to put awkward questions to footballers, asked him why he did it. It was a question that had been asked thousands of times before, like why do you *really* do it? As if he was going to be the first to receive the holy grail of a profound answer from football fans who questioned nothing and answered bollocks to most things. The establishment were deluding themselves if they expected any other sort of answer but their curiosity kept making them ask the same dumb question. What they got was 'Blah, blah blah larf innit . . . Blah fun . . . Blah

mates.' Scarrott wasn't about to expound on fans' disenfranchise-
ment and working-class isolationism.

'Cos I enjoy it, it's fun and anyway, would I be here on TV as
a bloody star if I didn't go around getting pissed and whacking
people?'

Wrong answer, Mr Scarrott, you are now the most reviled person in
England after Arthur Scargill and your sobriquet is Superthug. You
and your girlfriend will now be hounded by the tabloid press till the
day you die.

I heard a shout as a bucket of piss was deposited down the drain:
'It's like being on County Coaches on a bad day.'

There was Vince grinning.

During the first period of our remand they dispersed us around
different prisons, although Terry and I were on different wings in
the Scrubs. Information came slowly because each remand hearing
was set at seven days apart. Going to court was a bit of fun as we'd
all meet up again and hear stories from the lads who'd obtained bail.
After the Scrubs (as it's affectionately known by everybody) I got
moved to Brixton, a prison which has a high proportion of black
prisoners. It seemed to me as if they were given a harder time than
the rest of us. Deprived of their jewellery and clothes, a major form
of expression, incarceration sits badly on their shoulders. So what
did they do? They walked around with their belts undone to be
different. A fashion statement, even if it meant that their trousers
sometimes fell down. Plus the domino matches. They didn't just
place a domino on the table. No, they shouted at full blast at
their opponent sitting two feet away, then smashed the domino
down with such force that the table nearly broke and sometimes
the game had to be stopped because they'd scattered the other
dominoes. Quite a few laughed every time that happened. As they
put myself and Terry together, we talked a lot, although Terry's
attempts to teach me chess were doomed to failure. Terry also
seemed pissed off that I showed no interest in cards. We spoke

about matches and places we'd visited, laughing about different characters.

Jeff was proud that he had always managed to find a bar for a drink wherever he went. When England played Romania in Bucharest, his boast was finally undone as his search for a bar and a good time proved fruitless. He came moping back to the hotel, shocked that a city could be so completely shut down: 'That Ceausescu has a lot to answer for.' The square concrete boxes which had replaced the previous rustic-character buildings had severely tested Jeff's love of travel and culture.

'I wonder what Jeff would make of this place?'

'A wonderful example of Victorian ingenuity destroyed by modernist tendencies.'

'He might get a drink in here, though.'

Then a collapse into fits of laughter. Romania, May Day 1985, was the day that Ken Bailey came a cropper. The silly old twit used to dress up in a Union Jack suit then march around the pitch waving a shield. Some Romanian gypsy boys came up to the fence. When he went over, they grabbed hold of him and started giving him an absolute hammering, smashing him to pieces. The supporters' club people shouted to us. Having spent all their time sneering at us everywhere we met, they now needed us to rescue their quaint old friend.

'Help him, somebody help him!'

'You go and help him. He travels with you lot, not us.'

One day Terry banged his arm and that started him moaning about Miller, the Arsenal fan. Terry had gone with Miller and his little firm for a midweek League Cup match featuring Arsenal at Oxford. Miller had established himself as an ace Gooner face with Arsenal in the eighties and his firm was reckoned to be a bit tasty. That night they suffered the ignominy of being ambushed by Oxford and had temporarily scattered. Terry fell over a wall and broke his arm.

Because of the lack of recreation, the radio became my best friend.

Evening phone-ins were great, especially when they used to do football violence and Doris Disturbed used to ring in to inform everybody that she knew what football hooligans needed. Yeah, and I know what you need, Doris! In September 1986, the smell of Brixton meant that I was listening to my radio near the window. Chief Inspector Hedges came on the radio regarding police behaviour in London. A caller asked him about the Chelsea conspiracy and the six-year undercover operation, and why they didn't arrest the fans earlier.

Hedges answered uneasily, with a flustered tone in his voice. His answers astounded me, almost as if he wasn't sure of the ground he was covering.

When the caller persisted, Hedges said he couldn't give too much away and the caller was thanked for his contribution then politely moved on. But if the police were unsure of their case, what was I doing here? My legal team were on to it straight away and got a copy of the tape.

After the Scrubs, I never thought I'd find a prison as run down again, but Brixton was even worse. I think they built that place with rust. As well as the filth there was the overcrowding, which meant you had to be locked up in squalor 23 hours a day. No TV or gym or library, although they did let us watch a film at weekends. I requested *Escape From Alcatraz*, which went down like a lead balloon with the warders.

The only bright spot was the fact that you were allowed to have food sent in from the outside. Some of the lads organised a cash whip left with the cafe owner opposite and he used to send in a special every morning. The warders let it get cold and congealed before they sent it down to us. Perhaps some of them spat on it for good measure. Terry and I made a point of eating every morsel and giving the warders a 'Yum yum, that was delicious' expression when we passed them. Jeff had chipped in fifty quid then shot off to Mexico to follow England in the World Cup. While the rest of the world watched Maradona cheat England out of the World Cup with his infamous Hand of God goal, Terry and I sat in a cell reminiscing. In any other country's prisons there would have been a riot if they had dared not show the World Cup. Even in Argentina, where the state murdered its opponents, the jails dared not take the risk of not showing the World Cup.

Visiting was 30 minutes a day but not at weekends because the system, even for unconvicted men, is meant to oppress. Finally, I was moved to Pentonville, once a debtors' prison, where people were put because they couldn't pay their bills. I told the intake warder the drill.

'Lockdown 23 hours a day, no TV, no gym, weekend film.'

'Well, that saved me a job,' he said wearily. The place was depressing him. (I read that prison warders have the highest divorce rate in England. I can see why now.)

Terry and I shared a cell at various times, almost as if they didn't have the intelligence to leave us together permanently. Eventually, I was moved to Coldingly prison in Surrey. While being on remand is never pleasant, at least there I had a clean cell on my own, sheets which were washed regularly, access to showers every day and more importantly, somewhere with fresh air and reasonable food. Beyond the perimeter fence, the rolling fields of Surrey looked beautiful. Just a metal fence between me and freedom.

For seven and a half months they'd kept me locked up without charge. Now I had a court date. In less than a month I would be in court and able to put this behind me. The Coldingly warders were ex-servicemen who breathed clean air every day and they made life pleasant, recognising that many in the remand system often get released, so their job was to earn a living and lock you up but treat you with a modicum of respect. As I saw it, the warders at those London prisons had lost their self-respect as human beings, so they didn't know how to interact with people. Now, as the trial approached, I had long sessions with my solicitor, Bob Waddell. Here at Coldingly it was in a clean, airy, pleasant-smelling room, a lot different from the early chats we had at Brixton, in a grey windowless room where the smell of decay came from the putrification of the human spirit. In the centre of that room was a bare table with two grey plastic chairs that needed years of grime scrubbing off.

At Coldingly, I met my barrister Nick Price, a man with sharp eyes which noticed everything, even if he didn't seem to listen to some of what I said. We understood each other well. He grasped my personality, but cautioned me very early on that although there were serious flaws in the police case, my scrapbooks were a worry. Without those, I would be home and dry.

January. My first lasting memory of Chelsea was in the third round of the FA Cup. Every New Year is always greeted by the FA Cup third round, when David meets Goliath for the first time. The FA Cup is all about the David teams socking it to the big boys. The fact that we'd started our trial at this time augured well in our minds. We arrived at Inner London Crown Court and the transfer drill was explained to us.

'Don't bother, we'll soon be out of here,' I said with conviction.

The court prison officer looked at us with that look which said, 'Don't bet on it'. So the routine was trial, back to Brixton. And you were always waiting while the system appeared to run out of everything. Vans, drivers, pencils; you name it, they always seemed short of something. Everything except time, there was always plenty of that. Still, the more time we waited around, the less time we'd have in Brixton.

The waiting room down below the Inner London Crown Court was a grim, horrid affair. Once, many years previously, it had been painted. Now all it had were the years of neglect and graffiti as cargoes of human flotsam passed on their way to the courts above and left their mark. Many of those who'd left their graffiti tattoo couldn't spell, which is probably why they were here. Prisoners had burnt their names or other abuse on the ceiling using matches. The smoke within the room and the oppressive London pollution had long since turned the paint a horrible sand-brown colour. It was a depressing place. You left the room by a door on the call of the usher and went up a spiral staircase, where you came into the light. Even though we were on trial for our freedom, it was always pleasant to come into the court and see clean clothes and light in a room and smell furniture polish on wood.

So at last we were here. The lads who had bail were pleased to see us and asked how we were bearing up.

'Marvellous, best hotel Dougie has ever stayed at,' I remarked.

I had been to boxing matches where the MC announces the big fight. 'And now we have the main event for Court 1, Inner London Crown Court.' As we entered the court for the first time, the press benches were packed. These people were here to enlighten their readers about the shady world of football violence. People who'd never attended a football match yet spoke with utter conviction at their dinner parties about what scum we were and how we should all be locked up without trial. Their prejudices were about to be justified by our trial. After all, if we were innocent they wouldn't have been able to charge us, would they?

As we emerged into the court, Vince was humming the *Rocky* theme tune and he started bouncing like he was entering the ring. With the police, press and witness box to our right, we settled down in the dock in the following order: Terry, myself, Vince, Shaun, Toomsy, Dale, Willie, Dougie, with Young Peter furthest left. We stayed like that for the whole trial (kept the formation solid, to use our football parlance). In front of us was our defence counsel. The press box was packed on the first days (halfway through the trial we were down to one reporter) and they looked at us intently. We returned their looks scornfully. 'Wankers,' muttered Shaun as he looked over. Opposite us was the judge's bench. To our left was the jury. The public gallery was above our heads so that we couldn't see them. The chief usher sat in front of the judge. 'All rise,' he barked out.

Judge Schindler walked in and sat slowly down, not looking towards us until he had looked at the jury and the other side of his court. He finally looked at us. He was wearing those small glasses that pawnbrokers wear so that they can look at the objects they are examining then look at you over the top. He did that a lot. Read, look, read, look, only moving his eyes.

At the start of a big trial there is always something in the air. Barristers get up for a trial just the same way sports people get psyched up. They don't bash their heads against a wall like mad rugby front-row forwards, or clench their fists, or twitch like Olympic athletes immediately before a race, but they get tingles in their fingers when they put the papers into their briefcases, which look like overweight versions of normal cases. As the case goes on the cases expand, almost as if the briefcase is experiencing pregnancy.

The first morning of the trial was taken up by legal arguments. You could say that we all felt confident. One by one our barristers outlined our case and stated that the evidence against us was flimsy, circumstantial and not very credible. After our opening speeches, I thought that the judge would stop the trial then with the words: 'No case to answer. Go home, gentlemen, and enjoy the rest of the season watching Chelsea.' I waited but the words never came.

Instead came the case for the Crown. The prosecution had two main barristers. Alan Suckling, QC, was the head honcho, with a long, thin, accountant's spent-too-long-studying-balance-sheets face, who occasionally chewed his cheeks, slightly sucking them in. He seemed to have a mean demeanour about him, beyond concentration intensity. The second-in-command stood up. He appeared a cocky man, also thin-faced, with short black hair trimmed neatly, the way the police have it. His name was Brian Lett – nicknamed 'Toilet' by the graffiti artists downstairs (Terry and I surmised that Jeff would call him 'Eau de . . .' to give it a classier edge). He had round gold-rimmed glasses on and every time he felt he made a moot point, he turned his head around as if he was looking for applause. He was number two, perhaps he wanted to be number one. This was his moment.

'Ladies and gentlemen of the jury, you are faced by members of a worldwide terror gang so widespread and dangerous that they could be broken out at any time. These people are such a terrible menace to society that if it wasn't for the vigilance and bravery of the undercover police, who risked life and limb to apprehend these menacing people, we could be looking at serious loss of life.'

Then came the crunch: 'There were links to far-right organisations which have violent anti-Semitic and racist tendencies.'

I looked over at Schindler on the bench and he wrote something down. Surely the jury would see through that claim, as Willie was black.

I looked around the court, which had fallen into a shocked hush, then I looked at the defendants one by one. Ginger Terry was a solicitor's clerk who liked a bet, cards and a game of chess. He was 5ft 4in tall in his stocking feet, with smart red hair and was quiet, meek and mild-mannered, yet was being painted by the prosecution as some sort of King Rat leading a deranged gang of modern-day Borgias.

Then there was myself. My star sign is Leo, recognised as a leader of men – well, that's what a Brighton fortune teller once said. While I have been described as being ugly and attractive at the same time, all I had ever wanted to do was be numero uno MWG and earn enough to keep me in beer and foreign holidays.

Then the others. Young Peter saw himself as a young Valentino. Toomsy was a caricature pisshead, overweight, jolly and scruffy, who everybody enjoys having around them in the pub. Vince was a decorator (a bit of a tosher, not much good at paper hanging) who didn't smile a lot, while Willie was as black as the ace of spades but very quiet, with that smile showing plenty of pearl white teeth. While he was 6ft 2in tall and a big, powerful man who looked mean, he was a special diet cook at a London hospital. Dale was short and stocky, with a hard look about him. Shaun was 5ft 10in tall and an average man who didn't stand out. All of us were just excitable Chelsea fans. Dougie was really unknown but seemed simple and fun. He looked like the shaggy character from the *Scooby Doo* cartoon, with his long face and body, while his standard expression to almost everything was 'Bollocks' or 'More bollocks'.

This was the crew being put forward as destroyers of the English way of life, yet our demeanour in the court could hardly have been described as frightening. If this were a Sunday school outing, all the old ladies would sigh and say how nice we looked. We could have been an advert for Pears soap, we looked so clean and tidy. We had set out our stall. In America, defence lawyers use presentation advisers using colour tones to influence juries. Our advice was look smart and keep quiet.

The evidence started. I'd read all the police statements and had run through them and made my comments. I felt I'd done enough to show them up for what they were – pure fiction – but there was one area that worried me. My legal team had fought tooth and nail to have my scrapbooks excluded as evidence. I'd kept a scrapbook of all the press cuttings of violence since I started to attend matches. I had always intended to write a book about the football terraces because at that time nobody had ever done it before.

When you hear evidence, it strikes you how funny it sounds compared to those it relates to. When the police officers started talking about the Everton match at the start of the trial, we all started sniggering. The match in question was a midweek Milk Cup tie. Ironic that the scrubbed schoolboys were being described at a Milk Cup match. I hadn't gone to the match so I wasn't really involved in this part of the trial, yet as I saw it, any inference from this would reflect on us all. Before the trial, Terry told me what had happened.

During the match, Chelsea played well, won 2–1 and the usual shouts about unemployed and thieving Scousers were chanted – Chelsea equals jobs and prosperity. Liverpool as a city is dirty and inhospitable. Even those who live five miles out tell jokes about it or warn their children that if they are naughty they will leave them in

Liverpool. A general catechism among Chelsea fans is that there are more burglar alarms in and around Liverpool than any other city in England. After the match, Terry and a few others came out of the ground to travel home and the usual hard core of Everton lads were waiting for them. It's always lively up there and win, lose or draw, the Scousers always want a piece of the Cockneys. Stanley knife loves Cockney and bottle alley is never far away as you get near Lime Street station for the trip home. No pub is safe in Scouseland for someone with a Cockney accent.

As they came out of the ground, some lunatic charged through Terry's group with a fireman's axe. He swung and missed Terry by inches. Terry was terrified and went to run, but other Scousers had come in after the mad axeman. With the police in close proximity, the mad axeman disappeared up the road. Miraculously, he hadn't struck anybody.

Within seconds of the fight erupting, half the Merseyside police force had intervened. The lads went back to Lime Street and Terry got a punch in the nose from some irate Evertonian in a brief skirmish. It was an occupational hazard for a Cockney in a foreign country. Once, two mates, Keith and Mark, had travelled up to Newcastle to watch a Chelsea match, booked into a B & B, gone to the match and then gone into a nightclub where they both pulled local girls. As they went outside, local lads heard their accents and started on Keith, giving him a whacking. Mark ran over to help just as the police came along. They heard the accents, gave both Mark and Keith a slap, let the three Geordies go and then nicked Keith for being drunk and disorderly, despite the protestations of the local girl. A policeman present summed it all up.

'Listen, lass. The best advice I can give you is to get off home and ignore this Cockney rubbish.'

PC Alan Bell stood in the dock. The police, with their dark uniforms, crisp white shirts and notebooks held at the ready, make giving evidence look slick and easy, so you can see why their evidence often sounds good, especially when they pull their notebooks out. Like us they wanted to create a good impression. 'Would you mind if I read from my notebook, your honour?' And they always look at the jury when they give their evidence and extend certain words within their evidence. They always use the surname of the accused because it sounds harsher. Not Stephen Hickmott or Terry Last but Last or Hickmott, stated in austere tones.

PC Bell stated that he had infiltrated the Chelsea mob. Joined 2,000 Chelsea fans inside the ground, where the atmosphere at the match was volatile. Chelsea fans were making gestures to their Everton counterparts. Well, if you look down at the team benches or go along to any Sunday morning amateur match, people are making gestures and shouting at each other. People have been making gestures at football matches since the game was first started last century. Even the Corinthian Casuals, the most gentlemanly of teams in the world, make gestures at each other and shout, because it's football. It was hard to see what the police were getting at, but as PC Bell went on it soon became obvious.

He admitted that the Chelsea fans were kept in the ground for 30 minutes after the match, so it would be reasonable to assume that any Everton fans waiting around would be the aggressors. But no, PC Bell painted Last as a man who was looking to confront Everton fans. Bell and his colleague PC Kehoe managed to follow a group of 30 who walked towards the station looking for trouble, even though there was no other way of getting back. Then they overheard these conversations.

'A man I know as O'Farrell shouted: "Hold your fucking horses, let's get this organised."

'Last then said, "The Everton always wait for us here on the left. They go around the back and come up this side street."

'O'Farrell said: "What are we going to do then?"

'"Meet them and go through the cunts."

'Reid then shouted: "What's the plan of action? What are we going to do? If we don't get it organised, we're going to get a kicking."

'"Just follow Terry, he knows what he's doing. Let's steam into the cunts."'

I remember laughing when I first read this. When it was read out in court I roared, much to the disgust of Schindler.

'Last then crossed the street and shouted to his group: "Let's have the cunts, let's run them." He then ran back down Diana Street with his fists clenched and into a group of about 20 Everton fans. He was punching and kicking with both his fists and feet. A number of Everton fans were punching and kicking.'

The picture painted was one of pure chaos, of people so out of control that the fabric of normal evening life outside Everton Football Club had suddenly come to a halt. Life had been changed by the introduction of these unfeeling heathens. Bell continued: 'I saw two vehicles stop closest to the fighting. Both drivers got out and ran across the road, leaving their vehicles. A man and a young woman who were crossing the junction when fighting broke out were forced to run across Walton Lane in front of moving traffic to avoid being caught up. I just happened to be standing in the central junction with PC Kehoe, watching the fighting, and I could see clearly.

'"Where the fuck were you," Last said to O' Farrell.

'"You were too quick," replied O' Farrell.

'"Next time, get it fucking right," said Reid.'

It was like a terror movie. People so mad that they took their fighting onto main roads and stopped the symbol of the 20th century, the motor vehicle. In true Hollywood terror movie tradition, the car occupants had stopped and fled on foot from this terrible monster. Nutters so fighting mad they walked in front of moving cars. They also terrorised innocent passers-by, making them risk their lives in busy moving traffic and leaving them mentally scarred for life.

The prosecution barrister got up and asked a series of seemingly banal questions which even Dougie could have written, all of which just restated what had been said. Then he said, 'Thank you, PC Bell', and sat down. Terry's barrister got up slowly. They always did that when they were about to ask something profound.

'Now, PC Bell. Could you please explain whereabouts you were in relation to Mr Last, who was by your own admission at the front of the group?'

'At the back.'

'Of a group of 30 people walking along a pavement because there was traffic coming along the road?'

'Yes.'

'Some way back, a considerable distance?'

'Not that far back. Close enough to hear them talking.'

The barrister then went into a comical routine about distance, using exaggerated verbal mannerisms and expressions relating to distance using the yardstick of the back of the court and to what extent PC Bell could hear people talking in the public gallery, which, of course, PC Bell could not.

'And were these 30 people between you and the group of three talking or making some noise?'

'Yes.'

'So you must have remarkable hearing to be able to hear all these conversations verbatim, bearing in mind the distance between you and the group you are alleged to have heard the conversations between?'

'Well yes, I suppose I have.'

Terry's man turned to the jury and put superlative expression on his verbal delivery.

'Come, come, PC Bell, isn't this the hearing of a superman?'

Then he ended the exchange in mid flow. In the movies, the witness admits his mistake. In real life this wasn't the case. As quick as he won that point the barrister moved on, rather like a boxer switches the point of attack from the body to the head. Points were made that even if Superman had heard the early exchanges between Terry, Shaun and Willie, they could be explained away by the fact that these innocent Chelsea fans might be nervous of getting beaten up in a rough city, especially as those Everton fans had been waiting around for nearly an hour by the time the attacks took place.

'Do you not think, PC Bell, that the police should be using their resources to tracking down the people who wait for nearly an hour to ambush my client, who is merely attempting to get on a train in a violent environment back to London? I believe there is a law relating to loitering with intent.' The barrister created an image of people sticking together like cowboys being circled by Indians and only fighting to defend themselves.

Then we had the recollections of Anthony John Brady. I thought PC Brady had the face of a man who was squinty. He reminded me of my hamster after I'd dropped it into the sink when I was a kid and when I fished it out, its eyes were scrunched up. Brady's mannerisms made for a lot of laughs in the waiting room downstairs. Some days it was only him that kept us going with humour.

Brady prided himself on knowing not only the nine accused but others, too, whose names he would throw into the statements, making the evidence come to life by adding bit-part players. He didn't just identify us from the incidents we were on trial for – he recognised us from previous football matches. Essentially, he was claiming to be part of the furniture at Stamford Bridge, close to the gang's workings.

Brady once stated that he watched the accused involved in 'heavy conversation'. When the defence barrister heard this, he wrote something down. When he got up to cross-examine him, it was the first in a series of hilarious exchanges. The defence barristers immediately saw a chance to lampoon him – it was almost too easy for them.

'PC Brady, what imperial or metric equivalent would you attach to the tone of a "heavy" conversation?'

Right from his first appearance, Brady lacked credibility in our eyes.

Then PC Peter Kehoe got up and remarkably remembered exactly the same words as PC Bell. He relayed the same dialogue, adding his little bit of theatre. 'Last fought furiously' and the car drivers were 'obviously alarmed as they jumped out'. Kehoe then added his own piece of startling evidence, which made the judge look up as well as the jury. His rider was more than a startling fact. It was Stephen King frightening, a blood-curdling roar from the Hound of the Baskervilles, its delivery by a po-faced PC making its resonance so frightening that ordinary people should have received counselling before they were exposed to something so sinister. 'I saw Last receive a blow in the face from what appeared to be a large wooden mallet wielded by one of the Everton supporters. Last's reaction was to fight furiously.' So Terry, all 5ft 4in of him, sitting in the dock with the complexion of a 12-year-old choirboy who would fall over if you hit him with a feather duster, had not gone down when being struck full in the face by a wooden mallet but had fought even harder. What sort of people were we?

I saw something in that first burst of evidence. They were trying to expose the fact that we were not really harmless football fans supporting their team, but something far worse. This was how they were trying to portray us: 'Ladies and gentlemen of the jury, what we have here are people who turn into superhuman monsters at a football match, impervious to pain or suffering. Football makes these people so mad that their physical appearance bears no resemblance to their ability to fight against any foe, even if they are outnumbered 10 to one. Men so strong that even a savage physical attack full in the face with a wooden implement from a violent rival, which would leave ordinary mortals pole-axed on the floor, cannot stop them. It only reinforces their strength to fight harder.'

From MWG to SAS in one fell swoop.

Last is so powerful that he can continue to fight and win despite horrendous physical injury with a weapon. A leader as great as El Cid, who led his men into battle despite being killed the day before. Remember how insignificant and skinny Heinrich Himmler, head of the SS, looked. Physical appearances can be deceptive. That is why he is such a powerful leader and why men follow him into battle. He does not even need any hospital treatment from such a blow.

Suddenly, in a flash, we were no longer harmless MWGs, we were the bogey man on a late night horror film. If we were allowed to spread our disease it would be the end. HG Wells couldn't have startled the population any more with his *War of the Worlds*. The tone was set.

January 11. The lads sat downstairs. So far the police had displayed little in terms of evidence and we all agreed that each officer had his own stupid mannerisms. 'Clowns at the circus,' stated Vince. Surely the jury would not accept this? Uninspiring was how I saw their evidence. My barrister saw it differently.

Today we were going to sit through video footage.

'It's like Saturday morning cinema,' gushed Dougie, unable to concentrate for very long. At least the rest of us could concentrate on the detail of what was being alleged and discuss matters with our legal team. For Dougie it was interminable boredom because he had never been to any of these places.

January 12. The jury were shown the security camera video of three Chelsea matches.

West Bromwich Albion away in August 1985
Liverpool away in November 1985
Everton away in December 1985

There we all were on the tape, watching the matches and generally talking, waving our arms, shouting at the referee and chanting Chelsea. There, contrary to the gaming act, Terry was seen playing cards with Toomsy and some others.

The video lasted 30 minutes in court. It was compiled from 450 hours of video footage. I remember going out with a posh Roedean-educated girl once and she took me to a Brighton art gallery to look at modern art. It all looked like someone had spilt paint on the canvas while she gushed about the mood of the picture.

'No, Stephen,' she chided me, 'you need to look deeper to find a hidden meaning.'

Well, all I can say is that the jury would have had to look very hard to find a hidden meaning in that 30 minutes. More to the point was that they'd been videoing us for six months yet not one gesture or abusive action could be shown to the jury. Terry was seen winning £50 off Toomsy, whose posture and belly looked shocking on film, while Chelsea drew and lost the away matches. Eventually, they came to a part where I was up on my feet making gestures.

'Here is Mr Hickmott rousing the crowd into violence.'

The jury had all seen more offensive gestures in their local primary school playground. Even the judge looked perplexed. The scribblers in the press gallery looked exasperated.

Of course we had all seen the extensive video footage, and some of it pre-dated the period of the conspiracy, so watching the part where Shaun was seen wading into the Crystal Palace fans, clearing their end, made us roar with laughter.

'Remember that Shaun? 1975. Absolutely stupendous. I'll ensure a crate of beer is sent over to your cell,' I whispered to him. Shaun looked red-faced at his stupid behaviour of ten years previously, having been caught on camera throwing punches at Palace fans. You naughty boy, Shaun.

Just up the road, the really big trial of Winston Silcott and others accused of murdering PC Keith Blakelock was going on. This trial was billed by the popular press as the story of the breakdown of law and order Police talked of revolution on the Broadwater Farm estate. In reality, that was a trial to send someone away for life for the murder of a police officer. Sometimes I'd read a paper relating to the Blakelock trial and an interesting fact was that after the Broadwater Farm riots when Blakelock was killed by a machete blow (or hacked to death by a frenzied, braying mob, if you read the *Daily Mail*) the police cancelled Tottenham Hotspur's home matches for two weeks in case football fans and disaffected youths on nearby Broadwater Farm joined forces and engaged in further disorder against the police.

In terms of avenging the breakdown of the established order, the rationale at the two trials was the same.

In the waiting room before the day's proceedings began, we always used to try to start the day with a joke. Looking at us sitting downstairs, laughing and joking, it was hard to believe we were on trial for serious offences. One day we were chided for the noisy laughter.

'Listen, mate, after watching Chelsea struggle for years at some of the grounds we've visited, this is like a trip to a five-star hotel after a week in Butlins,' cracked Shaun, which elicited more laughter.

Then the door would open, we'd be called and a silence would come over us as we made our way up the stairs. Dougie never went anywhere without his copy of *Viz*. Most days he'd recount some of Johnny Fart Pants or Cockney Wanker to us. 'I reckon those coppers are all a bunch of fartpants,' he'd say. Gradually everybody in the courtroom took on the persona of a *Viz* character. Brady in particular became the butt of our humour. His statements included the line where he had to state his date of birth. Brady had put 'over 21'.

'I reckon he's exaggerating his IQ,' said Terry.

One of the barristers told us that it was common in a long trial for at least one policeman or woman to come through as a right nincom- poop (this had to be translated by Terry to the other lads as buffoon). It was often the only way some of the judges kept concentration.

The day after the film show we were treated to more revelations from PCs Bell and Kehoe, with their amazing superman hearing. Bell now brought Dale into the fray.

'On Saturday December 14th, 1985, Chelsea were due to play Sheffield Wednesday. I entered a crowded Swan public house with PC Kehoe. As I stood by the bar I was joined by three youths, one of whom was Dale Green.

'"There's no fucker in here," stated Green as he looked around the bar.

'"Give them a few minutes, we've got almost half an hour before kick-off time," said his friend.

'"The fucking Wednesday coaches will be coming through in a minute, there'll be no fucker to meet them. If they stop at the lights outside here we might have a chance of a bit of a knuckle. They're a game lot, the fucking Wednesday," stated Green.'

The lads finished their drinks and went outside, while the duo followed. Dale then put his hat on, which PC Kehoe said was part of an elaborate disguise ritual, quoting him as saying: 'What do you think, cunt (*to his mate*), I don't want to be recognised when I put the coach windows in, do I? I got stopped from having a bit of a knuckle by this copper a couple of weeks ago. He might be here again today.'

PC Kehoe continued: 'Green later pulled the scarf up over his face and later gave a V-sign to passing Sheffield Wednesday coaches and shouted "Fucking shitters". I then went back into the pub and made notes of what had happened on a programme.'

When we went back downstairs at the end of the day, we felt the evidence offered was a pantomime so we turned it into one as we mimicked Kehoe. You could say that we weren't going to take this seriously. However, the constant use of gratuitous swear words in evidence was giving an impression that we were all foul-mouthed morons. As if we would call each other 'cunt'.

Amazingly to me, PC Peter Kehoe heard and saw the same thing, but added he had heard Green saying, 'We've got to show the flag, ain't we [by smashing up the Wednesday coaches]. No fucking bottle.'

Our defence barrister could not resist this and was up out of his chair like a sprinter coming out of the blocks.

'PC Kehoe, you claim to have made notes in the Swan public house immediately after the conversation. Did you stand at the bar and write these down in front of everybody?'

'No, I was undercover. I wrote them in the toilet.'

'What, by the latrines?'

'No, in the cubicle.'

'How long were you in there?'

'Around 15 minutes.'

'You sat in there for 15 minutes and wrote your notes. Was the public house toilet busy at this time?'

'Yes, sir.'

'Rather a risky thing to do, don't you think?'

'It was important to write down the statements straight away.'

'Where did you lean?'

'On the wall.'

'What sort of pen did you use?'

'An ordinary ballpoint pen.'

The barrister then walked back to his desk, offered PC Kehoe something to write on and asked him to demonstrate to the court how he wrote leaning against the wall with the pen raised. And the pen wouldn't write properly because the ink in an ordinary ballpoint only flows with gravity, with the tip pointing down on the paper.

'Yet you managed to get all this down by sitting in the cubicle for 15 minutes, leaning against the wall of the cubicle?'

'Yes.'

The barrister then produced a picture of the toilets of the Swan at 2.45pm on an average Saturday when Chelsea played at home. It was not a pretty sight. One of the women on the jury went green around the gills. Even my stomach turned a little. Only Toomsy was unmoved.

The clerk called the landlord of the Swan. He wasn't in court. Schindler was beside himself with rage. A man leant over the front of the judge's bench, then scurried out when Schindler barked at him. The landlord eventually turned up. In the witness box he stated that there had been no locks on the doors of any of the cubicles for a considerable period, because they had been kicked off so many times there was no wood for the metal screws to grip on to.

'So not only did you claim to write on a slippery melamine wall but you also had to keep one foot holding the door shut while people tried the door to get in. Under these circumstances, PC Kehoe, I put it to you that you could not have written that in the toilet because you were never in that toilet.'

We smiled at each other. Shot down in flames. Mayday. Mayday.

The landlord of the Swan was told to report to the court again the next day to explain his late arrival. Now Schindler addressed him on his terms.

'Why were you late?'

'One of my deliveries was late and I unloaded it before I set out.'

'Do you know how much this trial is costing per hour? You have wasted this court's time. You will go to the cells downstairs until I decide you can go, to see how you like waiting in court. You will also be fined the sum of £250.'

When his licence came up for renewal later in the year, he lost his licence to trade as a publican.

The same day saw an Arsenal fan, Ian Lowe, jailed for 30 days for headbutting a police officer, with a fine of £100 or 14 days' concurrent for drunkenness. This depressed Dougie no end, because he was only in for throwing a drunken punch which hit a police officer.

9

SCRIPTWRITERS' DAY OUT

As the trial went on, it settled down into a pattern. One day would see some excitable parts, the next it would be rather boring and tedious as the barristers played what seemed like legal games with each other. The judge liked this bit because he was able to take an active part. Terry was at his barrister all the time, pushing him on a legal point, making sure that he'd push a certain matter back at the prosecution when he felt that Inman hadn't pursued it as far as he wanted him to. Terry was always thinking. If he wasn't doing the *Telegraph* crossword he was thinking about a chess puzzle. Time, which at the start of the trial had seemed so important, now became a blur. Once more I put in for a bail application and once again it was slapped down. I felt that the anti-Semitic references to our activities had turned the judge against me.

Some days the exchanges became reminiscent of Laurel and Hardy slapstick rather than a serious criminal trial. The police during their raids had discovered a Red Hand of Ulster badge on Black Willie's jacket. The prosecution tried to make a case that Willie was a National Front activist. Willie looked at Lett incredulously.

'But I'm black!'

'An interesting paradox, do you not think, Mr Reid? A black member of the National Front,' smirked Lett.

'I am black, therefore I oppose the policies of a party which wants

135

to deny me the right to live in this country, which is my home, and ship me back to where I don't come from.'

'So why do you have the Red Hand of Ulster badge, which represents a far-right paramilitary organisation?'

'I like the badge. The colours look good. It's a fashion thing. The colours look good on my dark jacket.'

We started laughing. 'He's pushed himself into a corner,' muttered Terry to me.

Lett seemed to choke. He then tried to pursue the point. Willie was not only opposed to the National Front, he used to go out with Harriet Harman, a future Labour Cabinet Minister, helping to distribute anti-racist literature. Harriet even offered to come to court to be a witness about Willie's work in combating racism. As it was, a letter from her was shown to the court outlining Willie's involvement in anti-racist politics. One by one the jury read it and nodded and looked over at Willie. From that moment, Willie was not guilty.

The prosecution wanted to show that we were bigots and that part of our activities was a far-right conspiracy revolving around attacks on Jews and blacks. They tried to link us with the far right, including Irish, Belgian and French paramilitary groups. But if we were racist, why were we mates with Willie? Trying to link Willie with the National Front was a bad day at the office for the prosecution.

Most days, Dougie spent the morning daydreaming. In the early part of the trial he made faces at the prosecution team when they turned to look at us, or tried winking at the women jurors. Schindler saw him doing it one day. Dougie clocked him out of the corner of his eye and sat up as the judge bristled. He seemed exasperated with Dougie, who shook his head every time it was mentioned that he was in our company. The judge didn't like this and scowled when he saw Dougie doing it. Terry and I were listening intently and we would often lean across to whisper a comment regarding a police officer's evidence. They were wheeling people in from everywhere. In the afternoons, Dougie would bring his *Viz* up to the court and start reading it. One day he burst out laughing at a Fat Slags story.

The judge jerked his head up and motioned for counsel to stop talking. A hush fell over the court. He looked at Dougie.

'Mr Welsh, you might be laughing now but let me tell you this: if you are found guilty of this charge, you will be punished with the full force of the law which I can give.'

Dougie snapped back: 'I shouldn't be here. I don't even know these people. I had never seen them before I was dragged down the police station. Nobody knows why I am here. What the hell am I doing here? This trial is a fucking laugh and they know it,' said Dougie, pointing to the police.

'You will be quiet in my court!'

'Right, that's it. I'm not sitting up here about something that is nothing to do with me.'

He stood up and went downstairs. Schindler looked horrified. He stopped the trial and summoned Dougie's barrister.

'You will go downstairs and tell your client that he will apologise or be in contempt.'

The barrister returned, as did Dougie to his seat. The barrister then apologised and the trial continued, albeit in a slightly tense atmosphere. Later Dougie told us what happened.

'The barrister came in and said I should apologise. "Bollocks, what can the judge do? Jail me? You want an apology, then you give it." So he did.' Dougie spent the next month refusing to come upstairs, sitting downstairs reading every novel he could lay his hands on – real escapist stuff like Sidney Sheldon or Harold Robbins. Every day the judge looked over the dock and saw only eight of us. I don't think he was impressed.

I remembered the colour of Young Peter when he got bail, the colour flooding back into his face. I felt a lot of jealousy. I tried once again. For a third time I was knocked back.

After a month of the trial, for some obscure reason, all bail was revoked. Now they had to transfer nine of us back and forth. This was far too much for their meagre resources to cope with, so they rigged together two cells, put in bunk beds and let us stay at the Inner London Court cells. It soon became an MWG social event, especially when it was realised that the court cells backed onto a park and we had windows to the outside world. Willie's black friends, who lived locally, used to jump down into a concrete recess and pass cans of beer, bottles of vodka and dope through. Nights became fun. One evening, Dougie sat there and said it was the best Tuesday night out he'd ever had. Willie used to get faceless drunk. One evening, Shaun berated him.

'Shape up, Willie, or you'll get us all nicked.'

It was meant to be tongue-in-cheek, which made its delivery even funnier, so he tempered it with: 'Okay then, give us a couple of cans.'

Young Peter's girlfriend used to pass McDonald's through the windows then sit there half the night talking to him. In the early morning all the debris was thrown out of the window. The warders didn't seem to suspect anything. Anyway, we weren't harming anybody, plus they really liked us because we were always laughing. They arranged a TV and discussed football with us. One Monday morning, Vince spoke to the warders with a completely straight face.

'I see the boys did well at the weekend.'

'Really?'

'Yeah, 35 arrested.'

More laughter.

The defence barristers love someone who they can mock or show up. It is intellectual bullying, or a chess match where one side has poor piece positioning and the opposition attacks. As Terry put it one morning: 'There is always someone in life, and it doesn't matter what he does or wears, he always looks stupid. Right from their first day at primary school, through secondary school, they are destined to be laughed at because of their crass stupidity. We had one at our office. He wore wide pinstripes and red braces and used to think that he was attractive to the girls. He used to slobber over them in the summer while they were working, with his little sweaty underarm patch. Even the men in the office used to cringe.'

We all looked at each other and immediately shouted out various names of the person we thought was fool of the week, then burst out laughing raucously.

One day Brady was subjected to a torrid cross-examination from my barrister. I bet this exchange has been told at legal dinner parties a few times.

'Mr Brady, you claim in your statements to know the accused personally. You recognise them and have been at away matches and have spoken to them using first names. Would this be a true statement of facts?'

'Yes, sir.'

'So would it be fair to say that they recognise you, because you are quite well known in the Shed End (*Shed End was explained to the judge*) for throwing people out?'

'Yes,' Brady smiled. The barrister had fed him the bait, he had bitten and was about to get reeled in.

'So, Mr Brady. How did you go undercover?'

'I bought a brown anorak.'

'You purchased an anorak. A brown anorak.' The barrister said 'brown anorak' the way Lady Bracknell pronounced the words 'a handbag' in Oscar Wilde's *The Importance of Being Earnest*. He then produced two photographs of Brady, one in uniform and one with the anorak.

'Quite a disguise, Mr Brady, (*subdued laughter in the court*). I can see no difference in these, yet you claim to have been able to get close enough to my client on numerous occasions and listen to his

139

conversations, yet he failed to recognise you. Does this not strike you as a little strange?'

'No, sir.'

The barrister then questioned Mr Brady about an incident which we were aware of at a previous Chelsea home match against Millwall.

'Mr Brady, I believe that not only are you well known to my client but during a match against Millwall a substantial part of the Shed terrace chanted at you.'

Brady looked at him rather quizzically.

We all started giggling as we half knew what was coming because we had briefed our barristers.

'Please could you tell the court what your nickname is as I believe you know of it.'

Brady mumbled something under his breath.

'Please speak up for the court, Mr Brady.'

Brady mumbled something once again.

'Mr Brady seems to have some problem speaking clearly. I believe that the crowd are chanting "Rat Face Brady, Hang Him, Hang Him, Hang Him." I also believe from my client that your sobriquet within the Shed terrace is "Rat Face Brady". Hardly a man who would be inconspicuous undercover wearing a brown anorak, would you say?'

I swear I saw the judge laughing. I know we all fell about, as did the public gallery. My barrister enjoyed his after-work glass of chardonnay that evening. Not that we had it all our own way. The clarity of the legal mind is always a revelation.

When Terry took to the witness stand, they were determined to go after him. Terry did not drink. The popular conception was that drink caused violence. So the fact that Terry didn't drink, or very rarely drank, might have been against them.

'Do you drink, Mr Last?'

'No, only orange juice.'

'Ah. You don't drink in order to keep your head clear for the real business of fighting or organising the fighters. You don't want alcohol to cloud your mind.'

They had declared their hand. No drink is bad. So we thought we'd get a step ahead of the legal minds on this. When Toomsy was asked the same question, he might say: 'Yeah, you bet, I drink between 12 and 15 pints.' Yes, Mr Toombs. This ensures that you are really fighting mad, able to take physical blows which otherwise would hurt you. Alcohol enables you to have superhuman strength.

We thought it over again. Same question. 'Two pints.' Very good. Just enough to get you in the mood for a fight but not too much so that you will have a cloudy mind. Still able to think but able to get a buzz from the beer.

By the time I got on to the stand, I felt I had the optimum level in my head.

'Four or five pints.'

'A good way to get fighting mad just before the alcohol stops you functioning effectively as a fighting machine, Mr Hickmott.'

That was scary stuff because it wouldn't have mattered what level of alcohol we had consumed, they would have to establish a causal link between their evidence of violence and our pre-match drink. If we'd have read the Bible before matches I am sure they would have shown this created a violent state in our minds.

Terry was an avid collector of everything he had ever done, as well as keeping a diary. The diaries were to be a main plank of the case against Terry and ultimately us all. The conspiracy had to be underpinned by some central pillar and it became obvious early on that an organisation had to have a leader. Terry, with his responsible job and chess skills, was put in as that leader. In reality he was an intelligent loner who kept his work, social and football life separate. He was interested in studying birds and often travelled out to the Norfolk Broads to watch rare species on the Fens. This threw the prosecution but they soon had this strange paradox down as a form of schizophrenia. Sensible, well-adjusted person goes mental at football. Terry had purchased a number of photographs from a guy nicknamed Plasticine, who took photos at football. His intention was to publish a book of photographs about lads at football. Terry felt that the notes in his diary would also have made for a good book, as football fans were a social phenomenon. One day, during Terry's cross-examination, the prosecution came in with a revolutionary discovery. They told the court that they had discovered books full of secret codes, so secret that they could not break it. Terry's barrister was up and at them.

'These secret codes are actually books of chess moves. Mr Last is a member of a chess club and, like all club players, keeps a record of his moves,' he said forcibly with barely concealed scepticism, like he was dealing with a fool.

Lett didn't flinch. For every action there is an equal and opposite explanation.

'You see, ladies and gentlemen of the jury, Mr Last is a cunning general. He moves his men around like chess pieces. The chess pieces are his foot soldiers and the code books are records of the moves of these foot soldiers.'

Terry stood out well in the box. For the rest of us there was the hilarity, generated by his obsessive collecting of all things Chelsea. One day the clerk came in with a bottle of Chelsea aftershave and the Chelsea record from the 1970 Cup final, 'Blue is the Colour'.

The clerk announced that he was introducing the appearance of Chelsea aftershave into the list of exhibits. This caused ripples of laughter all round while we roared, especially Willie as he saw that as rank bad taste.

'Where did he get Chelsea aftershave from and what does it smell of?' he sniggered. 'Splash it all over, splash it all over,' was heard mimicking the famous Brut TV advert. I was laughing so much that Schindler demanded silence in the court. Just admitting that you wore a football team aftershave would have been total humiliation in the pub. Schindler failed to see the funny side of it.

Terry looked at us daggers. He parried the questions so well for seven days that it beggared belief that the person in the witness box was the same one the police were describing. Terry's diary did mention confrontations with other fans but for the most part it was really a record of his life. He was an obsessive collector of everything, match ticket stubs, Bucharest tram tickets, etc, so it was very difficult for the prosecution to cast doubt on what Terry had been doing on certain days, because he would quip: 'I remember that well. I have the record of who attended in my diary.' There were quotes in the diary which the prosecution wanted to make hay with, but for the main Terry was well ahead on points.

They did numerous moves to try and throw him. One day the prosecution pulled in Terry's collection of a stuffed puffin and a guillemot.

'What is the relevance of these, Mr Last?'

Like, what the hell are you on about? Terry looked at him like Eric Morecambe used to look at Ernie Wise when Ernie would pronounce that he had written a play wot was the best.

'Relevance? They are stuffed birds. I am interested in rare bird breeds. I do not see taxidermy as a criminal offence. I purchased those from an antique shop.'

It was almost as if the prosecution were trying to paint Terry as an off-the-wall person who would be attracted to the abstract thrill of football violence. He was the mad colonel in *Apocalypse Now* who went surfing during the heat of a battle. Terry's bird-watching outings with a telescope were really a chance to plan violent strategies at future confrontations. Stuffed birds showed an interest in death.

Terry's diary meticulously recorded the punch-ups we had been involved in, recording the good laughs we'd had. 'Run the Derby, 35 of us done 200 of them. Done really well.' Harmless stuff, really. Then the prosecution asked Terry about the Spurs Auschwitz song in his diary. Lett asked Terry to sing it from the dock. Schindler wanted to hear it so Terry sang it, while we laughed.

> *Spurs are on their way to Auschwitz*
> *Hitler's gonna gas 'em again*
> *You can't stop 'em*
> *The boys from Tottenham*
> *The boys from White Hart Lane*

The effect of this on Schindler was lost on us because we were too busy laughing, unable to appreciate the seriousness with which a Jewish judge would view this type of humour.

The police had dredged around everywhere to find data on Terry. Once, coming back from Turkey, a woman called Josie Sykes had exchanged words with him on the aeroplane because she wouldn't sell him a programme. Her comments were put to Terry. Abuse of females was how it was presented, even though there was nothing in it. Then they produced different bank books, which they made out to be some sort of secret hooligan slush fund. Terry kept all his money separately from whatever he did. Perhaps some of the cash transactions he indulged in during his spare time with certain individuals were outside of the law, but that was not what he was on trial for. After seeing what had happened with Terry, Vince decided not to go into the witness box.

Dougie's humour was infectious, so we often told him some of our stories before the day's court started or during a lunch recess, especially during the month he stayed downstairs. There were times when we were not in the waiting room downstairs but somewhere in Europe, watching Chelsea or England.

Chelsea played Leyton Orient in the fourth round of the FA Cup in 1979. Fancy dress, everybody said. My brother was always acting the goat and one evening he turned up with a full gorilla suit.

'Don't ask me where I got it from,' he said, so I didn't. Dressing up at football is de rigueur nowadays, but in the seventies it was unheard of. I walked out of the tube at Leyton dressed in full gorilla outfit. Even though it wasn't that warm, I was sweltering inside. I gained entry with all the Chelsea fans, making animal noises. On the terraces I started jumping up and down when Chelsea scored. I was hauled out of the ground. The police told me that they were ejecting me for behaviour likely to cause breach of the peace. Sense of humour bypass, really. The picture of a gorilla (me) being escorted out by an unsmiling PC was reproduced in every Sunday paper. As I came out of the ground, some Chelsea fans waiting outside were being abused by a small firm of West Ham. The sight of a gorilla charging along Leyton High Street caused consternation among the West Ham ranks and they scattered in pure panic. I had the paper clipping framed with the caption printed underneath: 'Which One's The Monkey?' When the police raided my house they asked me about the picture and caption, although they never used it in court.

Terry had been in Greece in 1982 for the European Championship qualifying match. 'That was one hell of a trip. Twenty of us got a cheap trip out to Athens and stayed for four days. We set up shop in a local taverna. Athens hospitality is legendary and this taverna owner was no exception. We were offered everything he had except a night with his daughter, although had our intentions been honourable then I have no doubt he would have been happy to let us go courting with her. The international match was due to be played in Salonika on the Wednesday and the trip included a coach transfer on the day of the match. As we were in Athens on the Tuesday night, we decided to attend the Under-21 match. On the Monday evening the locals were so friendly. On the morning of the game we got some funny looks. Before the match, the tension in the air was palpable. As we walked towards the stadium, all hell broke loose.

'Bricks, bottles, stones came at our group. Standing across the road were hundreds of lunatics foaming at the mouth. "Don't you recognise some of them?" I said. "We were drinking with them last night." Forward they came. We retreated, then made our charge to make them back off. The Greek fans were throwing everything they had at us, including the kitchen sink. I remember looking across the road and seeing our friendly local taverna owner frothing at the mouth and throwing rocks in our direction. A man possessed, unable to recognise us in that state. I remember kung-fu kicking this mad, screaming Greek in the chest, which sent him crashing back against a wall. Even then he continued to shout obscenities at me, so I dropped him with a right-hander whereupon, on lunatic autopilot, he spumed more abuse at me.

'Eventually we fought our way to the entrance gate of the stadium and entered. Inside, the atmosphere was even more manic, with us being attacked from three sides. The only way to stem the barrage of debris was to charge the Greeks to make some space between us and, aided by the riot police, we managed to do this. Up close, the Greeks didn't want to know. As soon as a huge gap was cleared, good old Ted Croker, the Football Association chairman, came on to the terracing. Follow me, boys, to the safety of the seats? You're joking. Was Ted there to help us, to give us good advice? No.

' "You deserve everything you get, as we have told you not to travel. You are not wanted by us and you shouldn't be wearing those England shirts," said Ted.

' "Well, you bloody sold them to us, you old twit," someone chipped in, then people who'd been under attack for the past hour gave him a piece of their mind.

' "Thank you, good Samaritan Ted," added Jeff. Then as he turned to leave he was set upon by the locals and took a battering. Ted then turned to us, looking for help.

' "Bugger off, you silly old bastard, you're getting everything you deserve," shouted a fan, which made us all laugh, in between ducking more flying rocks.

'Fear comes in many forms. Here in Greece it was totally manic, then it upped a couple of levels when the riot police fired tear gas indiscriminately and started clubbing everybody who ran away, making a chaotic situation madness because the crowd then started stoning us and the police. God knows how the Greeks built an empire, if that was anything to go by. After the match we were kept in the ground for an hour, then transported by armoured bus to Piraeus. As soon as we alighted we were confronted by hundreds of locals with sticks, stones and bottles. Another battle ensued. Where's good old Ted when you need him?

'The next morning we travelled to Salonika for the full international and experienced something similar as England won 3–0. This time, we got into the stadium but couldn't hold our ground and had to leave and fight our way up on to a hill overlooking the stadium. We stood there holding the high ground, running the Greeks back down the hill throughout the match, even rolling huge boulders down the hill. Every time one of these boulders smashed into them we let out a huge roar, which caused the Greeks to charge again. Inside the ground, the West Ham lads rallied all the other fans and were fighting non-stop as the Greeks really went for it. With no other choice but to fight the Greeks, the West Ham led the lads themselves and they did it in true marsh man style, fighting their way out of the stadium, eventually being led around the pitch while the cameras bulbs flashed. The banner headlines in the tabloids shouted "England Fans Fighting Disgrace Again". The violence was exacerbated by the larger crowd present, combined with the riot police's determination to club everybody in the vicinity of a fight, regardless of who was getting attacked. Two lads from Oldham received nine-month prison sentences each for pushing over a police bike in the mayhem. After the match we came under a hail of stones and bottles. A typical Greek welcome, according to Jeff.

'On the Thursday morning we returned to Athens, with everybody smiling at us, and entered our local taverna. "Welcome, crazy English. Greek football not as good as England, eh?" the owner shouted. "Have an ouzo." He then poured out drink after drink like he was somebody else. We whispered among each other: "That was him, wasn't it?" Other customers came in and slapped us on the back and drank to our health – the same people who'd been trying to decapitate us on the Tuesday evening now invited us to stay with them the next time we visited Athens for an England match. Now that really was incredible.'

Although we had read the police statements before the trial and had some idea about what they were planning to say, actually hearing the evidence presented before a jury still had the power to shock.

On 20 January, the court heard from PC Michael McAree, who was on duty in plain clothes and happened to be in the King's Head. Terry and the boys used to have legendary games of cards in there before matches. Two weeks' wages and a season ticket have been won with a pair of Jacks blind against the board at three-card brag before.

'Green walked into the bar and peered into various cubicles which skirt part of the bar. He then walked to another part of the bar which is dimly lit. He appeared to be looking for someone. Green then sat down in a cubicle opposite the entrance door, having purchased himself a drink and some food. At 5.45pm a male who I know to be Terence Last entered the public house. He went directly to the cubicle where Dale Green was seated. The two shook hands. Last was given what appeared to be a pint of lager. At 5.50pm O'Farrell, along with Gerald Kelly and Michael Thomas Greenaway, entered the bar and sat with Last and Green.'

'Zigger Zagger, Zigger Zagger, Oi Oi Oi' laughed Vince to Shaun, referring to Greenaway.

'There were two other males in the group,' McAree went on. So far the lads had met for a pre-match drink. However, this was the start of something so incredible that we all felt that they had been watching too many Godfather movies.

'Last was sitting at the head of the table and indicated to the other persons present when they should speak by pointing to them.'

Terry leaned over to me. 'We were playing pontoon and I was banker so I indicated when they had to bet, because you know what the lads are like, they sit there chatting before a match when they should be concentrating on the cards.'

McAree continued: 'Last appeared to be acting as chairman. At about 6.30pm all the persons previously mentioned got up from the table and walked across the road to the Swan. Gerald Kelly took with him a glass of beer. I entered the Swan and I noticed that all those persons previously mentioned were sat at a table on the podium next to the stage. Again, Last seemed to be acting as chairman, pointing to the other participants to indicate again when to speak.'

'We took our card school over the Swan because the landlord was worried about the police tugging him about illegal gambling,' whispered Terry.

'At 6.55pm, a man I know as Douglas Welsh entered. He was greeted by members of the group. He sat down at the table, where the discussion continued with Last again appearing to act as chairman. Shortly afterwards I went towards Stamford Bridge with this group, who joined up with another group who had been lurking around Fulham Broadway station. Kelly, who had been standing in a window of a kebab shop opposite for 40 minutes keeping watch, joined the men. Inside the stadium we stood on the Shed. The match was between Chelsea and Oxford United.'

'I was in the West Stand seats,' said Terry.

'I and PC Pickard formed part of the group around Green, who stood with his back to the game.'

This was a popular myth printed in the press at the time, that many football fans never watched the match and stood facing the crowd or the away fans, hurling obscenities. PC McAree then relayed a remarkable series of statements relating to the group which brought others of the accused into play.

' "Toomsy will get a group visa and hooky passports." This was queried by a person unknown. "Don't be a cunt, it's fucking Russia you are going to, not a day trip to France," replied Green.' After all, he'd been at a meeting with the chairman only minutes previously. Some of the others didn't want to go to Russia but they were all up for the World Cup in Mexico where they didn't need visas. Toomsy was billed as the expert.

'Trust Toomsy with cash? He's not being serious. Give him your dosh and he'd go hunt down a card school,' said Vince.

PC McAree had heard more: '"You should have seen the Sunderland game, it was fucking magic. There was this cunt from Sunderland. I give him a good kicking before the match and would you believe it, the cunt turns up at the game covered in fucking bandages. You know, I felt sorry for him. He told me he had 17 stitches. I didn't have the heart to give him another dig," said Green.

'"Yeah, fucking good night that was, we fucking slaughtered 'em, you did a good job, mate, setting that up," said an unknown youth.

'"Get ready for Saturday," said Green.

'"Yeah, it will be all right. The man's a genius," said a coloured youth.'

When this was read out, all of us collapsed in fits of uncontrollable laughter. Judge Schindler was not impressed. 'You will control yourself.' I looked over at the jury. A couple of them were smirking. Despite the shout from Schindler, you sensed that he had a sense of humour. If it hadn't been for the anti-Semitism attached to our case, I felt that the judge would have liked our humour. Willie leant over and whispered in a mocking voice, like Lenny Henry does: 'Yeah. Who is the man? The fucking genius? Who is this shady Mr Big?'

'Green continued to hold court with his back to the match. At half-time, Green adjourned to a tea bar.

'"You should have seen this copper at Finsbury Park. We gave him a right pasting."

'"What about the cunt with the fire extinguisher," added someone else. Green burst into laughter.

'"I showed the cunt. Set fire to him then hit him over the head with a fire extinguisher," then laughed even more, adding: "The world's full of cunts." Just before the end of the match, someone asked Green if he had anything lined up for tonight.

'"How many have they brought, two?" stated Green.

'"Pity, I fancied a good kicking tonight," added another.

'"This lot will have come by car, won't they? There's no point in doing the stations and I reckon there's no coaches. I sent John to have a look for coaches but there isn't any," stated Green.

'"Still," added his mate, "there's always Saturday."

'"We've got something half worked out," added Green at the end of the match. At the final whistle I followed Green back to the Swan, where we sat near Green and a number of other people in his company.

'"Be ready for Saturday, boys," stated Green as he left the pub at 12.05am.'

PC Pickard heard the same words.

'PC McAree, you state that you stood outside the Shed. Could you please show me on this sketch where you stood and allegedly overheard these conversations?'

McAree looked and indicated a position directly below the tea bar.

'Known as the Bovril entrance at Chelsea?'

'Yes, that is correct.'

It was the part of the end next to the covered terrace, open to the elements. There followed a series of questions to ensure no ambiguity and enable the barrister to ascertain exactly where McAree had been standing. Going slowly back to his desk, the barrister collected papers which were the weather reports for London regarding the evening in question. Huge amounts of rain had fallen that evening. The court was told that whenever it rained, the practice was for everybody to crowd under the Shed terrace roof to seek cover.

After a pause, the barrister asked McAree how he managed to hear all this given the circumstances. The barrister didn't seem to be expecting an answer. McAree shrugged a don't know.

'No further questions.'

They might have been made to look stupid but what they had done was paint a picture of foul-mouthed youths who glibly talked about setting fire to people or giving them a kicking so bad that they needed 17 stitches – like Dale wasn't human.

My entrance into the conspiracy took a little while. When it came it was dramatic. Fact is often stranger than fiction – but not when it is being translated from some police statements in our case. For a match at Birmingham they managed to work in every aspect of our terrible behaviour. Deceit, cunning and violence. And I was like Macbeth making his entrance in the second act after the witches had dominated the stage.

At the match played at St Andrews on Saturday 21 December, PC Bell went to the refreshment bar at half-time, where he observed Stephen Hickmott standing with Douglas Welsh. Also with them was Vincent Drake.

'Good game was it, Dougie?' I whispered.

'Is St Andrews where the golf course is?' he replied.

Boy, as a football fan you sure do get offered some miserable choices. Greaseburger or no burger at all. Stale bread, ketchup bottles with two-week-old rubbery residues by the squirt nozzle. Warm stewed tea in polystyrene cups. Burned animal fats and stewed onions lingering in the air amid the sizzle sounds of the 98% meat-free sausage swimming in its own fat. Football fan catering; culinary excellence it ain't. What they haven't sold the week before is probably frozen down to be sold the following week.

As I remembered it, the Birmingham bar was closed that day, but anyway, Bell of the super hearing had overheard our cunning strategy.

'"We're leaving the ground early, there will be about 200 heavies so there will be no problem," said Hickmott.

'"Where will the Birmingham be?" asked Drake.

'"We'll meet them somewhere along the main road towards the city centre. We've got to go before the Old Bill get their act together.

Meet back here at about 4.25, then. Put the word about," said Hickmott.

'At about 4.25pm a large group of about 150 were by the exit gates, which were now open. Hickmott, Drake and one other walked into the centre of this group and a conversation took place. They left the ground to be confronted by a number of mounted police, who turned them back. Hickmott, Drake and the others then engaged in heated conversation. At the end of the match, myself and PC Kehoe were at the back of a group of around 50 who declined the offer to get on buses to go back to Birmingham New Street station. When the group was stopped, Hickmott and Drake pushed past the police officers, then rejoined the group. While they were waiting, Drake and Hickmott were talking to another group about football in general.

'"Do these lads know about the QPR game?" said Drake. "We're going to ambush the QPR at Ladbroke Grove at 10 in the morning. They are meeting there early and all coming to Chelsea together."'

Kehoe also apparently had the ability to see around corners and hear words that were spoken, had a vivid recollection of numbers and had managed to keep near enough to myself and Vince to hear our words. Amazingly, I was also judged so powerful that I could push past police officers with impunity. Almost as if I had some sort of mythical power, like Obi-Wan Kanobi in *Star Wars*.

Then we had the versions of plainclothes police officer Donnegan. He observed me not watching the game at all but 'getting information from other youths who were asking him what was happening after the game'.

'"We're meeting at the back," Hickmott replied.'

Later in his statement Donnegan brought Terry and Shaun into the affair and managed to link the forthcoming trip to the Mexico World Cup with gang violence, introducing the name of the Birmingham group, the Zulu Warriors.

'They were talking about the World Cup in Mexico and how they intended to get to Mexico and how much it was going to cost.

Another youth ran past on the outside of the crowd and joined Last's group.

'"Tel, are we gonna have a go at the Zulus or what?"

'"Yeah, no problem. Where were you earlier when we had a go?"

'"I was looking for you but couldn't find you."

'"When we get near New Street we'll break away from the Old Bill and get them in the town centre. They'll be waiting for us anyway," said Last.

'"How many have you got, Tel?"

'"I've got Shaun and Peter and about six more. Hickey should be up the front with a few, we've got more than enough for the Zulus. Peter, try and find Hickey and we'll have a go at New Street."

'Peter then went to the outside and ran off towards the front of the crowd . . .'

'Jesus, it's fantasy island, how could I run to the front when we were penned in by horses and half the Birmingham police force?' said Young Peter to Terry, shaking his head.

'It's a bloody John Wayne film,' said Shaun.

'"Shaun, hold on, let's stick together," called out Terry. "Slow down, let's get the firm together. We'll have a go at New Street."

'We were approaching New Street and were walking over an underpass. Below were a large group of youths. They were chanting "Zulu, Zulu."

'"Let's get the cunts," shouted Last, who then ran across the road and jumped up onto a wall overlooking looking the youths below, where he was joined by six others. A mounted policeman got them back into line. I again got behind Last, who was joined by O'Farrell.

'"Fuck that horse, we could have had a good knuckle then. Never mind, we'll get away at the station."

'When we arrived at the station the Chelsea fans were escorted on to trains.'

My concern that day was that our coach was not where it should have been. Robin had gone Christmas shopping and the crowds and traffic in and around the town centre meant that he was not at the rendezvous point. I had so many people coming up to me asking me what was going on after the match that I told everybody to meet at the back and follow me. Birmingham were one of the worst teams I had ever seen, so when they equalised everybody just wanted to go home. However, Chelsea scored late to secure the points, which made everybody full of beans. When the police unlocked the gates after holding us in for about 20 minutes after the match, they allowed me and one other person to leave the cordon to look for the coach then, when we returned, advised us to be escorted up to New Street because they didn't want us hanging around at the ground waiting for the coach. In the meantime, they would get on the radio and try to find out where the coach was.

For some reason, the police were out in force. If this was a Macbeth conspiracy then there were more than three witches stirring the pot today. On the witness stand, PC Hobbs said he continually observed Vince not watching the match. Hobbs had a nice line in chatty observation combined with the firm hand of the law. He added the personal touch with comments like: 'Remember, lads, we're from London and I can recognise you, so behave or we'll have you nicked. You arranged to meet the coach here [at New Street] just to cause trouble on your way back, didn't you?'

He was the nice guy bobby, firm but fair, and we would respond to this type of policing, so much so that he claimed I said to him: 'Are you coming back on our coach? We've got some juicy videos.' Hobbs said he had then read the riot act: 'When this coach gets going, it is not to stop until it gets clear of Birmingham. Is that clear?'

As it happened, we all got on board and 50 yards up the road the coach was attacked by a huge mob of Birmingham fans with bricks. Three lads on the coach were arrested for daring to complain about the police failure to give us an escort.

Nick Price pushed as hard as he could but could make no instant impact on nothing observations. 'Would you say that someone organising a coach would be asked questions as to where and when people were supposed to meet their pick-up, and would you say that you have not established any link between my client and any violent incidents, except to state in your own words that his party was the recipient of a vicious cowardly attack by a determined group of people calling themselves Zulus who were 20 times the number contained on my client's coach?'

One by one, all the police agreed. But we know that Macbeth comes along as an ordinary guy but turns bad later. A play needs to develop its bad guys as it goes on. The problem was that the jury were not taking this early stuff in. Who remembers how pretty the young girl was in the first scene of *The Exorcist*?

Derek Inman wanted some of the action regarding the comments about Terry.

'So you claim that my client's reaction to seeing a group of youths below him in an underpass, shouting, "Zulu, Zulu, let's all do the Chelsea," was to jump on a wall overlooking them. How much lower was the underpass? Thirty feet? Forty feet? Did you think that my client was seriously intending to jump 40 feet off a bridge parapet?'

'Well, no, not jump down at them, but engage them.'

'From 40 feet up? How could my client possibly do that unless he had the powers of flight?'

I loved it when they found a point to ridicule in the evidence because they always extended the expression on the word, then looked over at the jury with half an eyebrow raised.

'No, would not a better explanation be that my client, who was merely returning to New Street station, was subjected to an attempted attack by other people claiming to be Zulu Warriors – who I believe from history were very vicious soldiers, hence their nickname – and jumped on to a wall to escape a police horse which was charging around at the time. When he was told to get off the wall, that is exactly what he did.'

The police answers threw up more questions than they answered.

At last Dougie was in the frame. He had sat in court for two months without being involved. Not bad for a person who was supposed to have been part of a six-year conspiracy. Now his barrister finally stood up.

'Good morning. You have probably been wondering who I am,' he said with a jovial jauntiness. 'Well, I represent Mr Welsh. Please stand up, Mr Welsh, and let the jury see you.' Dougie stood up looking embarrassed, with his friendly grin.

Dougie's defence was that he wasn't there so his barrister asked if any of the other defendants knew him, which they didn't. Dougie smiled and nodded at this, as did we, but what else could the barrister do? Dougie was convinced that during the weekend he was said to have been in Birmingham with us he was actually under arrest for shoplifting in Horsham. However, this line of defence was denied to Dougie's legal team because, despite a thorough search, the police had no records of Dougie in custody and no police officer could remember the arrest, plus the store security video could not be located.

With there being nine of us, the cross-examination became a long and rigorous affair. Sometimes the police would get tied into knots and the judge would sigh to signify counsel to speed up proceedings. Ask them this question, then: so what happened on the following Saturday at Ladbroke Grove before the QPR match that we were all supposed to be talking about? Why didn't the police put together an operation to catch us in the act of affray? Nothing happened, because there never was a next Saturday ambush at Ladbroke Grove except in the vivid imaginations of the police. Let's get this show rolling because the jury will be convinced once our legal teams get their teeth into them. They're on the ropes. They are nearly finished.

Chief Inspector Hedges stood in the dock, all braid buttons and starch. This was a man I'd heard talking to the mystery caller on the BBC radio phone-in all those months ago on remand. A man who got flustered by one persistent questioner. Now, under cross-examination in the dock he started talking about the caller being a member of the National Front.

Step forward the caller, nothing to do with the National Front. Blind Jerry, who used to go in the seventies and eighties with his dog until he lost his sight completely due to his haemophilia. Alan Suckling for the prosecution tried to discredit Jerry because he couldn't defend what Hedges had said. Suddenly Jerry was on trial because he'd asked the police a pertinent question on a phone-in.

'Did you go on Mr Hickmott's coaches?'

'Yes.'

'How did you lose your sight?'

'Through being a haemophiliac.'

'Did you ever take part in the steaming-in of ends?'

'How could I do that? I was almost blind.'

Even though Jerry came out well in the box, Hedges' original flustered state, which I thought would be in our favour, seemed to be lost by the prosecution's tarring of all football fans.

Any conspiracy to cause affray by a group of fans travelling on a coach must involve the coach driver. Robin was a friendly guy, even if sometimes the old coach broke down on the M1. I lost count of the times we needed to get off and trek to the nearest train station, leaving Robin underneath the engine, covered in grease. See you next week, Robin.

The wonderful thing about England is the need to provide an instant cure for its problems. In the days of Empire if there was a problem in the colonies with the natives, Parliament used to dispatch a gunboat or shoot a few locals to calm their ire. This seemed to have been extended to curing football hooliganism. Trouble on the train? Ban alcohol. Shut pubs within two miles of the ground. Ban drink inside the ground. Well, Minister, they are taking their own and drinking it two miles and one yard from the stadium and getting into the ground tanked up. Right, make it an offence to have drink on any vehicle travelling to a football match. Once that came in, Robin obeyed the law. No more Wolverhampton 1,000-can raids. He would not allow any drink on to the coach.

Downstairs in the room where you waited for trial, many different people came and went. Inner London meets the Rovers Return, us the stars of a real life soap opera with different characters flitting in and out. One morning, in walked a very smart man. Suits that had a measured cut about them, definitely not off the peg. So sharp you'd cut yourself on him was Terry's comment. He was very suave and loved to chat with the boys. John Palmer was his name. The press nicknamed him Goldfinger. If we thought the establishment were after us, then it was nothing to what he was going through.

There had been a huge robbery of gold from the Brinks Mat warehouse at Heathrow. At the time it was valued at £26 million. The figure was rumoured to be even higher but the authorities played down the value. So much was taken it upset the whole gold market, so that it was almost impossible for the robbers to sell it back onto the market. Robbery is one thing but to upset the gold standard price undermined the Western economies.

We followed Goldfinger's trial with interest. He was being charged with melting down and laundering the gold from the Brinks Mat robbery. His explanation was quite simple. He had purchased coins (which you don't pay VAT on) then melted them into gold bars (which you pay VAT on), sold the bars on below market value and pocketed the 17.5 per cent VAT, which gave him huge profits. Whether he was melting the Brinks Mat gold was irrelevant – the Crown needed to show England and the rest of the world that stealing £26 million of gold would not be tolerated. Even now the popular press continually tell us that nearly all the money has been recovered, while others say that the money financed Canary Wharf and half the timeshare developments in southern Spain. During his exile in Spain dodging the English police, Goldfinger had made a fortune selling timeshare properties in Tenerife. He invited us to

Tenerife and have a beer with him, although he didn't invite us to stay for free, even if Dougie did ask. We all liked Goldfinger because he was a genuine, nice guy; plus he had something about him which made us sure he would walk. That man only needed a jury of all women to get a not guilty. You got the feeling he felt more comfortable in the company of women. Women liked the Latin looks and confident money swagger that he had. Sure enough, the Brinks Mat charges did not stick but they gave him a few years for the VAT fraud. I got the feeling that he saw that as a result.

Robin was called as a witness. He ran a youth club in Tunbridge Wells in his spare time and cut a diminutive figure. His humble bearing was of Dickens proportions: 'I'm very humble, Mr Copperfield.'

Lett got caned. He tried to antagonise Robin but it cut no ice. In the end, he cut and ran.

'So, Mr Grounds, you run County Coaches and transport these people around. You must have seen lots of violence?'

'No, sir. I have never seen any from the Chelsea lads.'

'Never any?' asked Lett incredulously, giving his neck a full 45-degree turn to the jury with his affected bemused face. Robin shook his head.

'No, sir. None at all.'

'Are you in fear of them?'

'No, sir, they are good boys. In fact, I'd have to say that they are the best behaved group I've ever had the good fortune to transport. I would have to say that I have more drinking and swearing from the youth club trips to Margate. I'd much rather transport the Chelsea lads.'

'*He doesn't include Boghead, Clifford or Viscount in that answer,*' I said to Terry.

They should have stopped it then because Robin was impeccable, never putting a foot wrong and dumbfounding the prosecution. When Lett sat down, he looked at his senior prosecutor. You could see him thinking, Why did we put him up on the stand? That man was middle England, a personification of reliability – Mr *Daily Mail*. Robin's evidence about our demeanour was diametrically opposed to that given by the police and it had a big effect on the jury. Just two more witnesses like Robin and I'm in the clear, I thought. I'll be out by mid February latest. FA Cup fifth round, with a bit of luck.

One morning Willie had some bad family news and he asked for his bail to be reinstated. Schindler dismissed his application as an irrelevance. Willie went mad and shouted at the judge.

'Don't you dismiss my family like that, you Yid!'

Schindler exploded. 'You are in contempt of court. You will apologise.'

Willie was sent downstairs and informed he was in contempt. His contempt would be dealt with at the end of the trial. There was now another person who needed a not guilty.

Occasionally, the prosecution would bring in a new face, similar to the way star guest actors pop in and out of soap operas on TV to give it some credibility. A fresh-faced bobby to show how many of them had witnessed our conspiracy. For the match against Tottenham Hotspur on Saturday 28 December 1985, they wheeled in PC Stephen Page and PC Morrison, who observed Shaun in a crowd and followed it around the streets for some time. Describing them as if they were ducking and diving, looking for trouble, they brought the Yid word into play.

'"Where are those Yiddos? Not a Yiddo in sight."'

PC Bell also spoke about his recollections of the Spurs match: 'I was with PC Kehoe for the whole time of my tour of duty from about 12.30pm on general observation duties of Chelsea supporters. As the Tottenham supporters entered Fulham Broadway tube station, I noticed a man I know as Stephen Hickmott with Vincent Drake. I crossed the road and joined this group with PC Kehoe.

'"We've got to have a go at the Yids, we can't do them over there (*indicating towards the station entrance*), there's too many Old Bill," said Drake.

'"We can't just let the cunts fuck off. We've got to do some of them," stated Hickmott.

'"If we go up here (*indicating to his right to a road called Marwood Road*) I know some of them get off buses."'

They finished their statements by adding that only clever policing had stopped us attacking the Yids – not Spurs fans, but Yids. Every time the police mentioned the word Yid, the judge looked up over his gold rims and gave us a cold stare. If any phrase wound that judge up, it was the use of the word Yiddo. I felt that the police put added emphasis on the way we were supposed to have expressed Yid like we were anti-Semitic. I wouldn't know a Jew if I was sitting next to one. For all I knew, Dougie could have been Jewish. It is a pity that nobody among us was, because that would have pooh-poohed that line of attack the way Willie's colour made the National Front angle look stupid. Terry saw the relevance of this and wanted Nick Price to hammer home the point that Yid was the same as Zulu, it was a simple name that fans had for their little cliques within the support of the team, like the Gooners or the ICF. The term was a reference to the fact that Spurs were predominantly made up of Jewish directors, but instead of being offended the Spurs fans adopted it themselves to turn it on their tormentors. The judge waved this away. As far as I could see, he still saw any reference to Yid in that context as a derogatory slur.

On 26 January 1987, the police raided a number of addresses and arrested a large number of West Ham ICF members. The marsh men even had their own calling cards. Under the two-hammers logo were the words: 'Congratulations you've just been done by the famous ICF.' The raids had been prompted by a fight on a cross-channel ferry when a small group of West Ham fans had battled with a larger group of Manchester United fans. When a news man asked one of the marsh men getting off the ferry what he thought of the disgraceful scenes, he was met with: 'Ten of us, 40 of them. Blinding result that was, mate.'

The West Ham fans faced the same charge as us: conspiracy to cause affray. The authorities seemed to have developed a pattern for arresting fans and keeping them in custody. The press informed everybody that once again police officers had used undercover surveillance to infiltrate and observe the West Ham lads. Not that I had any love for the West Ham chaps, but I wouldn't wish a dawn raid and arrest on my worst enemy. I just hoped and prayed that a few of the Chelsea lads had turned up at their remand hearing to give them a little wave off to the cells.

At court on the morning of 28 January, they wheeled loads of metallic torture equipment into the corridor. It had us puzzled. Into our waiting room bounced a middle-aged, slightly tubby woman with a beaming smile. Her name was Cynthia Payne.

'Hello, boys. Treating you well, are they?' This woman was like a breath of fresh air. She reminded us of your favourite aunt who comes over for Christmas dinner, drinks all the sherry then makes you roar all day and night with raunchy stories about your mum or dad. She made us smile and gave us a different perspective on what was going on upstairs for us.

'Don't worry about anything. I've had loads of upper-class types around my house.'

We failed to see the relevance of this until we started reading the papers and catching up on the details of her trial. We couldn't reconcile the lady we had met with the newspaper reports of a lady on trial for running a house full of prostitutes. One day we asked her what all the torture equipment was for.

'Correction procedures for naughty boys.' Then she smiled. 'Some are ex-public schoolboys and they have to continue their education into their adult life.' It was dubbed the luncheon voucher trial because many older gentlemen went round there and paid for sex with their luncheon vouchers. We could all see why people would want to go around her house, because you immediately felt at ease with her.

'Do you know something, Cynthia, when this trial is over I think I'll come around for a cup of coffee and a doughnut one afternoon at your house at Ambleside in Streatham, it sounds very quaint,' said Dougie.

'You do that, luvvie,' replied Cynthia. She had taken a liking to Terry.

'What about you, Terry?'

'No, I'll think I'll give it a miss. From what you've told us, I'll bump into half the legal profession and I don't like to take my work home with me.'

Cynthia came and went before she was found guilty, but for the brief period she shared the room with us we enjoyed the *joie de vivre* she brought into the room.

In *Hamlet* there is a long soliloquy while Hamlet talks to a ghostly apparition. It is the making of the play. When I was at school, my English Literature teacher used to rave about this and his whole life seemed to revolve around some King of Denmark having a long conversation with a skull. When PC McAree got up and produced the most extraordinary soliloquy recounting the most incredible dialogue with Terry and the boys, I thought I was back in 4a in Tunbridge Wells.

'On Saturday 18 January 1986, I saw a man I know to be Terence Last in the vicinity of Rolfe Street Station, Smethwick, where the police were controlling crowds departing from a football match which had just taken place. Last approached the main entrance and tried to explain that he wanted to get the train back to Paddington instead of Euston. After a heated conversation, Last and his small group were prevented from boarding the train they wanted.'

McAree now recounted a huge amount of dialogue which suggested that Terry's main motive for travelling back to Paddington was really a violent confrontation with the Zulus at Birmingham

New Street. The overheard conversations were with an unknown male.

'"Anything planned, Tel?"

'"Yeah, but it ain't gonna be a good knuckle with only five of us. Fifteen would be another thing."

'"Fucking trample all over the niggers, Tel boy. Anyway, where's Hickey?"

'"Hickey ain't interested anymore. All he wants is a punch-up and to make a few bob on the coach. Even then he only half fills it with divs."

'"Why don't you sort out something good for a knuckle. Hickey will come then," said Last.

'"It's in hand, boys. I'll sort something out for Earls Court, or Victoria or even South Ken [Kensington].'"

This remarkable dialogue continued for hundreds of remembered words and linked myself and Terry as some sort of colonel in chief and general, discussing the way it worked. It brought up the way the gangs were starting to link up for the forthcoming campaign in Mexico by introducing a connection with Scotty of West Ham.

'Who the hell is Scotty?' mumbled Vince. 'I've never heard of him.'

This caused consternation in the enlisted men around Last.

'"*Friends* with West Ham?"

'"Bloody sensible for Mexico. Not a bad call, Tel boy. Not a bad call."'

Terry leant over. 'Isn't that what Arthur Daley says to Terry McCann in Minder?' Christ, I thought, we've turned into a simple south London firm of knockabout TV rogues.

'"We well outmanoeuvred West Ham at the Arsenal. We had them good. We thought they would be at Victoria but we had them over. Anyway, boys, it's peace for the time being," said Terry.

'"When are we going to get a full firm out, Terry? It's a long time since we met firm to firm."

'"Well, I had big plans today but the Old Bill ruined it," said Terry.'

On and on it went, with McAree developing the script and characters to show how their evil words and plans were becoming a pattern of contrived violence. All this done by standing close enough to hear the words clearly, then managing to record them verbatim immediately afterwards. McAree might have been a Hamlet reincarnation, but the play he was developing for the jury was Shakespeare's *Julius Caesar*.

> Messenger: Prepare you, generals.
> The enemy comes on in gallant show;
> Their bloody sign of battle is hung out
> And something to be done immediately

To back it up, Sergeant Hobbs told how he had spoken personally to Terry and had informed him that he wasn't getting the Paddington train. However, the fact that Hobbs confirmed the earlier part of the statement without any other embellishment added some weight to what McAree had said. Now we had links across gangs with plans to make violent confrontations with other individuals – a huge gang network. Often in the press the police make statements that drug gangs are getting together to ensure total domination of our young people. In the *Godfather* movies, the gangs meet as a group to carve out territory and cause mayhem. For the first time Inman seemed to struggle, while Lett looked good. In all cases on the TV there comes a turning point where one side is seen to look bad. This happened here today. How can you deny a non-existent conspiracy without people believing that there must be something there? Terry likened it to the Allied landings at Normandy in 1944. Hitler was so convinced that the landing would be on the Pas de Calais that he thought that the landing at Normandy was a diversion to get him to send his troops somewhere else.

The next morning, Dougie asked about the West Ham fans and their love-hate relationship with the Chelsea lads away with England. Terry had some interesting theories.

'Essex man is derived from marshland dwellers and all their problems stem from the fact that the rest of England historically look down their noses at them. Plus they allowed some woman called Boudicca to boss them around long before it became fashionable to have a woman PM. Because of this quirk of history, they see England games as a sort of macho parade where they have to sneer back at everybody. Marsh is a very common name in rural Essex.'

The world according to Terry, warped but funny.

For Chelsea, watching England is great because we have never seen European success. That is why Chelsea always have the greater numbers. The West Ham always want to intimidate people and cause fights, so the northern lads have started ganging together to stop the West Ham fans.

'Remember that time in Romania when West Ham Taffy and a few others asked us if we would get together and sort out the Leeds boys?' said Terry.

I remembered it well and started laughing. Fifty per cent of the travelling lads were Chelsea. Also with us was Jeff, a man of subtle taste and intelligence.

'Are you wiv us against the Leeds or do we have to do it all ourselves? Call yourselves Londoners, you're a bloody disgrace!' shouted Taffy at our group.

'Excuse me, but do I detect an IQ problem here? Aren't you cursing us with a Welsh accent?' asked Jeff.

'We're not the IQF boyo, we're the ICF, and I can see that you lot are not up to much.'

'Bucharest was once described as the Paris of eastern Europe and you want to use this cultural experience to punch out some Leeds United fans. That's a bit damn personal, isn't it, as well as being low class?' mused Jeff, half laughing. With that, Taffy stormed off. Meanwhile Jeff spent the whole trip referring to West Ham as the ICF – Ice Cream Firm, while they glared at us with increased intensity every time they saw us. Jeff was playing a dangerous game because Taffy was a nasty piece of work, always looking for an excuse to really hurt somebody. Once, in Luxembourg, he'd slashed Charley Farley, a Chelsea fan from Tunbridge Wells, across the face, leaving him a nasty four-inch scar. Another inch higher and he would have lost his eye.

Terry felt that West Ham's resentment of Chelsea stemmed from the fact that Chelsea got bigger respect from the other England fans following the battle of Budapest in 1981 and from the press coverage regarding the trip to South America in 1984. A group of Chelsea lads decided to follow the England team on that tour, taking in the matches in Rio de Janeiro, Santiago, Chile, and Montevideo, Uruguay. It wasn't a cheap trip. Travelling to watch your country halfway across the world would normally be a cause for a pat on the back from the organising FA blazers, but as usual it was the us and them, you are not welcome syndrome.

The match against Brazil was brilliant and England won 2–0. However, at the airport there was a hold-up due to one of the England players, John Barnes, being stopped for travelling using a passport from his native land, Jamaica – at least that is what the lads were told by an FA official. The lads got to the aircraft first and were mistaken as the England officials and team. This is South America, where incompetence and corruption sleep side by side. One English accent sounds the same to a Brazilian.

'Are you with the England party?'

'Of course,' they replied, smiling. After all, this was a great wheeze.

They were then given first-class travel passes. It was only when they were sitting laughing and joking that they realised that they were right among the England players. When one of the lads shouted out a comment about Barnesy being stopped because of his passport, things became heated. The press people made out that they intervened to stick up for Barnes and were having a go for the comment that was shouted. That was all rubbish. What they were really angry about was that the lads had got the first-class travel vouchers while they had been left bickering in economy. The South

American flight crew were happy with the seating arrangements.

'Why don't you clear off back to economy and let us drink our champagne in peace?'

'But those are our seats,' protested the press.

'No, they are not. Possession is eleven-tenths of the law. Plus the fact of the matter is that if Barnes was proud to be English then he'd have been travelling on an English passport.'

Then one of the lads, who was a racist, added this: 'Anyway, black players' goals don't count, so England only won 1–0.'

Whether or not the others agreed with that statement was immaterial, because these lads were going to stick together, come what may. When the press got back they wrote the truth about this – as they saw it.

There is no better place to watch football than Eastern Europe. Even when the communist yoke was firmly attached around their neck, they had a passion for football which defied description. That invariably meant that on match days, any England fan was fair game to get attacked with brick, iron bar or fist. One such time was in Budapest in 1981. Both Hungary and England had to win to stay in the World Cup. Against the picturesque backdrop of the River Danube in the Nep Stadium, Trevor Brooking hit the most wonderful goal I've ever seen. He hit it with such power that it stuck in the metal net support stanchion in mid air at the back of the goal, seemingly suspending time. The sight of the wedged ball was the cue for the Hungarian fans to start digging up their concrete and shingle terraces and pelting us with the debris, plus anything else they could get their hands on. This continued as we exited the ground to be confronted by a huge, stone-throwing mob. After a hairy trip, the England lads on the underground were pretty fired up. The riot police were seriously pissed off at seeing their country beaten in the World Cup, so without warning they started putting tear gas through open windows. There was nowhere to go except out of the closed doors and windows, which got smashed in the exit rush. Normally mild-mannered people lost it. With English backs to the wall and the confined area favouring the England fans, the riot police backed off. Then a baying Hungarian mob appeared. How fearsome a sight the screaming, tear-stained English looked as they charged I will never know, but the Hungarians fled in terror to be met by the police reinforcements who were coming to help their colleagues. Thinking it was the English charging at them, the Hungarian riot police battered their own people. That is where the Chelsea boys took over, leading a two-mile march through the Budapest streets back to our hotel. We held the front line with the chant: 'Stand together, England and St George.'

Then, as they advanced, we charged them. 'Forward. Stand here. No back-off.' Then we held the line further forward as we regrouped. 'Wait, wait, charge!' While West Ham stood there scowling (with Jeff mocking them, calling them the pests of Buda), I led another group up some parallel sidestreets then really tore into the Hungarian lads, completely scattering them. Their horrified faces! It seemed to them as if we knew the geography of the streets surrounding their stadium. On the train back to Paris, all the lads were shaking each other's hands and laughing about the best organised offensive manoeuvre they had ever seen.

I'd organised a coach up to Southport, where my brother Sam and I were booked into a B & B on the Saturday. The coach was travelling on to Everton on the Sunday. As usual, British Rail had excelled themselves and trains were non-existent, so getting home by public transport would be impossible. A real MWG weekend for those in the know. Pub, nightclub, perhaps even a liaison with a local Southport or Scouse girl. Minimum, a good laugh. On the Saturday I'd arranged pick-ups at various points, culminating in the coach stopping at the Swan. However, once we arrived at the Swan it seemed as if half of London had arrived on spec to get on the coach. The centre of the pub was full of overnight bags piled high. I had to leave behind serious numbers because the police were by now observing us and stopping us all the time. When they couldn't find anything else wrong then it would have given them great delight to turf off people at the side of the road because of overcrowding. Leaving behind bodies is always a grim moment in the life of an entrepreneur like myself, but these things happen.

PC Kehoe was first up: 'On Saturday 15 March I was on duty in plain clothes with other Metropolitan Police officers keeping observation on Chelsea supporters in Southport, Merseyside. At about 10.30pm I saw a large group of youths.' He then picked out Terry, Toomsy and Peter as people he could identify. Terry was described as wearing a white jumper and jeans. 'The group were walking towards us on a wide pavement to our left as we observed them from the opposite side of the road, about 30 yards away. The group numbered about 30 persons, were rowdy and, due to their number, took up the whole pavement. Last, Toombs and Peter were leading at the front.

'"Come on," I heard Last shout as he raised his right arm like he was leading a charge. I then saw a group of three youths walking from the opposite direction on the same footway. As Last got level he punched one of the group, who had tried to move out of the way, in the face with his right hand, which he followed up with a punch to the body. As the youth crouched down protecting his face, he was kicked in the stomach. Other youths joined the assault. The three youths stumbled through the group assault then moved on.

'A few yards further on I saw two middle-aged women walking towards this group on the same pavement. As they moved nearer the group they took refuge in a shop doorway. As the group moved towards them, they began to verbally abuse the two women. One of the group snatched a hat from one woman – "That's a fucking horrible hat, you fat cow" – then threw the hat away onto the road. Both women were clinging to each other and crying, obviously distressed. The group, still being led by Last, turned right into an alleyway.

'After a short time I heard the sound of breaking glass, shouting and screaming, which seemed to be coming from the direction of the alleyway.

' "One less Scouse," shouted Last.

'The group, led by Last, then ran across the road stopping cars in their wake and halted on the other side.

' "Watch out for Old Bill, lads. They'll be everywhere once they find that div with a bit missing."

'"What are we going to do now, Tel?" shouted another.

'"We're gonna wreck this shithole. Come on, you lot."

'At this the group ran up a sidestreet in an intimidating and disorderly manner.'

According to the prosecution account, the group had progressed from being mad fighting machines when confronted by other youths to being callous, unfeeling human beings who showed no compunction about attacking innocent people walking along a street on a Saturday night, or abusing innocent women who were just minding their own business. The abuse of the women really stuck in the mind. I believe that this had a huge effect on the jury, with its seven women.

Everything that happens in any event has a purpose. Whatever you do, you can influence the outcome by focusing attention on events. Chi masters claim to be able to project the human life force with thought power. Athletes claim to be able to win races in their mind before they actually do. If they don't win it in their minds then they will not win the actual race. Jury selection had seen a jury given a female bias. The terrifying significance of this dawned upon me.

Not that some of the Chelsea lads didn't owe young Stanley a taste of his own medicine. They could dish it out themselves. One Saturday after an away match, some lads returned to Kings Cross and walked up towards the local pub on the Euston Road they sometimes drank in. It was early evening in December and it was dark. Up towards Euston they saw a small group of fans. Thinking nothing of it, they continued to walk.

'Cross over, lads, they're Scousers,' someone said as they got closer.

Then from nowhere came the attack. 'You Cockney bastards,' they screamed. They didn't know they were Chelsea. Any London fans would have done. One of the Chelsea lads didn't see the sickening blow on the side of the head from a house brick taken from a builder's skip. Legs buckling, wobbly giraffe, lights out, going down with a dull thud. The other five Chelsea lads ran. After a hundred yards, the Scousers gave up the chase. They ambled back along the road until they came to the prostrate Chelsea fan, kicking him a few times.

'Give him Stanley.'

'Noughts and crosses.'

So they gave him a Stanley, striping through his shiny black leather coat with a new blade, giving him a cross in the box around his shoulder blade. Two hundred stitches. They did the same to a West Ham fan later in the season: 116 stitches. The fact that an Everton fan received six years in jail for that doesn't take away the anger you feel for those who do that sort of thing. Chelsea were well known for only taking on those who wanted it, not innocent people. But another officer told of how he had heard us discussing the events in Southport, reinforcing the prosecution account.

They called in the Southport victim who was thrown through the window and a number of his friends, but they weren't able to identify anyone conclusively.

Their final witness was a police officer in training who stated that he had recognised me attending the match, sitting in the front of the coach. The match in Everton and the trip to Southport really set the scene, but even though the barristers gave Kehoe a hard time in the witness box, the constant repetition by police witnesses of foul-mouthed, violent rhetoric was turning things in their favour. I had seen the expressions on the faces of the women jurors. Hickmott had organised a coach of the worst elements of Chelsea fans. Their aim was to travel up the evening before the match with the intention to attack innocent passers-by and abuse women then leave them clinging to each other terrified. They were the lucky ones. Those who were not spared were maimed for life. Hickmott and Last are the co-ringleaders in this plan.

The fact was that there had been trouble in Southport the evening before Chelsea had played at Everton, but this was Saturday night and as our barrister pointed out using arrest records, there were always fights on Saturday night in Southport when the pubs shut. Yet the jury were being asked to consider that the London police present stood by and watched all these serious violent incidents then did nothing – and were subsequently unable to produce any conclusive witness identification at a later date.

I remember Terry coming over to our guest house on the Sunday morning to meet two of his mates but they went to a different pub to the rest of us. Terry, who had been up half the night playing cards, and the two lads he met at our guest house were off to another serious card school. I never enjoyed playing cards, at least not the way Terry played it with its minimum bet of £2 blind.

The coach was due to leave Southport railway station on the Sunday. Everybody filed aboard laughing and joking about the previous evening's fun – a real good MWG night out. I think one or two of the boys even pulled birds and got telephone numbers for the following season's excursion. Just as we were about to pull away, the police charged on, only to be confronted by Viscount Lindley the dog food eater. He used to eat a can of Pedigree Chum for lunch. Nobody went too close to him and he really did have dog's breath. Needless to say, Viscount hadn't pulled the night before. Despite the shock of seeing Viscount gobbling Chum with extra liver, the police insisted on searching everybody before pulling off two blokes for offensive weapons. 'Why don't you pull Viscount off for offensive habits?' one wag shouted. During the search I was asked about trouble the previous evening. I looked around then shrugged my shoulders, because that was the first we all knew. If there had been trouble among any of those on our coaches, it would have soon been common knowledge.

One Monday morning, Dougie's barrister entered the court with a plaster cast. The judge looked up and asked the barrister what he had done.

'Broken my arm, m'lud. Skiing accident.'

'You haven't attended any Chelsea matches over the weekend, have you?' Then he let out a loud guffaw and laughed towards the jury.

I was seriously angry about this. There we were on trial for very serious offences and the judge was implying that someone going to a football match risked serious injury.

There were three matches mentioned in the original charge. The last of these was the Full Members' Cup final at Wembley on 23 March 1986. I had arranged to go with a mate and meet my brother outside the ground at the pay gate, those being the days when it was still possible to pay on the day. The funny thing was that if there really had been a conspiracy to have violence, then this probably would have been the match to organise it for. At the time Manchester City had a firm who called themselves the Young Guv'nors – Liam Gallagher of Oasis actually claimed to be a member of this gang. One of their main faces, Mickey Francis, who is currently banned from every football ground in England, and 17 of his mates went to prison for varying periods for violent disorder. The YGs were up for it that day, no doubt about it. Only a few seasons ago Chelsea had been up at Maine Road, Manchester, for a Friday night match and had reduced their lads to quivering wrecks in their backyard.

As it was, I travelled up from Tunbridge Wells with my friend Martin and attempted to find my brother at the pay turnstile. Just as I was trying to get in, an uncoordinated fight broke out between a mob of Chelsea and some Manchester City Young Guv'nors. From my theatre in the standing stalls, I watched Chelsea boss the Guv'nors.

Into the witness box came Kehoe, who had been on duty with Bell at Wembley in plain clothes. The thread of the play had come full circle. These men were reciting *Henry IV*:

> In thy faint slumbers I by thee have watch'd
> And heard thee murmur tales of iron wars.

By now the jury could hardly remember the actual events of the evidence at Southport because it was over a month ago, but every time the police trotted out the supposed swear words or violence it must have struck a chord in their memory. Kehoe described a match where there had been minor disturbances inside the ground and also in the refreshment area.

Kehoe continued: 'After the match we stood between the twin towers on the concourse close to the Olympic Way flyover and watched the crowd of Chelsea fans leave the ground. I spotted a man I know as Vincent Drake with two other men I do not know.' Kehoe then added his descriptions of the youths with their long hair and clothes colours. 'I noticed that we were being followed by a group of about 30 youths, which soon grew to about 50. I was joined by PC McAree and we managed to position ourselves immediately behind Drake.

'"We'll have a look at the station," said Drake as he looked around at the group. "We're bound to meet some City there. We'll give them a fucking good hiding. We've got enough with us now."

'About 100 yards further along Olympic Way the group stopped and looked around.

'"Where are they?"

'"We're wasting our time here. Just follow me."

By now the group had grown to 100, with Vince 'in the lead', according to Kehoe. I looked over at Vince in the dock and made eye contact. Vince was grinning all over his face. You could say that we were not taking it seriously. Vince as leader of 100 Chelsea geezers defied belief. He struggled to organise himself a clean pair of underpants every morning.

Kehoe continued: 'Drake again stopped the group and addressed them: "We've got a nice little team now. We'll get the Manchester bastards on the coaches." With this he carried on leading, mustering his men with various calls which showed that he was the leader and his troops would follow. Suddenly Drake came across O'Farrell and Hickmott, who led 30 youths in their firm.' Kehoe being close enough to hear because he had kept himself close to Drake.

'"We're going to do the City coaches. Are you going to join us?" said Drake.

'"Yeah, we were going to do that anyway. The only problem is that we have got about 30," said O'Farrell.

'"Okay, Hickey?" asked Drake.

'"Yeah, hold on," replied Hickmott as he continued to talk to three other youths, then walked off, with PCs Bell, McAree and myself in pursuit.

'"Stop, stop!" shouted Drake further on. "No carry on, too many police."

'"Okay, lads, on we go. Not much further, my beauties, we'll soon be fed," shouted O'Farrell.

'The group was then joined by a group of 30 led by Douglas Welsh, who started conducting operations, telling the others where the coaches and Old Bill were situated.'

To us that was comical in itself; having spent time with Dougie, we knew he couldn't lead a dinner queue.

Kehoe continued his account.

'"This is it, lads," shouted Drake. "Have the coaches."

'Our group, which numbered about 250, started towards the coaches. The group was being led by Drake, O'Farrell and Welsh, all of whom were grunting rhythmically. I saw a brick thrown at the windscreen of a minibus, which did not break but cracked.

'"They're sitting fucking ducks! Have them, have them," shouted Drake.

'"Have them, have them!" repeated O'Farrell, shouting.

'At this the mob began indiscriminately breaking the windows of the Manchester City coaches. I saw Welsh with his fists clenched. "Kill the Bill, kill the Bill!" he shouted. I saw a man round on a police officer who was attempting to effect an arrest. Welsh was one of this group. At this point, I ran after the head of the group, who had now run up back towards Olympic Way. As we queued for the train, I heard Drake say: "We'll have them again at Euston. The rest of the lads are meeting at the North London tavern. We can go from there and cut the bastards up when we're in force."

In came the coach driver for some Manchester City fans. His coach had been the recipient of a tear gas canister and a stun grenade which blew out a window. When asked what he would like to do with the persons who'd perpetrated that act, he replied that he'd like to take a machine gun to the whole lot of us. Our laughter could be heard as far as Manchester.

One by one, the defence barristers questioned the evidence we'd heard.

'So, PC Kehoe, you were in attendance with PC Bell at the match against Sheffield Wednesday, where you observed my client close enough to be able to hear him?'

'Yes, sir.'

'And I believe that the phrase used back in your colourful evidence was "Remember the Fat Man" and "Watch out for Old Bill". Is that correct?'

'I believe so, yes.'

'You have also told the court that you spent some time in the crowd at Birmingham marching back to New Street and also at the Spurs match. I also believe that you claim you were on the streets for some time at Southport, where you claimed to have seen events so close up that you could identify people and hear words spoken clearly.' The barrister had started calmly, yet now an edge came into his voice, almost like controlled anger. 'Now you are telling the court that yourself and PC Bell followed this group and stopped on numerous occasions, and remained close enough to hear conversations, yet not once did anybody recognise you. Does that strike you as a little strange? I know it strikes me as strange.'

'Not really.'

The barrister looked at his papers, but it was all for effect because he knew exactly what he was going to say. He then asked questions relating to the way the fans were supposed to talk to each other and whether they had spoken to the police in the same way. After all, the police were supposed to be undercover, so conversations must have gone on between them and the fans. The use of the differing forms of language was made, to try to create doubt in the minds of the jury – the barrister using perfect Queen's English then suddenly changing tempo and throwing in a slang reference like 'organising knuckles' to try to throw Kehoe off balance.

So it went on. One by one the police came up and one by one, from my vantage point, the accused's witness box theatre, they were shot down. For a moment I was back in a duck shoot at a fairground. Pop, clank, pop, clank, down went the metal ducks. At the end, the fairground attendant gives you a voucher for a prize. Here the prize was my freedom. Our legal team seemed to keep on hitting their targets, but would we be awarded the prize of freedom by the jury acting as fairground attendant? The police, in their case against me, didn't seem to be establishing a conspiracy except to say that I had been at the match. Some of their statements struck me as contradicting themselves.

Real life was even more amusing. My pal Martin had been pulled at the ticket barrier for trying to dodge his fare and the crowds were so dense that I missed him coming out of Wembley Park station. The same crowds where Bell and Kehoe had been able to pick out Vince and Shaun at will. As I approached the stadium pay gate and the fight broke out on the grassy bank, I turned to watch it. Just then, I was approached by some police officers.

'What are you doing up here?' they said. 'This is the Manchester City end.'

'Sorry, lads, I was looking for my pal Martin and my brother and thought I would purchase a ticket and catch them in the ground later.'

'Go to the other end or we'll nick you.'

'Sorry.'

I can see the headline now. Superthug apologises to police for going in wrong stadium entrance while his friend says sorry for fare dodging. I entered the Chelsea end, watched the match, which Chelsea won 5–4, and then, after Chelsea paraded the cup around the ground, made my way down Olympic Way. So it was only the Full Members' Cup, but it was still a cup and I felt good about the victory. On the way down I was chatting to three guys about the match when Sergeant Hobbs walked along from the station back up towards the ground.

'See you Saturday, Hickey,' Hobbs said, smiling.

'I'm not going.'

'You'll be there, it's West Ham.' He then walked off. After the match I travelled home back to Tunbridge because I'd had a couple of late evenings and felt tired. I arrived home at around 8pm. Find a conspiracy in that lot. Yet still they tried. And the more they tried, the sillier they looked to me.

Because I thought the police case was weak and because I held the stupid notion that my sharp mind was on a par with their legal brains, I was determined to have my time in the box. My barrister had discussed it with me and I felt that it was in my best interests to speak up. Also, I still had the problem of the scrapbooks, which my legal team were fighting hard to have excluded as evidence. The judge listened to the arguments then ruled in the prosecution's favour. Once the scrapbooks were allowed in then I had to take the stand, although secretly I wanted that time in the witness box anyway. I loved a crowd, loved sitting at the front of my coach, being recognised and acknowledged in and around Chelsea. Even the marsh men's abuse was a form of compliment. Weren't all the great leaders masters of oratory? Didn't Mark Antony turn the crowd after the death of Caesar? I come here not to praise Lett but to bury him. After all, apart from the accusation that I'd organised a coach to Southport, the police had not really shown a case against me. I stood in the dock feeling confident. Lett stood up slowly then gathered speed as he came across the floor at me.

'Hooligan!' he barked loudly at me. 'You are a hooligan!'

'Pardon?'

'Mr Hickmott, you are and always have been a hooligan.'

'I beg your pardon?'

'Mr Hickmott. Do you have problems with your hearing, because you seem unable to hear the question in order to be able to give me an answer?'

'No, nothing wrong with my hearing.'

'So you are a hooligan?'

'Oh, I see. Dictionary explanation. Hooley family of Irish descent from south London around the turn of the century, famous for fighting. It is where the word hooligan is descended from. No, sir, I am not related. I am a Hickmott.' I turned around and grinned at the other lads, who were falling about laughing. 'Under this criterion, I would prefer you to address me as Hickmott.'

'You are a thug.'

More pardons and verbal exchanges about my hearing.

'Oh, I get it. Thug. Thuggees. Indian bandits where the word comes from. No, I'm not related to them either. I am still a Hickmott.' More laughter.

This went on for quite some time. The judge looked up at me a couple of times over his little glasses but in the main kept his head down. Lett would ask me a question then, as I went to answer, interrupt and throw something else in to try and stop my train of thought. Finally, I snapped.

'Didn't anybody ever tell you that it is rude to interrupt people when they are talking?'

Lett loved it. All he wanted to do was get me angry so that I would lose it. At the end of my first day in the witness box, I thought I'd done well. In terms of an exchange in the public bar I suppose I had, but this wasn't the public bar of the Roebuck in Tunbridge Wells, this was the legal premier league. As I sat down, Nick Price turned to me.

'Why did you do that?'

'What do you mean?'

'Wind everybody up with all that babble about Hooley and Thuggee bandits. It doesn't go down too well to be seen to be cocky and irreverent about the law and its applications.'

The next day I tried to get my answers out without rising to their bait, but try as I might, I couldn't resist a bit of fun.

'Mr Hickmott, I understand that you were involved in an incident at Newcastle where flares were used?'

'The only flares in this court are the ones being proudly worn in the picture the jury saw of PC Brady in his discreet disguise.' I looked across at Schindler. He looked down and shook his head. He was trying not to laugh. The whole court collapsed into uncontrollable fits of laughter, including the jury.

To extend the conspiracy they had dragged up two names from the 1982 World Cup in Bilbao, although they never produced the two men called Styles and Fairbrother who had supposedly seen me organising arm-wrestling contests between Chelsea fans and other people. I could barely keep the ridicule out of my voice. As I looked over towards the lads, they were smirking while Nick Price's face was thunderous. Then I came in for questions about my fake passport. The explanation was quite simple. What I'd done was changed the date of birth on a one-year passport, which could be obtained at the time from post offices, to enable me to get an under-26 cheap European rail travel card. But all roads eventually ended up back at my scrapbooks. It was an Achilles' heel which the prosecution hammered away at.

'Why would you want to keep press cuttings of violence, Mr Hickmott, if you are not indeed a hooligan?'

'Because I intend to write a book outlining the biased reporting of the tabloid press.'

'So you are a distinguished writer?'

'No.'

'But you keep clippings of violent incidents at matches?'

'Yes.'

'Now, if we come to the match at home to Liverpool, I see that you have a clipping under the title "Match of the Day". Could you please tell us where you were that day?'

'In the North Stand.'

'Where the violence was at its fiercest, Mr Hickmott. I believe it was described as a savage charge by the Chelsea fans.'

Then they came to my previous convictions. Put in context, they were not too bad. Even Saint Peter would struggle to stay clean if he'd been to as many away matches against some of the rough types I'd encountered.

1973, Sheffield United; wrongfully convicted of robbery.

Ipswich away, 1974; drunk, whacked some local carrot-cruncher.

1975; fined £10 for swearing at Bristol. Jesus himself would have sworn that day if he'd seen how badly we played.

1977; criminal damage. Only trying to correct a spelling mistake, your honour.

In 1978 at Liverpool I came out of the ground and some lunatic was brandishing a piece of wood. He was screaming that he was going to decapitate me, although not put quite so politely. I got the piece of wood off him and proceeded to chase him, battering him about the head to see if he liked it. He didn't enjoy it one bit. As I was walking back, some Scouser in the passenger seat of a car called me a Cockney wanker so I threw it through his rear window. I was fined £250 and given a six-month suspended sentence.

Later in the season I was in a fracas at Birmingham when a police officer got hit by a brick. I was charged with assault on the police officer. Found guilty, ordered to serve the suspended six months plus another six suspended. I was in Winson Green Prison near

Birmingham for a few weeks before my appeal came up. I won the appeal and received £190 compensation.

Derby 1981–82; bound over to keep peace and fined £100, although throwing milk bottles was better than the alternative facing me in a dead-end street.

February 1986, Chelsea v Spurs. A policeman let loose his dog on the crowd and it bit me, so I kicked it. I then asked the officer if his wife was as ugly as the dog. After being held over the weekend, I was charged with using threatening words and behaviour and received 14 days in Pentonville – but no answer to whether his wife was uglier, so I must assume that to be true.

At the end of five days in the witness box, I felt I'd given a good account of myself but Nick Price was not so sure – it might have appeared that my cockiness and confidence indicated that I felt above the law. He was worried about the scrapbooks and the reaction of the jury when I was questioned about my previous convictions. Everything else was negotiable.

In retrospect, it was probably a mistake to get up there and mix it with the legal eagles. Vince said he had nothing to gain from getting up there and declined. His barrister didn't try to persuade him one way or the other. Dale, Willie, Toomsy and Peter also declined to go in the box. Shaun went in and acquitted himself very well, being reverent and very humble where he had to. None of us really came out better than the prosecution because we were playing Fourth Division stuff, learnt from shouting banter across the pub bar, while they were in the top division of the legal bar. Plus, what did it matter if they didn't get a result? They would still be drinking with their fellow barristers then catching the Friday night seven o'clock train back to their big houses in Sussex. We should have all just left the police case thrashing about on the rocks. Nothing to say, dickheads. Prove it. Without us in the dock, the police case would have floundered in the swirl of rhetoric, leaving it helpless as a stranded whale on Brighton beach.

* * *

The Farmers Rest pub incident in Newcastle was very serious. For all the evidence the prosecution produced, none of it showed anything other than lads being stupid, making threats. There was never any real link to us carrying out the attack, but this was different. Chelsea fans at Newcastle face premier league hatred. They don't just want to hit you, they want to hurt you because you are from London with money and a job, plus Cockneys are flash.

Standing across the road, one Geordie gave the wankers sign, really giving it the full-on verbals: 'Yeah, Cockney, I enjoyed slashing you London trash, especially when your girlfriends are watching.' Then he really mouthed it off at Walshy, knowing that there was Old Bill everywhere and that he'd be hard pushed to have a real go. He was using the coppers as his protective shield.

'Afterwards, come up the Farmers Rest if you want your face rearranged, you filthy Cockney slag.'

Walshy gave him that demented, half-mad stare. I don't think Walshy watched one second of the match, he just kept talking to everybody who wanted to do it to stick with him after the match. Then he spent the rest of the game telling everybody that he had a hand-picked firm going up against some Geordies who'd seriously damaged some Chelsea boys. And anybody whose resolve looked shaky was told exactly what was expected.

'Well don't come then, you shitter, these are the Gremlins, tooled-up tasty boys who really fancy themselves as a calling card gang.' A gang who thought nothing of stealing your clothes if they caught you for a Geordie welcome. A leather jacket, Cockney. That will fetch a score up here.

The Newcastle police didn't notice 40 Chelsea boys slipping away from the escort. Outside the pub, Walshy looked for the choppsy Geordie bastard. When he wasn't spotted, the rest attacked their little mob outside the pub just before 5.30pm opening time. With no police sirens coming to the rescue, there was time to let them know they'd met the Chelsea nutters. The sound of a knife slicing flesh sounds like an orange being squeezed until the outside skin bursts and the juice squirts out. But the lads who were there didn't hear that, all they heard were the screams of two grown men begging for help and screaming for their mums, then their lives, as the Kilburn CFC surgeons did a real slicing number on them with surgical scalpels – faces, arms, legs, shoulders, stomach. Martin Stretton and David Hall were sliced to pieces with a calculated, chilling remoteness; hundreds of stitches, blood everywhere. The Gremlins were nominated and met the monsters of their worst nightmare.

Back at the railway station, some of the lads described it with hushed tones as awesome – they even used weapons from the antiques shop next door. It would go down in the annals. I was not sure. It's one thing to sort out a few unruly Geordies, have a punch-up, an MWG scuffle, but the surgeons had just taken it too far. I wanted to get out of Newcastle, because any Chelsea fan hanging around was going to do for this attack. As we were the last group left in Newcastle, the whole coach party was arrested waiting outside the station. You could see by the looks on the faces of the police that they were visibly shocked from the details of the attack. The police threatened to hold us until we confessed. Nobody cracked, even those on our coach who were involved in the attack. We were held for three hours then released on bail pending enquiry.

Nobody ever got convicted for it. Terry was promoted in the court case as the leader. That wasn't true, although just being a Chelsea fan in the same city as Hannibal Lecter-types made us culpable. When one of the Newcastle fans was brought into court with his horribly disfigured face, someone gasped. When the pictures of the other slashed Newcastle fan was shown to the jury, two looked away, one gulped in breath loudly while others turned a pale, sickly white. We sat there impassively. That went down badly, even though the Newcastle fan in the witness box was asked and then answered that he didn't recognise any of us.

Dougie appeared in the dock looking as impassive as ever. He had really prepared well for this moment – he'd read the *Viz* Christmas annual. Dougie's barrister, having had to sit around for months doing nothing, didn't hang around with fancy introductions as he strode forward across the floor to prove his client's innocence, but he was like a Shakespearean actor with no script to work with. The premise that someone was on trial for a six-year conspiracy with people he'd never met was so far-fetched it didn't bear thinking about. It must have been one of his more difficult cases.

He did his best for Dougie without attacking the police. After all, we believed Dougie so why shouldn't the jury? Dougie came down that evening shrugging his shoulders, happy with what he'd heard.

At the end of five months, the judge started summing up. Whether or not he was biased from a legal point of view is hard for me to judge. Once I wanted to jump up and shout, 'Lies, you're repeating their lies!' but my barrister had told me not to do that under any circumstances. Notwithstanding that, I didn't feel he gave us any slack and a couple of times I saw Terry's knuckles whiten as he gripped the wood in front and mutter 'Garbage' under his breath. The case as the judge saw it was that the jury had to decide whether or not there was a conspiracy to cause affray and whether or not the police were correct in their recollections of the conversations.

One by one the jury filed out. I looked at them, trying to get eye contact to show them that I was innocent. Now time really started to drag. At the end of the first day we decided that the length of time was a good thing. Then came the second day. All of us were feeling the strain.

'Some innocent, some guilty,' reckoned Young Peter.

'*All* innocent!' I said forcefully. 'We're all going home today.'

Then the jury came back. They couldn't agree on a verdict. The judge said he would accept a majority decision. Our confidence soared. We were all looking forward to that pint in the pub across the road. I hadn't had a proper drink in 10 months. Suddenly it was announced that the jury was ready. They had been out for nearly three days – perhaps they had got bored after deliberating for over

15½ hours. I went up those spiral stairs with a real sense of purpose. My heart was thumping. Was I going to give that McAree a giant V-sign in about 20 minutes? The jury filed in. None of them looked me in the eye. I had a huge panic attack; suddenly my stomach felt wobbly. Then they started reading out the charges and the names.

Shaun O'Farrell, not guilty all charges. Well done, Shaun. He smiled and clenched his fist.

Peter Brown, not guilty all charges. Peter could hear the cheers from behind him in the public gallery where his family were shouting, punching the air and clapping wildly.

William Reid, not guilty all charges. Willie looked impassive and just bit his top lip slightly. He had expected that but even so, his relief showed. Schindler still had him back in court for the contempt as well as possession of cannabis, but he never served another day.

Stephen Toombs, not guilty all charges. Toomsy gave a big grin. 'Large lagers all round tonight, lads.'

Terence Last, guilty on the conspiracy charges. Also guilty of an additional affray at Everton on December 10th, 1985.

Stephen Hickmott, guilty on the conspiracy charges. Shit. Why? Why me? What have I done? I turned to look at the jury but they were not looking at me.

Stephen Hickmott. Possession of a false passport, guilty.

Vincent Drake, guilty on the conspiracy charges.

Dale Green, guilty on the conspiracy charges.

Douglas Welsh, not guilty on the conspiracy charges. However, like a *Viz* cartoon situation, Dougie was not allowed to go free because he was going to be sentenced for the assault of the police officer which he had pleaded guilty to, thinking he was going to get a £100 fine, over ten months ago.

The time was getting late. We would be sentenced on Monday. Judge Schindler had a sickly smile all over his face. I swear he gave a special look towards Dougie. He left us in no doubt that we should come to court ready for a stiff custodial sentence. What did he think we'd been doing for ten months on remand? Terry looked destroyed.

Once before I'd seen a dead body, with the lifeless grey flesh. This was the pallor of Terry's complexion, turning white before the grey death descends. His eyes looked like someone had got a vacuum cleaner and sucked out all the life, they just stared ahead with a dark, lifeless look. His cheeks were sucked in where he had been biting them, trying to hold back the tears. Terry didn't look so young anymore and shook his head slowly. Our lives were ended. All of our plans, our youth, had gone in that courtroom. Infamy then ignominy in the time it took us to walk back down the spiral stairs while the other lads walked to freedom. As I went down, I turned and saw the happy faces and I was jealous as hell. Terry looked like I felt, as did the others. I don't suppose I looked any better, but all of our thoughts turned to Dougie.

The press said that Terry stamped all the way down to the cells while Vince kicked the door on the way out and Dougie said 'Thank you' to the judge. The lads could have recited the first verses of *Twelfth Night* and I wouldn't have heard, I was in so much shock. The others who were not guilty were ecstatic but did not want to leave us. They shook our hands and wished us well, doing a locomotion-style dance in the air to go off to their celebrations, which would somehow be muted by the fact that we should have all left together.

'Good luck, lads,' said Toomsy. For one awful moment I was back on the Shed in 1970 with someone shouting 'Do your bird'. It didn't seem such a funny remark now. We had the whole weekend to think about what had happened. How could some of us, and not others, have been found guilty?

I lay awake that Friday evening going over the evidence. How could they have found me guilty on that flimsy rubbish? Surely the fact that four had been acquitted must have cast considerable doubt. Judge George would see that, wouldn't he? On the Saturday afternoon I listened to the radio as Chelsea drew 3–3 with Liverpool. An omen, especially as it coincided with 26 Liverpool fans having their extradition to Belgium over Heysel blocked. Draws all round. I

189

might get off with a couple of years and be out in six months. I slept on that thought.

Perhaps it was my false passport. Well, as a fan of the earn-a-pound brigade, how else was I supposed to travel around Europe? The false passport business had come from my desire to go to different countries as cheaply as possible. I changed my date of birth in order to continue to obtain an under-26 half-price rail card. Football is fun but sometimes following England got a bit of a chore, so my summers were taken up with the T-shirt business. Big rock concerts equals profit. Get a picture or design and reproduce it on a good T-shirt. Undercut the official licensed stuff, which is always overpriced. Moving 200 T-shirts in an evening equals a grand clear.

On Saturday 9 May, while the five of us lay locked in our cells, England took its revenge. On behalf of every citizen who'd been inconvenienced by football fans, right down to the old lady who'd had her TV schedules changed so preventing her from seeing her favourite soap opera, the papers all wallowed in the victory of good against evil. More frightening was the fact that we had not been sentenced. Judge Schindler would be reading this, so he knew he had a duty to make an example of us because England expects and Schindler would do his duty as required. We were the most dangerous group of plotters since they put Guy Fawkes to death. I know that the screws read some of it because we received some barbed comments from them. Sitting cocooned in the court system, isolated from the outside world, I hadn't realised how big this case had become. The reaction of the press showed how frightened of us England was. From tabloid trash to the highest, they murdered us in print.

The Times, page 3: **Jail Ends Reign of Terror by Chelsea's Soccer Thugs**

The *Daily Mirror*: **Soccer Psycho** Baby face Terry Last loved chess, birdwatching and weekends of bloody soccer savagery.

Meanwhile, the *Sun* ran two stories: **Evil General led soccer**

warfare and their real story, **Gay Yob's Girl in AIDS Agony**, which made out that Dale was a poof. They spent a whole page explaining why his tearful girlfriend would be taking an AIDS test after the police put out the story that Dale was in bed with another man.

The *Daily Mail* had **Salute of Hate** next to a picture of Terry and me singing in Istanbul when England won 8–0. 'Their hobby is not football. What happens on the pitch is of little interest to them. Their only goal is violence . . . Their game was finally smashed after police infiltrated the gang and even arranged for Turkish police to photograph the ringleaders as they delivered their Nazi salute. Last's arm is in a plaster. He broke it at Oxford attacking a fan. (*He'd fallen over a wall accidentally.*)

'Only a series of arrests in March 1986 prevented a party of Chelsea's most feared thugs from travelling in force to that year's World Cup in Mexico and trying to wreck the competition. A mass of National Front literature and anti-Semitic badges and flags were discovered in the swoop, along with a horrific array of weapons.

'Such was the gang's indifference to football that they played cards during matches. They had no idea that the police held the trump card that would put an end to their violent exploits. These men held responsible jobs, had wives, girlfriends and secure backgrounds. Cash was never a problem when they organised their trips of terror in Britain and abroad. Hooliganism was planned with military precision, even giving ranks and specific duties to the leaders. Last was the general. At night he would go to bed surrounded by his collection of Teddy bears. He kept a pet terrapin named Kerry Dixon after the Chelsea striker.'

That was the fix that middle-class England needed, we were control freaks with quirks in our character that made us different. Perhaps we were all closet poofs. A general who slept with a teddy bear. Then the *Mail* portrayed the brave police.

Caught in the crossfire – the brave police who joined Terry Last's army. 'We all knew that if we made a slip and were found out we would have been in trouble. They would have given us a good beating.'

The *Daily Telegraph* reported it all for the benefit of Judge Schindler's coterie. Here, Last was a field commander. One hundred and one prosecution witnesses. 'Even within the violent world of football gangs, the "Chelsea Headhunters" had a reputation for brutality with only a passing interest in the game. Between them they could mobilise 400 designer-dressed hooligans. They thought themselves untouchable . . . left calling cards: "You have been nominated and dealt with by the Chelsea Headhunters."'

We weren't the Headhunters, we were the Chelsea Nine, but why let the truth get in the way of a catchy name?

Then came the police backslapping. 'The overall officer in charge of the plan was Superintendent Mike Hedges, then working at Fulham police station, a stone's throw from the ground. He was concerned for the safety of the undercover team, knowing that if unmasked they faced serious injury and possible death.'

Death in the afternoon. Shakespeare, Hemingway, Siegfried Sassoon, the heady verbose speeches shouted from the parapet allowing the police to luxuriate in the gore of the bullfighter's kill.

'You have to balance the risks against the public good. In the end I believe we demonstrated to people in soccer violence that we will do anything in our power to stop them. Two days later when Chelsea played West Ham, what was normally hooligans' day of the year was recorded as one of the quietest. The lesser hooligans were running around like chickens with no heads. Their leaders were gone and they didn't know what to do.'

At the bottom of the page was a picture of David Hall who had been attacked at the Farmers Rest pub in Newcastle where he thought he was going to die. Terry's diary entry was linked to this. 'We done a pub load of Geordies. We done well against the Geordies. They were terrified.' Whether it was the Strawberry, the Farmers Rest or some unknown pub in the middle of nowhere made no difference now.

Then it was like the court case as they brought in a new name for added authenticity. Detective Sergeant Barnard, key co-ordinator of Operation Own Goal. 'The hooligans don't mind getting hurt or battered, they just want the pride of being the first ones there.'

PC McAree wallowed in his glory, stating how easy it was to infiltrate the gangs but of course they felt the sniff of extreme danger. 'I still believe that there could be the possibility of reprisals by other gang members and as a precaution none of us will be photographed. Last was the linchpin, even though he was a thin, bespectacled man. When he lost his temper, his malevolence showed.'

The *Telegraph* was not finished with Terry. To make matters worse, they had devoted the whole centre page to us, right next to the leader comment. This was the opinion formers' page. Thatcher took notice of what was said in the centre pages of the *Telegraph*. This was the Conservative government's pulse. I had this horrible vision of Schindler reading it over his Saturday bacon, egg and sausage, then going out to his garden bench to write his sentencing speech, adding another year every time he read each gory paragraph, finally adding another two when he saw the picture of the Newcastle fan.

'Last became obsessive about soccer and the potential it created for violence. Last called Spurs "The Yids". He recorded in his diary the singing of the gas song at a match at Tottenham.'

> *Spurs are on their way to Auschwitz*
> *Hitler's gonna gas 'em again*
> *The Yids from Tottenham*
> *The Yids from White Hart Lane.*

I believe that piece added another five years to mine and Terry's sentences.

I walked into the custody holding room on Monday morning and shouted, 'Appeal! We'll bloody well appeal, and we'll win. The press are in contempt of court. They even got our photographs wrong. They made it up, just like the police did. We weren't the Headhunters. That's a different group. We were the Chelsea nine.' Terry looked at me like I was a sandwich short of a picnic, the same way we'd spent the trial looking at the police constables and Lett, with incredulity.

'Who will we get to believe us the second time around?' he replied quietly. 'How will any football fan ever get a fair jury hearing after what they wrote about us?'

Dougie sat with his copy of the *Sun*. Still phlegmatic, he was laughing about what they'd written about him. Gang member Welsh, a labourer from Crawley, Sussex, was described as a man who would fight anyone. A detective said: 'Even at his funeral he'll probably reach out of the coffin and punch a mourner.' Dougie hadn't punched anybody prior to his Wembley punch since he was at primary school.

Judge Schindler was certainly perky on Monday morning. He had a glint in his eye. What had he been given over the weekend, a Gutenburg bible? He wanted a piece of us on behalf of the rest of civilised England, as well as himself – he'd listed football as one of his hobbies in *Who's Who*.

'The traditional British game of professional soccer has attracted as camp followers some of the nastiest, most vicious men to whom violence seems a way of life. As a result of this evil conspiracy many people were badly hurt, some scarred for life, absolutely petrified by horrific experiences that may be with some of them for the rest of their lives. The stench came from the hideous viciousness which sometimes accompanies the game in this country and is known and feared world-wide. They used football merely as an excuse to indulge in violence before and after Chelsea football matches at home and away. They used ambushes, diversions and other tactics to avoid the police.

'You are ruthless, violent and nasty men who used football as an excuse for violence. You have actually instilled great fear in very many law-abiding citizens who used to support, and bring up their children to support, the national game and their favourite team.'

Schindler was in full flow. He wanted Terry. After all, was this not a man who had links with the National Front, which expressed anti-Semitic tendencies?

'You are undoubtedly endowed with gifts of leadership but you used your talents to gratify your lust for violence. Although you were only 18 at the beginning of the conspiracy, you have learned quickly from the older men, more experienced in violence, until you became an undoubted ringleader, acknowledged as such by the Chelsea mob.'

Terry looked around, unable to believe that Schindler was actually talking about him.

'Last, you might give the appearance as meek but close to the surface lay a seething cauldron of violence which could be released at will. By 1986 you could be seen strutting around like a tinpot leader whose arrogance knew no bounds. You abused your talents to gratify your perverted lust for violence. You will receive ten years for the conspiracy and five years for the affray at Everton.'

Then he came to me. I, too, was a principal ringleader. He seemed to reserve a special sneer for me. Terry, after all, was just a violent tinpot dictator while I was his anti-Semitic lieutenant, so I felt he was goading me, trying to get me to shout something obscene at him so he could really wallow in the glory of sentencing. He told me he had considered giving me life. No, Mr Judge, watching Chelsea is for life. So he gave me ten years with another three months concurrent for the false passport. I smiled at him and thanked him.

Vince took it on the chin, unsmiling to the last. He was just a little lower in the set-up. Seven years. Dale got a special little mention in dispatches because he'd been a naval cook who'd served in the Falklands. What had made him be recruited by such vermin after serving his country in its hour of need? Five years.

Finally, the judge came to Dougie. So Mr Welsh had dared to complain about the judicial process being unfair and sworn at me, then treated me with contempt? Dougie had shown contempt for the whole legal process by refusing to sit in the dock for four weeks.

195

Dougie had even had the temerity to stand up in court and tell the judge that he didn't even know these people. Dougie had been heard to shout 'Kill the Bill' before being arrested by the brave policeman. Were that to be repeated, then it would mean the breakdown of law and order as we know it. So for your cheek for reading *Viz* in my courtroom, Dougie, six years.

'Take them down,' ordered Schindler with obvious contempt. Lett and the policemen were pleased as punch.

'Oi, Terry, do I have to salute you from now on?' quipped Dougie. Despite getting the roughest deal, he was still laughing. 'Bollocks to 'em all, lads.'

In the *Telegraph* on the Monday it was reported that Maggie had decided to name the date for the next General Election. She'd won last time thanks to the Falklands War – perhaps she now saw the defeat of the football hooligans as some sort of omen. Also reported was the rampage of the Leeds fans along the Brighton seafront where they had terrorised local day-trippers, stolen clothes worth £3,000 and set fire to four motorcycles. On the same day as our sentences, raids were carried out on 16 Millwall fans. Two of the men arrested and charged with conspiracy to cause affray over a nine-month period were Keith Wilcox and Simon Taylor. While it was the end of our beginning, I wasn't to know that their arrests would be the beginning of the end of the mass arrests of football hooligans.

10

CONVICTED

As I descended the stairs, I had a terrible feeling. Someone had hold of my arm and put me into a room. The officers who had looked after us during our time at the court knew something seemed out of place. They liked us, they were almost apologising. As I went in, we passed an officer holding a cup of coffee. The smell wafted under my nose. It smelt good. I didn't want that smell to leave me, for I didn't know how long it would be before I tasted freedom and fresh coffee again. I was suddenly back in the Italian cafe at Kings Cross where we had passed many an hour away.

On the wall was a picture of Juventus FC and Lofty had nick-named the Italian owner 'Spunk' when he told us he had seven children. He loved to tease us.

'Chelsea no good. Juventus number one club in the world.'

'Just shut up and serve us some tea.'

Then he would serve up the strongest tea I've ever tasted, with stewed tea leaves that woke you up after a night in the coach. You could practically stand your spoon up in it. Sausage, beans, eggs over easy, beans, fried slice, two toast and Italian salami as an extra. I loved our visits to that cafe. That cafe was Kings Cross for me.

In that cafe were the flotsam and jetsam of life in and around Kings Cross. Prostitutes and pimps after a night, alongside railway workers and other drunks and dossers who frequented the area, yet we all sat together enjoying tea that was strong enough to revive the dead. It probably had more caffeine than was allowed by the British Medical Association, but who cared when you needed waking up. Spunk was proud of his genuine Italian cappuccino machine that gurgled like an exploding volcano when he heated up the milk.

Suddenly Terry spoke and snapped me out of my misery.

'They really did a number on us.'

'I wonder what the others are doing now?' said Vince.

Dale looked at his watch. 'Toomsy will be on his third pint today.'

Dougie looked shattered. Six years for hitting a copper. If they couldn't get him on the conspiracy, then the assault would do.

The English prison system hates those who try and buck the established order. From the moment I was convicted the whole system seemed to come down on my head, especially when it became known that I intended to appeal. Once the English system gets a hold of you, it doesn't move too quickly. Once a mistake has been made it is hard to rectify it. Schindler may have roasted me in court, but he had not refused me leave to appeal. I had to look to this route, even if the chances of success were very limited.

On my return from court I was allocated my own cell. Every prisoner serving ten years or more gets a single cell. I preferred that. On Monday evening I was summoned to go before the guv'nor. On his desk was a copy of Saturday's *Daily Telegraph*, so his views on me and Terry were fixed. But he seemed okay. Stiff upper lip, very British. He was born a hundred years too late, judging by his demeanour. He said he ran a tight ship at Wandsworth. It seemed to me that he ran a ship which was so dirty and disgusting that the rats actually wore prison uniforms. If we kept our noses clean, we would be okay. Our celebrity status in the newspapers cut no ice inside prison. We were just one of many. 'Knuckle down and you'll be okay.'

'An educated Sergeant Hobbs,' was how Terry put it. Arsehole, I thought, he believed every word that was written in that *Daily Telegraph*.

For the first few days I sat and worked out how long I would be likely to serve. Hopefully, I'd get a bit of time off for good behaviour, so I could be out in six years' time. But I was determined to appeal. In prison everybody is innocent or there because they are unlucky, so nobody wanted to hear about my case except my solicitor.

Bill Buford was an American who, in the late eighties, enjoyed huge influence among the writing, chattering classes due to his position as editor of the magazine *Granta*. It was the trendy magazine to which writers among the literary clique used to get invited to contribute. Being a good writer doesn't necessarily mean that you will get reviewed or make sales, but being a part of the *Granta* dinner-party set ensured maximum exposure from the *cognoscenti* backslappers over canapés and small talk. Buford was fascinated by football hooligans as only Americans are, seeing them as quintessentially English, and wanted to get close to our feelings. The editor of the *Sunday Times* invited Bill to write about the trial in May 1987. The subsequent article undoubtedly helped many of the literary classes to enjoy sexual fantasies about football thugs, because 'Bill really knows these people'. His piece about me described how he had been nearby when I'd chased 'a small group of rival thugs':

> What happens when one of its dominant members disappears for 10 years – one so frenzied and so mad that the other members regarded him as a little strange?

So the *Sunday Times* reinforced the prejudices of the writing classes, while Bill was told what an eye-opening article he had done. I'm sure he was never there. My solicitor was appalled. He immediately wrote a stern letter which was reproduced in part in the *Sunday Times* on 31 May.

Unfair to the defendant
Had Mr Buford attended any part of the trial, and the general

tenor of his article suggests he did not, he would have realised that this description (red hair, soft baby face) could not apply to Mr Hickmott.

Bill Buford then stated that Mr Hickmott, upon hearing his sentence, shouted, 'Bastards! It wasn't me. It was the others,' and further stated there is some truth in it. I was present in court, and can state that there was no such outburst by Mr Hickmott, nor by any of the other defendants. Indeed, Stephen Hickmott was well behaved throughout the 18 weeks of the trial and in strongly denying the charge of conspiracy brought against him, he at no time suggested that any of his other co-defendants were involved. To describe Stephen as frenzied and mad is a gross distortion.

Robert Waddell
Solicitor, Stephen Hickmott

The *Sunday Times* declined to publish the parts of the letter about the acquittals. They were happy to print the lies about us, though. My mother bought the *Sunday Times* to read the letter. Next to it was the birthdays column. She saw the ages of Mike Gatting, England cricket captain, 31, and Bob Champion former jockey, 39, suddenly realised that I would be missing these years and burst into tears. I felt for my mother. She'd sat in court for many days during the trial. My sentence would hit her hard.

During my remand period I had also thought about Claire a lot. She had worked so hard to keep things going, making sure the rent on my flat was kept up to date as well as making sure all other matters were attended to, getting another courier to cover my work, keeping open as many options as possible so that upon my release I would be able to get back to work of some sort. After a few days' thought, I sat down and wrote the hardest letter I have ever had to write.

Dear Claire

Now that the unimaginable has happened I have to face reality and we must face facts together. I never thought for one moment I would be writing this letter and I thought that we would be on holiday somewhere in the sunshine. For the three days that the jury was out I was reading an article about Thailand. I saw this wonderful beach and I imagined you and I sitting there watching the most glorious sunsets one could ever wish to see.

However, the facts of the matter are that our previous life was ended the moment that sentence was read out. I understand that you have waited for over ten months since they took me away and that your strength has kept me going during some difficult periods, but now the time has come for you to take stock of what you are going to do. Unless a miracle happens (and they don't happen in here) you will not see me again for seven years at the earliest. Looking at the way they have pilloried myself, plus my determination not to admit my guilt, they may ensure I serve the whole 9 years 2 months left on my tariff.

Under these circumstances you must look to make a new life and future for yourself. I have no doubt that you will meet someone and I know that you were keen on starting a family. I will not be sending you any visiting orders because for us to see each other will cause no end of heartbreak and at the moment I need to keep my mind on coming to terms with what has happened to me.

I will be close to forty when I come out. Do not waste your best years waiting for me. One day I will make that beach in Thailand. You must go ahead and make it in the meantime without me.

Thinking of you.

All my love, Steve

Prison is boring. There is nothing to do except sit and wait. In prison you are always waiting for something. Waiting for a door to open, waiting for food, waiting for mail or visiting times or waiting to empty the chamber pot in the corner of the room. If it became necessary to have a shit at night in the cell, then it used to get wrapped in paper then pitched out of the window into the yard. Every morning the turd-covered yard used to get cleaned up by the sex offenders from G, H & K wings. They were nicknamed the 'Bomb Squad' by the other cons and as they cleaned up the yard with their buckets of water and brooms, the shouts of 'You dirty nonces' would echo around. We were proper prisoners in for real sentences, not filthy sex crimes.

Wandsworth operates a very restrictive regime because the people who run the system have no imagination. Ronnie Biggs escaped in 1965 by climbing on a rope ladder and jumping onto a converted furniture van parked conveniently outside. Two prisoners were rewarded with £500 each for holding off the prison guards. To this day Ronnie Biggs has enjoyed his freedom in Rio. So the stock-in-trade answer is that if they relax the regime, then Ronnie will escape again.

Every so often there is a riot and an inquiry is held. Recommendations are made, yet within a few years the system reverts back to the way the Prison Officers' Association wants the prison to be run. And to those inside it seems the people who administer the system love to allow the POA to brutalise prisoners because it saves them the bother of actually thinking about what they have to do to run a decent system. Seeing the warders in Wandsworth with their shades and keys on dog chains, it reminded me of the warder in *Cool Hand Luke*. Yes, they all appeared to me to be on a power kick. In their lives they were nobodies yet here they were able to order people about. That seemed to me to be the limit of their toughness.

I was better than they were because I was here because the government had decided to crack down on hooligans. Hadn't the government and the police stated that they would do whatever they had to do to get hooligans locked up? Yes, I was a political prisoner. In the early days when I was very down, I'd think back to my remand days at Pentonville and the man in the cell next to me. Loranne Osman had been on remand in that disgusting place for five and a half years by the time I left for Coldingly. He had the dubious distinction of being England's longest-serving remand prisoner, eventually earning the status of being a question in Trivial Pursuit. He was being held for embezzlement in Hong Kong. Eventually, he was extradited back to Hong Kong after serving eight and a half years on remand. An unconvicted man locked up for 23½ hours a day, allowed just one shower a week. People talk about the fantastic democracy that is Great Britain, yet here was living proof that our system is far from perfect, and who is feeding us this trash? A media dominated by the establishment, who pillory anybody who dares to suggest the status quo needs changing. I never heard that guy moan the way others did. His dignified and polite persona humiliated the judicial system which kept him incarcerated for all that time.

Exercise was a welcome relief from the general monotony of lockdown. The sound of feet springing down the metal steps into the exercise yard for an hour's walk around the yard was a pleasure even when it was cold and wet. Some Saturday afternoons, Terry and I would stand by the walls straining our ears to try and hear the cheers from Stamford Bridge, which was only a couple of miles to the north. The boys who got out used to write to us. Letters came from many different people whom I'd met over the years.

Some mornings, Terry and I would walk down the steps and be questioned by the other cons.

'What are you two doing here?'

When we explained, they looked at us incredulously. These were men doing sentences for murder and armed robbery or really hurting people. They couldn't fathom what we'd done wrong, unable to see the severity of our crime.

Sometimes we would see someone with an evil scowl. 'I bet he's

West Ham. Look at his miserable face.' While we'd laugh, it was always said so he couldn't hear it. It wasn't the done thing in prison to mock someone else. Everybody was just keeping their heads down doing their time.

Everybody had their own ways of relieving the horrible monotony. I missed the banter that we'd had at the Inner London Crown Court, so Terry and I relived away matches during the exercise period. Exercise became a giant away match. We'd swap stories and banter. I remembered a League Cup match at Arsenal in 1976 because it was the night that a 17-year-old Brian Bason broke his leg. I had played against Brian at school football, he went to Thomas A' Beckett school in Crawley. At the age of 15 he was a man. Once he scored five goals past us and he'd win most matches single-handed. He broke into Chelsea's first team at 16 and looked to have a massive future, but that broken leg finished him. He drifted down the leagues, finally ending up washed-up at Plymouth. It was in a challenge with Sammy Nelson that he broke his leg. Sammy was a hard player, he was to Arsenal what Ronnie Harris was to Chelsea. The terrace fans have always loved a hard man because they could empathise with that. It was also the night that the Battersea boys went along the train queue pulling out Arsenal fans and giving them a friendly slap.

Not that it was all fun and games among the lads in prison. Dale ended up on the same wing as two marsh men, who mocked him about being a poof. Dale chose his moment on the hotplate and threw hot tea in the face of one and chinned the other.

One night after lock up, I heard a bang on the door and a voice from the other side.

'Oi, you Chelsea bastard! Not so bloody hard now, are you? You're gonna get it!'

It disturbed me a little. The next night I was waiting for it.

'Chelsea wanker! You looked a little frightened today, walking down the stairs. You're going down, mate. Remember the Farmers Rest pub. Watch your face, wanker!'

I recognised the accent – Geordie. The Farmers Rest pub; when

Geordie met surgeon. This was a particularly nasty gang who carried surgeon scalpels and used them when they got the chance, then threw them away. One of the lads was a hospital orderly and used to steal them every week. As they walked away that day, one of the lads mimicked the Amex TV advert of the day. Holding up the scalpel, he said in mocking tones: 'Says more about you than a cosh ever can.' Then he laughed. The Geordies had been looking for it and what they got was more than they bargained for. Perhaps it was this bloke's mates? Perhaps he'd run and left his mates to cop it?

I saw Terry the next day. He, too, had received the threats. This went on for about a week, with the threats getting worse. One day I was walking along the landing when someone came up behind me and tapped me on the shoulder. I practically died from a heart attack. Everywhere I went around the prison I was on my guard. Watch your back, keep it tight, Chelsea, don't show fear. Easier said than done lying in a pitch black cell with a mysterious voice coming from behind a closed door. Every night I waited for the threats. 'Hello, Cockney, I'm Geordie. Soon, very soon. You won't know what hit you. Won't feel a thing.' After a while, the nightly threats ceased.

We weren't the only football fans in for conspiracy. On the other wings were some Arsenal lads who had been convicted of conspiracy to cause affray as well. In 1982 an Arsenal fan had been stabbed to death by West Ham outside Arsenal tube station. The next season the Arsenal planned their revenge and waited outside Finsbury Park tube for the ICF. All the Gooners were tooled up. But all they got for their trouble was three-year prison sentences.

Every day Terry and I would be at a different away match. Wolves in the South Bank, Manchester in the away end with the Mancs throwing plastic cups full of piss down on you, or Luton where the local lads used to pelt you with fruit and vegetables from overhead bridges then run like Olympic runners. We all agreed, nobody ever caught a Luton fan in full flight. The wing we were on was short of football fans. Serious criminals don't have time for football.

Although most Chelsea fans reserve their hatred for Tottenham, West Ham became the butt of our humour. 'We are evil, we are evil,' West Ham used to sing. So did other fans, but the way West Ham used to sing it meant that they always extended the E so it was Eeeeevil. Every time I spotted a misery guts, the thought that he was an 'Unhappy Hammer' crossed my mind.

Some days we'd relive dodgy days out. Every fan has one place which gives them a sleepless night before they go there. I'd heard from Arsenal fans it was Liverpool in a midweek match, while for me it was Bristol City. While the Arsenal fans I knew could tell me every terrifying step of their runs across Stanley 'Knife' Park, I always remembered the time some giant coloured Bristol lad in a group of five pulled an iron bar out of a sports bag and smashed me across the skull, putting me in hospital. Ambushed by idiots with stupid accents.

Terry mentioned 'Binnsy' one day. Binnsy. Just the mention of his name made me smile. What a wally. The ticket tout who used to fancy himself as a bit of an Arsenal ace-face leader. Once in the early eighties he came into the North Stand with his little firm of around 40 geezers. They were all about 10 years younger than him. We watched him walk up the steps one cold February afternoon. He was dressed in the fashion of the time, woollen jumper tucked into his jeans with gloves. Binnsy was big on fashion and posing, low on fighting. The Chelsea lads stared at him as he walked the long concrete incline up to the North Stand terrace.

'Look out, lads, it's that pop group Binnsy and the Nippers,' said a Chelsea Northstander disdainfully.

'What is he like? With those double glazed bins and all those kids with him,' said another. He was doing his confident, swaying from side to side walk. In reality he looked like he'd forgotten to wipe his bum and the shit was making him uncomfortable.

Binnsy walked right to the top of the walkway at the back of the North Stand, where the burger stand was, and said to the Chelsea firm, who he, for reasons best known to himself, thought was Arsenal: 'Where are all these Chelsea North Stand Boys I've heard so much about, then?' The first punch hit him square on the jaw, sending him straight down, sending his bins flying, his limbs and mouth trying to get it together, floundering like a boated mackerel. His firm of kids scattered everywhere without throwing a punch in anger while he grovelled on the ground on all fours as three or four attempted to stamp on his glasses. Eventually they smashed, so they gave him a good kicking. The police took him out. His jumper was torn to shreds and he held his mangled glass frames in his right hand, with everybody laughing at him – even other Arsenal fans. I never saw him over at Chelsea again except to sell tickets always saying that 'Business is business, no hard feelings.'

Losing yourself inside your imagination was the only way to survive Wandsworth. No day was better than any other, as the whole shebang was about keeping you static. An austere regime, similar to the way the upper classes learn about co-existence at Eton and Gordonstoun – no wonder they apply the technique so rigidly. The whole system was all about creating a blandness which could be controlled – no wonder we had become unruly at football if this was the limit of the imagination of the administration classes. This was the fate they had in mind for society in general – no wonder they were so petrified of us.

I was on D Wing, fourth landing – the top landing, which was all single cells. One visit every month for 15 minutes. One shower a week for one minute, then your weekly change of clothes. Wandsworth routine: 6.30am, doors open. Out on to landing, empty piss pot, back by 6.45am. 7.15am, breakfast of disgusting porridge. Back to cell. 10am, outside for 45 minutes' walking. Back into cell. 11.30am, lunch. Back into cell. 4pm, food. Door opened at 6.30pm for evening tea. You had to apply to go to the library, apply to go to the gym. Nobody bothered. Sometimes they would open up cells. They never opened mine. For visits the screws really gave the visitors, parents or whatever a hard time, so I told mum not to bother.

One man bucked the whole prison system and it was terrified of him, so they kept him moving around. Feed him, move him, sedate him. No wonder he was crazy. What could you say about a man who'd changed his name by deed poll to Charles Bronson, of *Death Wish* fame? Everybody is frightened of nutters but this guy was so crazy even the nutters took refuge in the sanity wing when he walked the landing. Warders who loved to boast how tough they were and could break any man refused to go near him. Having built his physical strength up with a fanatical obsession, he was almost as wide as his 5ft 11in height, with a huge neck and arms and a long moustache. He held the world record for press-ups and strength tests. During his incarceration he had been involved in numerous hostage-taking incidents where he asked for a cheese sandwich and a strawberry milkshake plus a plane to Cuba. He came on to the wing when I was working as a cleaner. On the first day he arrived, I was cleaning and I heard a lot of smashing noises. Charles hated furniture and Wandsworth had given him a cell with furniture in, so he smashed it all up. His cell door was never opened by any less than three officers. In the exercise yard he used to march around every day the opposite way to everybody else. The officers were absolutely terrified of him, and when he wanted food he just used to put his hand in and take whatever he wanted.

One day Stirling and I were cleaning the landings when Charles approached us.

'I need some soap.'

Shit, I thought, this guy's gonna kill me if I don't buy him some soap.

'Not the pansy stuff, the carbolic soap.'

A couple of days later I managed to get him a long block of carbolic stuff which you clean the cell floor with. The officers opened his door at my request and I handed him the soap. He looked me right in the eyes.

'You see this?' he said, pointing to the carbolic soap. 'This is what real men use.' Before I could say okay, Stirling piped up in a Scottish accent: 'I use Camay myself.'

For one awful moment I thought he was going to kill me. I was glad to get out of that cell. He was a funny man, with hundreds of stories which I used to listen to when he shouted them out of his window. He has been in nearly every prison in England, only starting out with a three-year sentence yet now he has accrued over 18 years. I never asked him which football team he supported and I doubt whether he will ever get out.

After six months I was allocated a prime job on the hotplate dishing up food, which I enjoyed, having spent so long locked up all day and night. It meant that I was out of my cell earlier than others as well as not being locked up all day, so I was moved on to landing one. With the food I dished up banter to all those who wanted to talk football. One day I noticed a screw watching me. The next day he sidled over.

'Hello, Chelsea. Still getting the late night threats?'

I looked at him, giving nothing away. 'No, they've stopped now.'

'Good laugh, wasn't it? I enjoyed that. Getting my own back on you Chelsea boys.'

I smiled at him. He'd had his moment of glory. Over the coming weeks he seemed determined to tell me his life story about the club he supported. He even told me what time he caught the trains from Kent, where he lived. Later some of the boys went down to Charing Cross station and waited for him. They took his picture and terrorised him for a few weeks, following him around the London underground and staring at him. Once, one of the lads said he was a surgeon and they reckoned he wet himself. He didn't seem to like the boot on the other foot.

As a political prisoner, I decided to make my cell the focus of my case. I wrote down everything I could remember about the trial. Every word which had been spoken by the police was indelibly etched in my memory. I made a sign and put it up on the wall: 'YOU CAN'T CAN A CHELSEA FAN' in memory of the ban badge. Chelsea had been banned from attending away matches after the incidents at Luton, where they set the trains alight, and Charlton, where they had smashed up the ground. Our last match of the season was at Wolverhampton and we needed a draw to go up. Thousands were intending to make the journey, so British Rail laid on two special trains for the travelling fans. Thatcher would have been proud of their entrepreneurial spirit in providing transport for people who were defying the rule of law. As the match approached it became obvious that the Wolverhampton locals and assorted London touts had bought up thousands of tickets and were quite happy to sell them on to Chelsea fans for a small profit. Consequently, hundreds of Chelsea fans were in the Wolverhampton end, myself included, punching it up with the Wolves fans during the match. The pictures of the celebrating banned Chelsea fans were even shown on the evening news that night. Ken Bates was quoted in the paper saying that there had been no trouble at the Chelsea end of the ground where the police had opened the turnstiles to let thousands in to see the match.

I also put up a sign saying 'I HATE WEST HAM'. This was ironic because at the trial, the prosecution had made great hay about the stupid 'I HATE' badges which they had found in my loft, along with loads of other football paraphernalia. The 'I HATE' and 'I LOVE' badges were a fashion thing in the early 1970s. It seems stupid now but everybody wore them. I remember the 'YIDBUSTER' T-shirts which people wore down at Stamford Bridge mocking the Spurs fans, until someone was arrested and brought before a stern-faced magistrate to be fined for anti-Semitic behaviour, even if it was just lads having fun.

I had until the second week of June 1987 to lodge an appeal. When I received the lawyer's synopsis of my chances, I suddenly realised how Binnsy felt that day on the North Stand deck, grovelling around on the concrete trying to retrieve his glasses.

REGINA and STEPHEN GEORGE HICKMOTT
ADVICE

Having given the matter a great deal of thought I have been obliged to conclude that there are no reasonable grounds of successfully appealing the conviction of one count of conspiracy to cause affray. It is quite clear from the other verdicts which were given that the evidence of the undercover team of Police Officers was not accepted by the jury and it was for that reason I wanted to review the evidence with great care to ensure that there was no inconsistency in the verdicts. It appears that the guilty verdicts were given where the evidence came from Police Officers who were not part of the undercover team or where the evidence was corroborated by other evidence.

I then considered whether there were any misdirections by the Judge in the course of his summing up. Bearing in mind the extraordinary length of the trial it has to be said that the review of the evidence was accurate. (*Not from where I sat it wasn't, I thought reading this.*) Such adverse comments made on the defence evidence came within the scope of the Judge's discretion permitted by the law, bearing in mind that the Judge did make it clear (as they always do) that the jury was free to accept or reject those opinions if they do not accord with the view taken by the jury. From the not guilty verdicts it is manifestly apparent that the jury accepted some views expressed by the Judge and totally rejected other views.

It was always acknowledged by Mr Hickmott that we had an uphill task in seeking to cast doubt on the totality of the evidence against him. I well understand that it must be particularly galling for him to find at the end of such a trial that only ten of the jury felt that the prosecution had proved their case, but majority verdicts have been permitted for many years now and one has to accept that for the purposes of testing a conviction a majority conviction has the same weight as a unanimous one.

There were two main issues in the trial where we sought to have excluded prejudicial evidence, arguing that any prohibitive value was outweighed by that prejudice. The first related to the question of the scrapbooks. We have always feared that their inclusion would have a potentially devastating effect, bearing in mind that they were filled with articles devoted to football violence and violence at other sports. Although the Judge at first was prepared to have excluded those cuttings which fell outside the scope of the conspiracy, once he realised that they were in no particular date order it became obvious that it was unrealistic and impracticable to delete some and include others. The inclusion of those cuttings was permitted on the basis that they tended to show the state of mind of Mr Hickmott. One must concede that such a ruling was within the scope of judicial discretion and although I always felt that there was a very arguable case for their exclusion, I must advise that I cannot find justifiable reasons for praying that decision in aid of an appeal. I might add that Mr Hickmott's comments as to the general veracity of such reports from the tabloid press has been wholly vindicated by the disgraceful inaccuracies which appeared in the media concerning this trial, about which Mr Waddell and I have had long discussions. I was gratified to see that the *Sunday Times* did publish Mr Waddell's letter of protest, albeit in a truncated form.

The second issue was the admission of Mr Hickmott's convictions. As Mr Hickmott knows, it has always been my view that there was not the slightest realistic prospect of keeping these convictions out of the trial, bearing in mind that our defence necessitated an attack on the veracity of the prosecution witnesses. Although Mr Coningsby fought long and hard to have them excluded it has to be said that the battle could never have been won.

Thus, in brief, I must advise in writing to the same effect as my oral opinion expressed to Mr Hickmott immediately after the sentence. While I appreciate that this will come as a disappointment to him, I know him well enough to believe that he is a realist: it would be both unfair and unkind for me to hold out hopes which are unfounded.

The far more difficult decision comes in relation to the matter of sentence. I have come to the conclusion that we are justified in testing it, but wish to stress the scope within which the Court of Appeal operates. The higher court will not interfere with a sentence unless it is considered to be one which is either wrong in principle or manifestly excessive. That means that there is left a residue of discretion on the part of the trial judge with which the Court of Appeal will not interfere. The view is taken that the trial judge has had a far better opportunity to assess a sentence in any particular case and that such discretion is unfettered unless it comes within either or both the two principles set out above.

The most glaring difficulty comes from the very nature of the wide scope of the six-year conspiracy. As we are unable to go behind the blanket verdict we have no way of knowing what the jury found as proved and what they did not. I cite for example the Newcastle Farmers Rest matter. It was not charged as a separate affray and thus it may be that the jury was not satisfied that Mr Hickmott took part: such a conclusion would not invalidate the verdict, but there remains that doubt. On the other hand, the judge is then entitled to conclude that the verdict did include Newcastle, and thus sentence on that basis.

I have made a note of the sentencing remarks. It was made clear that it was regarded by the Judge that a six-year conspiracy struck at the very heart of football attendances, that the very national reputation we have to endure as 'football hooligans' stems from 'organisations' such as this and that by

213

such conduct countless numbers of people have been deterred from watching what was described as our national sport. It is a fact that the wide coverage of the trial carried with it an inevitable consequence, namely that there were bound to be sentences which were both condign and deterrent. We have to accept that by the verdict Mr Hickmott was bound to be labelled as a ringleader and organiser. We must also accept that because of his age and number of convictions he was to be treated in the same way as Terence Last, who is that much younger and whose record is very much less serious, in the balancing process of attempting to find parity between defendants whose distinctions weigh adversely against Mr Hickmott and are counterbalanced by the view taken by the Judge that Last was the main ringleader.

If leave is granted by the Single Judge we will have an opportunity of perfecting the grounds at a later stage and can do so in conjunction with Counsel for Last if an appeal has been advised in his case.

Nicholas Price
The Temple
London EC4

So having said all that, Mr Price then sent through a general synopsis of my grounds for an appeal against the sentence.

1. That there was no direct evidence Mr Hickmott ever actually indulged in violence himself.
2. That it cannot be suggested that Mr Hickmott was involved in this conspiracy throughout the whole period, the six years from 1980 to 1986.
3. That the indications to be taken from the prosecution evidence point strongly towards the conclusion that he was becoming less involved as time progressed.

214

4. That although he is somebody with a considerable number of previous convictions, he served only one sentence of imprisonment and that was for a very short time, within the scope of this conspiracy.

5. That the evidence clearly demonstrated that he was not someone who attended matches for the sole purpose of creating trouble but was certainly a person who had a passion for football in general and Chelsea FC in particular.

6. That there was no evidence whatsoever to suggest Mr Hickmott ever carried or used any offensive weapons.

7. That the verdicts of not guilty relating to the other defendants is a clear demonstration that the evidence of the undercover team was not accepted. It follows that evidence adduced by that 'team' of Officers relating to the allegedly overheard conversations could not (or should not) be relied upon in sentencing.

8. That although it is acknowledged a deterrent sentence was appropriate, a sentence of ten years is an unnecessarily harsh deterrent.

9. That by reason of the above matters, the sentence was manifestly excessive and wrong in principle.

I thought it wrong that there were no grounds for an appeal against the conviction, but as Nick Price stated, I was a realist. When my brother Sam read the appeal data, he laughed. 'Watching Chelsea is grounds for putting someone in a mental home indefinitely. Ten years, you got off light.' It was the sort of black humour that football fans display to each other.

The Judge granted leave to appeal against the severity of the sentence. With luck, I'd be out for the European Championships which were being played in Germany in June 1988.

August 1987 was a difficult time as the new season started with me still in Wandsworth. For the first time in many years I'd missed the opening match of the season. For the West Ham lads, and also the

Chelsea lads who had been arrested (in 'Operation Own Goal Two'), it must also have been difficult. The West Ham lads had been raided in 1987 with all the dawn raids and TV camera crew exclusives, followed by obligatory remand as urban terrorists, probably held somewhere in sunny Essex. With memories still fresh from our tabloid mauling they must have feared the worst. The same went for the Chelsea lads who were now Headhunters II, part of the most feared football gang in the world. Chris Henderson was being dubbed chief Headhunter, the leader of that gang. We all knew him as Chubby Chris for obvious reasons, although his nickname became Combat Chris to some because he was once the lead singer in the punk band Combat 84. It was nothing to do with Combat 18, the far-right paramilitary organisation, which at the time of the band nobody had heard of. There was no doubt in my mind that the press were going to have a field day with the Combat nickname if they got found guilty.

The press reported the police tactics, which seemed the same to me. They claimed to have infiltrated the gangs at operational level, yet all they were producing were overheard conversations and a few calling cards. But look at it from the jury's point of view. Somebody was committing these acts, so why not those in front of the courts?

New Year 1988 came and went with me listening to the BBC football commentary in the afternoon and music in the evening. Only another seven to go if my appeal failed. My 12-foot by 8-foot cell seemed to be shrinking in size. I must have started to look down in the mouth because I was offered some drugs one day by a well-meaning fellow prisoner, but I wanted nothing to do with that. Drugs were for losers. I was determined not to be dragged down to the level of losing my time in a drug-induced haze. It amazed me how many drugs were available inside prison. I knew that people took drugs on my coaches but I turned a blind eye; after all, it was their body they were abusing. Inside prison the sudden high must have been replaced by terrible lows, such was the way of prison life.

For those who are guilty it is an occupational hazard. For myself and other innocent people, prison time goes slower – better to keep on an even keel.

A week later I received a letter from the lads who had been released. Many people wrote to me. Chelsea's form wasn't improving. The letters kept me going, as did my impending appeal. The lads were soon transferred out. Dale went to Blunderstone after four months, Terry followed after 14 months. For Terry, Blunderstone in Norfolk meant he was in his element, being out in the countryside. Vince was transferred to the Isle of Wight after 12 months. They just left me to rot in Wandsworth because they were reading my mail and knew I was planning an appeal and believed in my innocence. The system doesn't like people who won't admit their guilt. Dougie waited 10 months before drawing the short straw once again and was transferred up to the horrible HMP Full Sutton, just outside Leeds. This meant incredible hardship for his mother in travelling to see him and he ended up serving his entire time without visits. Perhaps Dougie's simple, 'I am innocent, bollocks' philosophy frightened those in control and they were worried somebody from *Rough Justice* might take his case up and make him a *cause célèbre*.

With the first trial out of the way, Thatcher let loose her midget Minster for Sport, Colin Moynihan, who ran around like a deranged terrier snapping away at all and sundry. In January he announced that English clubs, who had been banned indefinitely after Heysel from European competition, should not be let back in until after the June European Championships. The media, meanwhile, were running scare stories about groups of hooligans from England, Germany and Holland arranging pitched battles at the tournament.

In January the legal establishment ruled out an appeal by the Birmingham Six within minutes of it starting. Lord Lane ruled the new evidence highly unsatisfactory, branding the Six unconvincing liars. Like Dougie, they claimed not to have been in Birmingham on the evening of the blasts.

Meanwhile, Millwall played Arsenal in the FA Cup and disturbances broke out during the match. Moynihan called for an enquiry. An Arsenal lad told the true story.

'A mob of us were in the Arsenal Tavern just sitting around on the stage watching *Saint & Greavsie* around 1pm. The Millwall must have filtered in in ones and twos because before we knew where we were, an almighty row went up. "No one likes us, we don't care. MILLWAAAL!" The Millwall guys in the pub gravitated to that sound. They congregated by the bar and started doing the optics, pitching pint glasses over the bar. Three blokes then started whacking every Arsenal fan in sight with pool cues. Then the grunting noise which people make when they are on the ground getting punched and kicked, and noise of people running away in a crowded pub, girls screaming, people going over tables, glasses smashing, chairs breaking.

'A girl jumped up on the pool table and started directing operations. She was the traffic warden. "Three in the far corner." Pointing. "Over there, blondie and his wanker mates . . . Two trying to slip out . . . Four going into the toilets." Shit, she was the most frightening woman in England.'

'*You ain't met Essex Edna, the outside girl,*' I thought.

'All you could hear was the sound of glass smashing underneath bodies and the horrible noise of people shouting and screaming in pain as they rolled about in the glass on the floor. Then they put the chairs through the windows from the inside. Suddenly the girl jumped down and they were gone. In their wake they left the noise of pain; girls screaming, guys moaning on the floor clutching themselves, with horrible glass gashes to the arms and head wounds where glasses and chair legs had been smashed over them.'

Moynihan stated with some conviction in *The Times* that these thugs would be stopped. 'What the hell did he know about pub brawls?' added the Arsenal fan.

On 27 January six Millwall fans started their trial. Once again it was a conspiracy set over a period of six months with five under-cover officers. The fans had been acting together to act unlawfully to fight and to make affray between August 1986 and January 1987. The police said they mingled with thugs. Give the trial a fancy name, make sure the press shout out loud the gang nickname, in this case the Millwall Bushwackers. Fast forward, next group of fans please.

The Times was cock-a-hoop. Maggie Thatcher's determination to crack down on football hooliganism had won support from the police and football authorities. Maggie was winning. The fans were on the run. Now bring on the heavyweights – enter the marsh men.

In January 1988 the West Ham lads' trial came to court for the theat-rically named 'Operation Full Time'. It was set down for Snaresbrook Crown Court. That made me chuckle for a start. Snaresbrook, in East London, had the highest acquittal rate in the whole of England. Perhaps it is down to the fact that East Enders are a little bit villainous or perhaps they have a healthy disregard for the law. Whatever, I wished the West Ham boys well. When the trial started, suddenly I was back at my own trial again. The press eulogised the police evidence about the ICF with a descriptive, almost thriller writer's flourish. I didn't know at the time but three of the officers who were on my case also worked on the West Ham case.

The Times, Wednesday 3 February 1988. 'Seven undercover policemen posed as hooligans to trap a gang of youths who wrought havoc at soccer matches for more than six years. The heavily armed gang organised fighting in and around grounds with military-style precision. Some of their weapons were ball bearings used to hurl at mounted policemen. (*A new tactic, an appeal to the disgust in the English psyche about cruelty to animals. Nice one, that.*)

'The constables infiltrated the ranks of the notorious ICF, a group of hardened criminals devoted to violence. During raids, police seized weapons including a machete, spring-loaded truncheons,

Stanley knives and a scarf loaded with a weight. Travelling on trains with these thugs, the police took notes . . .'

I wondered out loud to myself whether in order to travel with the ICF the police had taken special lessons on how to look miserable! I knew from past experience that almost nobody infiltrated the ICF because they were the tightest group in London. They all had history together, even more so than us. If any outsiders had come along they'd have been on them like a shot.

Eleven alleged ringleaders had been rounded up. I looked at the list of names: Cass Pennant, Andrew Swallow, Bill Gardner, Ted Bugsby, Del Legg, Danny Daly, Harvey Cutling, Martin Sturgess, Paul Dorsett, Kev Shroeder, Peter Dickey. Some of the names I knew, even if my opinion was that you can't take a group of guys seriously who sing about blowing bubbles, pretty bubbles in the air (the West Ham song). I knew the way they operated as I'd come into contact with them on numerous occasions at home and abroad. Not a laugh between them. On the way back from Luxembourg in '84 there had been an exchange after we'd declined their offer of a partnership to really cane the Manchester United boys on the platform of Luxembourg station.

'There might be 50 of you but you haven't got one ounce of bottle between you,' mocked Swallow. The usual abuse and threats were uttered by them but we had a different view towards other fans at England matches than did West Ham. Some of these northern lads were our friends. What the West Ham wanted was an assurance that if we wouldn't join them, we'd stay neutral. 'That Taffy's like Von Ribbentrop meeting Molotov to get a non-aggression pact,' mocked Jeff, a historical allusion that was lost on almost everybody.

'Watch your step or I'll stuff some of my socks into your luggage,' added Billy Mathews. So the unsmilers marched along the platform and punched out the Mancs first, then any other northerners in their path, while we stood around laughing about the havoc that had just been meted out to Luxembourg city centre. Plenty went home with Rolexes or broken ribs, depending upon the company they kept.

Nothing pleased the West Ham lads except being known as the guv'nors, the toughest in the manor. Even when they went to Turkey they moaned. They flew down to Anatolia for a few days' R & R but ended up back in Istanbul bitching and upsetting everybody else. Ain't no sunshine when they're around. Most of them had abused me in person or via my ansaphone at some time or another. The police might have got some of the ICF (though perhaps they also had an innocent Dougie among them) but once again for all the wrong reasons, because the basic doctrine of a democracy is that you catch people while they do it or prove beyond a reasonable doubt that they did it. Reading what the police offered up on the ICF, I doubted that they had any more on West Ham than they had on us. The strength of the ICF was their togetherness – the marsh man mentality. If anybody could win it was the tragedians.

Mr Vivian Robinson, QC, prosecuting, told the jury that the ringleaders organised other supporters at British Rail stations in London, shouting instructions about what to do when they arrived at opponents' grounds. What, bloody Persil himself? They must be joking. Once again the police had overheard conversations. This time they had heard arrangements to get weapons for a 'bit of back up' and discussions about the best places to launch attacks on rival fans. I wondered if they had overheard Cass discussing his strategy to corner the market in soap powder packets. The jury was shown a video. However, all it showed were the miserable faces of the West Ham fans. Put that picture above your child's bed and they wouldn't dare get out, not even on Christmas morning to open their presents.

The funny part was that the West Ham lads had agreed to appear in a fly-on-the-wall hooligan documentary for an American TV station. In return for money they hammed it up for the cameras, taking the rise out of the characters they were supposed to represent. One of them was Cass Pennant. On the video he stated that the lads met in 'pubbies'. He meant pubs. For the American TV audience, though, Cass explained that the ICF acted like Rambo. They even

221

looked for confrontation with foreign paramilitary forces. They saw it as a challenge to take on armed police abroad. He was comical on the video – a real natural in front of the cameras – especially when he likened football violence to the Falklands War. He even introduced himself as a retired football hooligan on film.

'Really, Cass, you should get out more,' was Jeff's comment.

The trial was expected to last four months. Very soon the press got bored with the constant revelations, failing to see a grown man with Persil rail vouchers in his back pocket as frightening news for the general public, so it settled into the same pattern as ours.

Pretty soon the Metropolitan Police were making more 'football gang violence' related arrests. On 4 February, 19 Arsenal fans were arrested. One of the Gooners was shown in a national tabloid newspaper against a backdrop of a picture of Terry on a board in his room. Under the Words 'Gooners – The Herd' was a newspaper collage of events, including Terry's mug shot under the headline 'Soccer Yob Jailed'. Personally, I would have preferred to see the *Daily Mirror* headline: 'Beast of the Bridge'. Terry would have liked that because he once went £30 blind then opened up to find he had three jacks, winning over £300 then refusing to buy a round of drinks. Jeff described him as a beast. Magnificent, but still a beast. Pictures showing the Arsenal fans' intention to travel out to the European Championships in Germany were put on display.

When they arrested a large group of Crystal Palace fans on the same conspiracy charges as us, you had to pinch yourself to believe it was real. Perhaps it was a *Blade Runner*-type script where the mutants that nobody else knew about were hiding somewhere in Croydon. Scraping the barrel sprang to mind. Conspiracy? Conspiracy to run, more like it! While most London fans had other London teams as their most hated rivals, Palace had Brighton. Everybody wanted to play Brighton in the summer or spring months because that meant a great night out, but fighting? No, the police must have arrested the wrong people. The only thing that was terrifying about Palace were the seats they had installed, which meant that anybody above a 26-inch inside leg ended up with their shins crushed under their chins. Next to Chelsea, Palace had the largest site in London. But while Ken Bates was determined to develop a football club, Palace sold their freehold land to a supermarket.

On 23 February, 20 Liverpool fans being held in Brussels on manslaughter charges relating to the Heysel disaster were granted Belgian bail. Not that it did them much good, as they had to remain in the country. Every day I would scan the papers looking for someone to get a not guilty. It must have been like this in the Second World War when British people looked in the papers every day hoping for one small victory against the Germans, yet every day brought stories of further German victories. In March there were further conspiracy arrests of Luton and Wolverhampton fans, although the West Midlands force showed their police canteen sense of humour by naming their operation 'GROWTH', an acronym for Get Rid of Wolverhampton's Troublesome Hooligans. Even I laughed at that one.

Running in conjunction with the West Ham trial was the media-nicknamed 'Headhunters' trial going on at Knightsbridge Crown Court. Eight Chelsea fans were up on the same conspiracy to cause affray charge. Police had called this Operation Own Goal Two. Now this trial did cause some consternation in the media because of the use of calling cards. One of the lads at Chelsea had devised a particularly fetching design using a Nazi death-head skull and crossbones, under which he had printed 'You have been nominated and dealt with by the Chelsea Headhunters'. It was black humour of the roughest kind. The type which other fans appreciated, even if they feared the call of the card. Jeff had sung a witty line one day in the Imperial to the tune 'Ghostbusters', sung by Ray Parker Junior.

There's some ICF
In the neighbourhood
Who you gonna call?
Headhunters

I liked the name Headhunters. I felt it had a ring to it, and it was no wonder that the public picked up on it. ICF was miserable sounding. Even the ICF calling card was grimness personified: 'Congratulations, you have just met the Inter City Firm from West Ham.'

Then things settled down. My prison routine became one of waiting for news from one source or another. The showers took on the persona of the Watford toilets. I remember the first time I went to Watford. I arrived at the ground five minutes before kick-off, then the police sent me on a three-mile route march around the biggest allotment I've ever seen. By the time we got there the first half was nearly over. I went to the toilet and it was the most disgusting thing I'd ever seen. Green mould was growing up the walls. A Leeds fan had scratched 'Service Crew' on one wall above a rotting green copper pipe, although doing that was risking one's health. It looked like nobody had ever cleaned them, let alone serviced them. The toilet was open to the elements, so cleaning was done by the rain. In August the ammonia stench coming from stagnant urine in open drainholes was indescribable. I nicknamed the Wandsworth shower block 'Watford'. Not that it was dirty, we just didn't see it often enough and our smells needed a nickname and that seemed apt. The first time I went to shower at Wandsworth, I saw prisoners frantically soaping themselves down before the water was switched on. Idiots, I thought. The water was switched on and stayed on for exactly 60 seconds. While the others managed their wash, I was left with soap and frothy shampoo in my hair and no water to wash it off with. A horrible looking man with a ginger beard, which looked like it still had last month's breakfast in it, appeared.

'Right, you lot, fuck off. Your time's up,' he barked in a Scots accent.
'I haven't washed off the soap and shampoo yet.'

'You can do that next week. Now fuck off, before you're put on a charge.'

He was enjoying that. Quite what sort of upbringing he had that made him do what he did baffled me.

On 20 April 1988 the two Millwall fans out of the group of six who had gone on trial in January received custodial sentences. They were Keith Wilcox, 27, of Peterborough and Simon Taylor, 20, from Upminster. But something happened during the police-named 'Dirty Den' trial which made people sit up and take notice. Keith Wilcox was convicted on an 11 to one majority but the one dissenting voice would not be silenced. He stopped the trial when he stood up in court.

'Scapegoats, bloody scapegoats. It's bloody true, that's what they were,' he shouted.

Taylor got three years and Wilcox got a four stretch, while the juror found himself in contempt of court and got seven days.

I wasn't to know it but at the same time, the West Ham fans were telling their defence barristers that the police notes were incorrect. Not only that, but the same togetherness which had given us Chelsea lads such a hard time over the years was making the West Ham fans a formidable force to prosecute.

March 25th, 1988, was my second anniversary of incarceration and I was turning into an old lag. I had passed an A-level in German and also a welding and sheet-metal fabrication course. Hickey the Porridge they'd be calling me next time I attended Stamford Bridge as a middle-aged git. When I got older I'd be the codger on the tube.

'Don't smash that window, sonny, or they'll lock you up for 10 years, no reason.'

'Clear off, you old codger, when you was a kid there were real hooligans, not wankers like you.'

I waited for the noises of the warder coming along, the rattle of the keys and looked forward to getting out of my door with my chamber pot full of piss. Emptying it had become a highlight. I knew how many seconds it took me and how much was left of my day until night would come again. I was reduced to remembering that I'd seen Reggie Kray in prison and felt honoured. After all, here was a man who'd served over 30 years for killing a fellow criminal in a gangland fight, yet something made the establishment fear him. Child killers served less time than him.

In Maidstone, where I went after Wordsworth, everybody used to shout 'nonce' at Wayne Darvell. He was a simpleton who'd admitted to the horrific killing of a woman in a sex shop. However, he'd also admitted to every killing in Wales that he'd been asked about by the police. Whenever he was spotted, the shout 'nonce' went up. He would shout back in a broad, slow Welsh accent, which made everybody laugh: 'But I'm not a nonce.' And I thought I'd had a rough deal. I was down to go on a painting and decorating course. In the meantime, on to my job on the hotplate dishing up food and one-liners. Yes, I was happy to be allowed to work on the hotplate. I'd become a simple machine in the prison factory. How much would I deteriorate before I tasted a flat beer in the King's Head again, or saw Chelsea get dumped out of the FA Cup by some lower division team?

Wednesday 10 May 1988 is the most significant day in my football fan's justice calendar. People walk around America saying that they remember exactly where they were when they heard Kennedy was shot. Well, I remember that I heard the key go on my cell door and a warder stood there with an interesting expression.

'Some of your mates were on the news last night.'

'What do you mean?'

'Big trial was halted yesterday involving West Ham fans.'

'Those tossers aren't my mates.'

Notwithstanding that, I was intrigued. Page 3 of *The Times* put me out of my misery.

Judge halts trial as police files discredited

'Scotland Yard last night launched a wide-ranging police internal investigation after the trial of alleged football hooligans collapsed with the prosecution counsel saying he no longer trusted the police evidence . . . New material has been received which bears upon the integrity of the logs.'

I read it so fast that my eyes had to skip back and forth making sure that it was true. I can imagine lottery winners do this with their winning numbers, unable to believe what is written down in black and white. My heart was thumping so much that the whole prison must have been vibrating. Had they put a cardiogram on me at that moment, they would have had to sedate me. Suddenly, in my mind I was in the court with those happy Hammers. I pictured them jumping up and down singing the West Ham song.

> *I'm forever blowing bubbles*
> *Pretty bubbles in the air*
> *Come on you Irons*

Chanting at the police:

> *You're just a bunch of wankers*
> *You were Eeeeeasy*
> *West Ham took the Judiciary, la la la la.*

The Times reported the celebrations rather more sedately: 'As the case collapsed, the defendants cheered and left the dock and shook hands with Judge Hitchings. (*I could picture Swallow leaping the front of the defendants' box like he leapt a barrier once at Chelsea when Vince tried to take his head off.*) Some of the men were held in custody for one year before the trial.'

Judge Hitchings made his comments and instructed the jury to find the defendants not guilty. 'It has been made quite clear from the outset that an issue has always been, and remains, the integrity of the officers and their logs in respect of these matters. It has been made quite clear by the defence throughout that these documents were not safe and satisfactory to rely on.'

Bill Gardner threw a wobbly outside the court: 'The police framed up innocent people and it has been proved today. This case has given me arthritis. I'm going to sue. I want at least £100k.'

Shut up, Bill. Everybody knows that Essex man suffers from arthritis because he's fifty years closer to marsh life. Essex has the highest incidence of rheumatism and arthritis in England.

It's the same as the Persil vouchers. Those West Ham always know the next scam, the crafty bastards. We were so busy thinking that we were innocent that we missed the angle of a handwriting expert. Two days later, Judge Hitchings made a scathing attack on the police – 'I would have ordered the police to foot the bill if I could' – while awarding costs to the West Ham fans.

From Snaresbrook Crown Court to Knightsbridge is around eight miles as the crow flies. Justice took eight days to arrive (it was a slow coach). This time it made the front page of *The Times*. My old friend Brian Lett tried to get a retrial before he was left to announce the grim news that irregularities had been discovered in eight of the 94 pages of records kept by undercover police in that trial as well. Judge Lloyd instructed the jury to acquit all eight defendants. In court Mr Lett said: 'In the exceptional and totally unforeseen circumstances which occurred at Snaresbrook Crown Court last week, it was considered appropriate to have a scientific examination undertaken of the observation logs. The examination disclosed that there were "certain irregularities" which in the present climate was bound to leave the jury in doubt as to the accuracy of the logs. In the circumstances and after every careful consideration, I have been advised that the prosecution offers no further evidence in this case.'

Now it was Chelsea's turn to take the judiciary.

We are the famous, the famous Chelsea
Prosecution wank, wank, wank

The judge turned to the lads, telling them they were free to go, and the boys in the public gallery went berserk, turning the place into a nuthouse. For a few seconds the court was the Shed as the boys surged forward to be near the centre and touch each other. All together again. Chris Henderson was out of his seat, jumping up and down.

'To the boozer, boys! The champagne is on me.'

Over the road they marched into the Tattersalls Tavern, ordered champagne and lager by the bucketload and drank away, spilling out on to the street to tell the news reporters that 'after us, Hickey, Terry and the boys are next. We ain't forgotten you, lads.' Three female members of the jury joined them. That fact was reported in the papers the next day. The Hickey comment wasn't.

The Times: 'It is understood that about six officers based near Upton Park, West Ham United's ground, and three officers who infiltrated the alleged Chelsea gang will be the main focus of the investigation.'

Who were the three mysterious police officers, I wondered? I didn't have long to wait. The three policemen in the Knightsbridge case were Sergeant Brian Donnegan. PC Michael McAree and PC Michael Morrison. I stared at these three names for five minutes. McAree and Donnegan's statements which made Terry and I something akin to *Marvel* comic superheroes were still etched indelibly on my mind. Yes, I remembered the tabloids telling their story, how for five months they had lived the hooligan life. Weren't these the same two who had compiled damning evidence of our 'board meetings' and boasted how easy it was to infiltrate our way of life, how to gain our trust they'd sprinkled their conversation with four-letter words and gone along with our racist remarks? These brave men who had been 'under no illusions about the risks they were running'.

The miracle had happened. Into the long dark tunnel with my head out of the train window shouting 'I am innocent' for two years three months, and now suddenly there was a light up ahead. For the next few days I half expected the news to come that I was being set free. It never came. I should have known better. Chelsea were relegated after losing a two-leg play-off to Middlesbrough and in the match at Stamford Bridge, the Chelsea boys lost it and ran onto the pitch to fight the celebrating Boro fans. Twenty police officers were injured and 102 Chelsea fans arrested. Ken Bates made a comical statement: 'Chelsea fans would win the European Cup for support if there was one awarded.' Well, they'd have to win it in the Second Division the next season. Meanwhile, I devoured the pages of the same middle-class press which had castigated Terry and me. When Wimbledon won the FA Cup beating Liverpool, I knew it was the year of the underdog. The same month, the midget for sport confirmed that the ban imposed on English clubs after Heysel would continue. I lay in my cell with visions of Schindler picking over his food reading his *Telegraph*.

'The Metropolitan Police Commissioner Peter Imbert [later to become Sir Peter] said: "At this stage we do not know whether there has been deliberate misconduct or simply mistakes."'

Then underneath, printed bold enough for Schindler and everyone involved in my prosecution: 'Solicitors for Stephen Hickmott are planning an appeal. There is already an appeal against sentence in place, but plans are in motion to widen this to include the conviction itself.' I opened my window and shouted the words on to the forecourt: 'Well, I bloody well *know* I am innocent.' I shouted loud enough so that it would carry the few miles to the Court of Appeal.

The *Telegraph* wasn't finished: 'Mrs Thatcher's War Cabinet on football hooliganism, formed after Heysel, put enormous pressure on the police to round up gangs. This serious blow to police morale has caused serious internal embarrassment to Scotland Yard, who developed the techniques which have been used as a blueprint by forces all over the country.'

Then the *Daily Mail* chipped in – the middle England megaphone for the police and the fiercest critics of Terry and me.

Two Own Goals by the Police

'. . . the pressure on the police becomes more persuasive. Indeed, the Home Secretary must satisfy himself that this inquiry is as thorough as it should be. For two own goals by the men in blue are by any standards a team effort of which to be ashamed.'

They were so appalled that they devoted a leader column to criticism of the police.

When the police get too eager

'When the person who first prompted the police to divert more attention to the problem is the Prime Minister herself, speaking through banner headlines, then the pressures on officers to succeed are obviously much more intense.

'Two expensive trials in successive weeks have had to be abandoned by the prosecution. In both trials, electronic scanners which can detect alterations, erasures or additions showed that the police logs contained irregularities.

'The obvious issues to be examined in the Scotland Yard fiasco are the level of supervision and its quality and the assumptions held by the supervisors. To whom did the officers report and how often? Did the supervisors have sufficient time and expertise to provide effective supervision? Was the evidence which they collected consistently challenged?'

But at the bottom, lest England be allowed to forget that deep inside there was still badness they added '. . . don't forget the men went "Sieg Heil" outside the court.'

The editor of the *Police Review* wrote the police obituary. 'It is a sad culmination to a hard-nosed campaign to sort out rowdyism and violence prevalent at football.'

On 24 May a third trial collapsed. 'Operation Dirty Den' at Southwark Crown Court involving five Millwall fans was quietly dropped. On the same day, the reports flooded in about the violence at the England v Scotland match. There had been 220 arrests, with 90

231

people needing treatment. One man had died after falling from a train.

On 30 May, Douglas Hurd, the Home Secretary, announced yet another crackdown on soccer thugs. He didn't announce an amnesty on the five innocent Chelsea fans wrongly convicted. I wondered if he knew who we were or what tricks our minds were playing on us. I doubt it, and I doubt he cared.

Outside the jail, legal moves were afoot and over 70 statements made by a number of police officers, plus their logs, were being examined by Christopher Davies, MA, D Phil, forensic scientist. Still no bloody release date. What the hell is going on? I sat down and wrote a long letter outlining the parts of my trial where evidence had come in which I felt could be challenged. I started at 8am and I was still writing at lights out. I had been blessed by the light of the moon, so I used it as I sat in my cell writing all night. By the time the sun came up around 5am, I sat there exhausted with eight pages of legal points. I could hardly wait to get it to the mail room for posting. Then nothing. On 28 July, Dr Davies presented over 300 pages of examination of statements and logs. Eventually, I received a letter from Bob Waddell telling me that he had been over the points and had summarised them in a letter to the Home Office.

In November 1988 I was informed that I was being moved to Maidstone prison. This was a sign that the authorities were getting ready to release me as far as I was concerned. In the van during the transfer, I sat there grinning like Chelsea had won the FA Cup.

'What are you looking so happy about?' asked the transfer warder.

'I'm going home [to Kent] and very shortly I'll be home for good. I'll be there in January at the third round of the FA Cup this season.'

'Dream on, that's what they all say.'

'Yeah, the difference is that this time it's true and I'll be there as an unconvicted man sticking two fingers up to the Old Bill.'

He smiled at me: 'We'll see.'

Like the British army in 1914 on the Western Front, I expected it to be over by Christmas. But like the Front itself during the Great War, this was real trench warfare. Every yard would have to be bloodily taken. On 24 December I received bad news from Bob regarding the exchange of letters which had been going on. He told me that the Crown Prosecution Service had written to say that 'there is nothing in the material we have received which is likely to provide grounds for appeal against conviction'. He replied saying he would be continuing to appeal.

The FA Cup third round came in the first week of January and I was still inside, albeit in Maidstone, a much better nick, surrounded by plenty of Chelsea fans. No marsh men in Maidstone. My spirits were high – the whiff of justice was in the air.

My mother now got involved in the campaign to get me released and wrote to the then Attorney General, Patrick Mayhew, QC. Bob took up the letter and set out the case to him, applying to see the forensic evidence, 'particularly in the light of subsequent trials against alleged football hooligans which were not proceeded with by the prosecution in circumstances which attracted considerable press publicity at the time. Of particular interest was the trial at Knightsbridge Crown Court as two of the officers in that case were common to the trial at Inner London Crown Court.' He concluded:

It is still not clear the basis upon which the earlier trials were discontinued and the reasons why the evidence was considered unsatisfactory. It may well be that there is nothing which will assist Mr Hickmott's appeal but if the evidence of the two or three officers common to both trials was so unsatisfactory, it ought, in my view, to be disclosed to those representing Mr Hickmott, in order that a full valuation of whether there may be sufficient grounds to mount an appeal against conviction can be made.

Early in February I received a postcard from Torremolinos.

OKAY, HICKEY – WE'VE OPENED THE BACK DOOR, NOW IT'S TIME FOR YOU TO CREEP OUT.
  ICF ESCAPE COMMITTEE.

Very West Ham, that, telling me to creep out the back door, although I thought it was a nice touch from the marsh men, who were sunning themselves and probably indulging in lager by the bucketload and the three Ss.

When the fourth round of the FA Cup came and went, along with a number of letters, I suddenly realised I was climbing Everest with no oxygen – the authorities were sucking the air out, trying to asphyxiate me. I would have to claw myself up the rockface inch by inch, using only my strength of will. The establishment were going to be there every step of the way, trying to kick away my foot and hand holds.

On Tuesday 24 January, the two Millwall fans, Taylor and Wilcox, stood in the Royal Courts of Justice facing the Lord Chief Justice of England (Lord Lane) and two other appeal judges. Lord Lane's judgement stood up for football fans.

'The evidence against the appellants consisted essentially of conversations overheard by undercover police officers. In subsequent, similar proposed trials, the prosecution were unable to proceed, a decision having been taken that reliance could not properly be placed on the evidence of the police officers concerned.

'The prosecution take the view that the same consideration is relevant in the present cases and have notified the Court accordingly. There was no other evidence to support the convictions. In those circumstances the convictions are unsafe and unsatisfactory and the appeals are allowed.'

In the time it took for them to sing 'No One Likes Us, We Don't Care' the Millwall Two walked out as free men.

Now it was: Free the Chelsea Four! But did we have a high-profile team shouting our innocence? Did we hell. I had Sam, Boghead and Toomsy getting slaughtered every Saturday, raising their glasses to the day when I'd stand my round once again in the King's Head. Meanwhile, Bob Waddell was getting frustrated at the slow progress.

This was intolerable – death by a hundred acquittals. First West Ham, then the Millwall Two had walked free on appeal. All we had to do was get up in front of the appeal court to walk free. Perhaps I'd be out for the sixth round of the FA Cup? Once again I set out the position. I now had a copy of the *Telegraph*, which seemed to have been leaked information regarding the case. I was pounding up and down in my cell whacking my palm on my thigh. Keep it tight, Chelsea. Hold it together now. Don't lose it now the light is getting bigger. Finally, on 8 February 1989, Bob Waddell wrote to confirm he had received the forensic evidence we had been waiting for:

I have received a large bundle of material from the CPS. This consists of statements of a Dr Davies, a forensic handwriting and ink examiner from the Metropolitan Police laboratory, together with a number of photocopies of original handwritten statements by various Officers in your case.

I have not had the opportunity to consider the material in detail. However, it is clear from the preliminary findings that the statements of certain officers have been written in different inks and impressions of other pages of statements are apparent.

But even as late as 2 March, my team had not been supplied with Dr Davies's conclusions or the results of the internal inquiry.

I then received a wonderful piece of advice from Nick Price, written as only barristers can. I sensed from the tenor of the advice that his teeth were sunk in and he wasn't letting go (if he ever gets reincarnated, he'll be a Plymouth police dog). He used the phrase 'Delphic in its obscurity' to describe a judgement – a surefire sign that a barrister is in the ascendancy. In direct sales, when people waffle in a letter without using facts they are called weasel words. This was the opposite, with my legal man using his lawyer-speak 'expectation' words. I was being told not to raise my hopes but people in the nick had noticed a spring in my step. Close that sale, Mr Lawyer.

In the FA Cup fifth round, the knockout process went on . . .

In Maidstone they sent me to see the prison psychiatrist, as they did everybody. He asked me various questions about life and football, then asked me why I did all the violence. When I explained to him that I didn't do it, he persisted, asking why I continued to protest my innocence. He then informed me that I wouldn't be eligible for parole as long as I stated I was innocent. Until I admitted my guilt and apologised, they would never consider parole for me. So that was the system: all the filthy sex monsters admit they are sorry so they are let out early to re-offend, while people protesting their innocence get left to rot while the system grinds them down. I vowed to send him a card calling him an arsehole when I won my appeal.

In mid March, my stepfather, Roy, died. It was a devastating blow to be in a cell waiting to be released, unable to be there for my mum even though I was taken to the funeral, handcuffed to a police officer with two others in attendance. I was returned to Maidstone immediately the service ended. On 5 April I received more bad news from Bob. He had received a reply from Mr Kirkwood at the CPS. They stated that they would not be disclosing the details of the internal police enquiry, would be opposing any appeal, would not assist with any bail application while the appeal was awaited, and finally, the most incredible statement my solicitor has ever read – as far as he knew it had never happened in any other case – that the police forensic scientist, Dr Davies, had not drawn any conclusions from the hundreds of pages, nor was he asked to do so. What my legal team now had was 370 pages of forensic analysis: faint impressions of the first two lines . . . line two were written together . . . line four different inks. So while Hickmott burned, the CPS were intending to continue fiddling.

On 15 April 1989 I was sitting in my cell listening to the Saturday afternoon football. The radio crackled from Hillsborough, which was the scene of the FA Cup semi-final between Liverpool and Nottingham Forest. The match was kicking off at 3pm in glorious sunshine in front of a shirt-sleeved 53,000 crowd. I had a sneaking suspicion that Forest would do it even though they were playing a powerful Liverpool team.

The police officer in charge was controlling his first big match. Hillsborough is the home of Sheffield Wednesday and at one end is the Kop, then a huge bank of covered terracing, while at the other end there was a small cramped terrace in front of a seating area. Liverpool have twice as many supporters as Nottingham Forest but the police allocated Liverpool the smaller terrace at the Leppings Lane end. Like Heysel the crowd was going to be around 50,000. I remember one of the Gooners telling me that he hated that small terrace at Hillsborough and how the design of it meant that you were squashed behind the goal even though there was plenty of room higher up on the terrace to the side.

The game kicked off and I remember the commentator saying that there was some crowd trouble behind the Leppings Lane goal. After a few minutes' play the match was stopped and like many others in England, I listened as the news gradually filtered of dead bodies. Slowly the death toll mounted. The final number from that fateful afternoon was 96. The relatives and surviving friends still remain among us as living dead. Early the next week, the *Sun* was printing the lie that Liverpool fans had robbed dead bodies.

The authorities had put up their rigid metal cages to stop fans running on the pitch while the police had received all their extra powers to curb football crowds' excesses. Power to smash that innocent man and his son at Chelsea to the ground, to leave Terry, Vince, Dougie and me rotting in our cells (Dale was out, having served three years of a five-year sentence). All the cages had succeeded in doing was creating ready-made coffins. That night I lay awake thinking about those fans who'd gone to a football match never to return, and the poor mothers of those fans waiting to hear if their children had survived the Hillsborough lottery of life. Perhaps now I was the lucky one, lying here?

In May, Chelsea were promoted after winning the Second Division by 17 points. Next season they would be back in the big time. I hoped to be there to see it. Ken Bates, meanwhile, was having his own trials and tribulations, fighting his mammoth legal battle with Marler Estates who wanted £40 million for the Stamford Bridge freehold. Our struggles mirrored each other. We were both fighting like mad for justice and just needed a bit of luck to get out of the mess we found ourselves in.

4 May: I received further advice and draft Grounds of Appeal. I had read all the material so many times that I knew it off by heart. Nick Price spent three pages outlining why he thought the Crown case was in tatters, then concluded: 'It is contended support the allegation that the said statements contain matters which seriously impugn the veracity of the said Police Officers.' I seemed to be in Coleridge's sea becalmed. I knew that I only had to get in front of the Appeal Judges, yet the wind wouldn't blow me forward. I racked my brains to find out when I had killed the albatross. It had been a year since the famous collapse of the other trials, yet I was still here waiting.

One day in Maidstone, a Scots fellow called Jimmy from Aberdeen approached me and, after asking if I was Hickey, started to regale me with stories from Chelsea. I asked him how he knew the various lads and he explained that he used to be in the Rhodesian commandos, as well as the South African Army. At the time Rhodesia was a magnet for all types of mercenaries. Ex-French Foreign Legion, American special forces, Aussies. The Americans loved to talk about old regiments. When they were signing up, an American asked the lads what regiment they were from.

'Chelsea.'

'Is that Chelsea Special Forces?'

'Nah, mate. Stamford Bridge, Chelsea North Stand. We used to fight for Chelsea.'

One day they were camped out in the bush waiting for some guerrillas to come through the bush when they heard a motorised vehicle. Keeping their heads down, they thought it was an armoured personnel vehicle and decided to ambush it. They fired a rocket-propelled grenade and scored a direct hit. When the firing had died down, they discovered that it was in fact a tractor which had been sent by the viewers of *Blue Peter*. The Rhodesian soldiers could not understand why the Chelsea lads fell about laughing.

Jimmy told me hours of stories which put my exploits into perspective. We had done nothing compared to these guys, although the way they told it their firefights in the bush sounded remarkably like an afternoon fighting Arsenal in Earls Court. But then they didn't have the luxury of standing with their backs to the wall drinking lager to prevent getting a bayonet up the rear.

I hate summer. When the football season ends, you have to put up with cricket, a game loved by the authorities who put me behind bars. The stupidity of cricket and those that administer and watch it was summed up by the *Telegraph* wetting itself during a West Indies tour when the demon fast bowler Michael Holding was batting against the diminutive (a posh word for 'doesn't get many wickets') spin bowler Peter Willey. Preceding the series the *Telegraph* letters page had surmised what would be said if this happened. Sure enough, the BBC commentator said, 'The batsman's Holding, the bowler's Willey.' For the next week the *Telegraph* letters page was filled with hilarity. The fact that England's batsmen were going down faster than a Somme infantryman cut no ice. Listening on my radio to England getting turned over at cricket, thinking how the judiciary and establishment were more interested in a cute phrase rather than substantive matters, summed up my predicament.

At least in Maidstone my mum could come and see me regularly now. Every time she came she'd say the same thing: 'Home soon, Steve. Your room's ready.' Summer dragged that year. Even Maidstone acquired a body odour smell, a fact which took me back a couple of years to the disgusting London remand prisons. On 1 August I looked forward to the start of the football season, hoping to be out. Nothing seemed to be happening. I sensed it was getting closer, even if I was becoming a lag conditioned to my routine. Every day the cell lock clanked open with no news of immediate release. I began to think I was being forgotten. The cricket season ended with more optimism about the future. Cricket summed up my predicament – God, that was an awful thought. Hickmott, like the English cricket team, waiting for a bit of luck and everything would be rosy. Meanwhile the old farts sat in the pavilion quaffing their gin and tonics, not really caring if matters did change.

GRAHAM & GRAHAM SOLICITORS to S G Hickmott L45620, HM Prison Maidstone
21 August 1989
APPEAL
I enclose copy letter from Registrar's Office confirming the appeal will be listed in October. A final date has yet to be fixed.

I now enclose a full set of the documentation provided by the CPS consisting of the statements of Dr Davies, the forensic scientist, together with copies of the original manuscript statements of the Police Officers he examined and schedules of his findings. Dr Davies simply gives statements of facts to his findings without drawing any conclusions or forming any opinions, without which little sense can be made of the findings. The fact that there are impressions of other statements on the paper does not mean much in itself as there could be a number of innocent explanations for this.

However, there are other points of concern; in particular, in a couple of the statements, names have been omitted and the letters 'A' and 'B' appear in the original manuscript statement, but full names have been inserted in later typed versions which we were supplied with for the trial.

Please add your own notes as you probably have far more detailed recollections than either myself or Mr Price.

You bet I did and I sat and wrote out everything again. I'd had two years six months to mull it over in my mind. I would not leave any stone unturned. My pen was my jemmy, making sure that if that door had shut slightly I would be able to prise it open again. The marsh men had shown what could be done if you only looked at the police statements hard enough. Then I received a letter stating that the full appeal would be heard in Court Number 4 on Tuesday 14 November. I prayed that evening that it would be a good month for democracy. The next day I read *Papillon* again. My escape was near. Soon I would be sailing away on the coconuts.

11

REGINA V HICKMOTT

On Friday 10 November 1989, Europe and the rest of the world awoke to a different place. The Iron Curtain had been swept aside. East Germany had opened its borders and over 100,000 had walked across. People who had been under the Soviet yoke in eastern Europe were free. I knew how grim it was, I'd been there watching England. The next day Chelsea won 1–0 at Everton, with Steve Clarke scoring the winner to take the club to the top of the table. I thought back to the opening exchanges in the court nearly three years before when, at Everton, Terry was painted out to be this mad man, and saw this as the omen I needed. I had been cautioned not to raise my hopes but I was now convinced we would be winning.

As I left Maidstone, the warders wished me luck. Vince had no such luck, receiving only abuse from the warders at Parkhurst. 'Poxy Pompey fans who think Parkhurst is Alcatraz,' was how he described them. It was good to see Dougie again, even if he had lost a lot of weight and looked painfully gaunt. He had served his time with no visits yet still had his irrepressible sense of fun and his obligatory copy of *Viz*. Vince also looked thin while Terry just looked ill and a lot older – no more the baby face.

Downstairs once again, waiting for our time in court. I remembered what they had said to me before the original trial: it might last six weeks. It eventually finished after five and a half months. Somehow this seemed different, plus the cleanliness of the waiting room contrasted with that of the Inner London Crown Court, almost as if the stink of corruption would be cleaned away as well.

'All rise.'

Vince, myself, Terry and Dougie stood up and smiled at each other. Sitting directly in front of us in court were the top dogs in the legal firm: Lord Chief Justice Lord Lane, and alongside him Mr Justice Waterhouse and Mr Justice Allott. The Crown weren't going to lie down like they had with the others and the Millwall Two. To our left was the public gallery, packed with family and friends giving us the thumbs-up. The press box below them was strangely empty – our shock value had long since passed – then below that were the lawyers. The prosecuting counsel sat in front of us, along with the police officers. Our friend Brady was there; Vince gave him a Millwall-style growl when he turned to look at us.

Then, after the excitement of getting into court, tedium as for one whole day we sat and waited while the barristers argued away in rooms. By the end of the first day I was going mad. I paced the cells. 'Sit down,' said Terry. 'You're giving me the jitters.' Dougie had his *Viz*. I looked at it and turned to the Fat Slags page. I couldn't read it, couldn't concentrate, I was too tense. I slapped the walls.

'We're close, so bloody close I can taste that beer.'

Then, a sleepless night back at Maidstone. The others went back to Brixton but had requested not to be put in a cell with Hickey if we went to the same jail. 'He's going mad,' they all said.

Day 2. Dr Davies got into the box. Our counsel wasn't sure how they would go after him but the prosecution treated him in a hostile manner, even if they held back from treating him as a hostile witness. In very correct, scientific language, he stated that in his expert opinion all was not as it should be. An understatement if ever I heard one. The Crown went after him, trying to make out everything was okay with our trial. I wanted to shout, 'There's doubt, so much bloody doubt a fool could comprehend. Thomas in abundance, my learned legal friends.'

By the time Terry's man, Blunt, had finished his questions, even the staunchest believer had doubt about the reliability of our convictions. As I saw it, our barristers were using the victory phrases – the previous day our legal teams had been confident but cautious.

Suddenly, Price's Spitfire verbal delivery awaited its victory roll, the lost caution reflected in the body language of the opposing sides. Lett had a humbler, more submissive expression.

The boxing commentary was on – the Crown case is on the ropes, Price strikes one to the solar plexus, one to the head. The Crown wobbles, it's down, it's down. The referee is counting. The referee is counting the Crown out. The crowd are up on their feet shouting. The MC jumps up into the ring. The fight is over and the winner is . . .

Lord Lane and the barristers went into a room at the back. Thirty long, agonising minutes later, he emerged and made his judgement.

'New evidence demonstrated that it was highly probable the statements about the movements of the alleged soccer thugs were not written by the officers on the day they were purported to be written. These statements are unreliable and the creditworthiness of the officers involved in the making of them has been destroyed.

'The Crown had sought to uphold the convictions – against Last, particularly – on the basis that there was other evidence. In Last's case, there was a diary of his activities. But once it had been demonstrated that police evidence was unreliable, the jury could not have been satisfied that they could safely convict. The original evidence was not available at the first trial. The case was worrying and the Court of Appeal could not uphold the verdicts as safe.

'HICKMOTT, LAST, DRAKE, YOU ARE NOW FREE MEN.'

The next morning, Schindler would read that on the front page of the *Daily Telegraph* over his bacon and egg. Perhaps the original words he spoke about me and Terry would stick in his throat, making swallowing difficult. He might even choke on them. I doubted that, so for now I stood up with both arms raised and lived for the moment. This result was the equivalent of Chelsea winning the League, FA Cup, European Cup and World Club Championship all in one day. This was a thousand goals hitting the net in one go. Nobody could deny us our moment. In the public gallery, the noise of clapping and cheering raised the roof. Sam was hanging over the edge shouting

'Yes!' in between hugging my brother Martin and Mum, who I could see crying. Nick Price turned to me.

'Well done, Steve, it's over.'

I had waited so long for this day, spent so much time thinking about how mad I would go. Now it was here I just sat there stunned, unable to believe it was over. I clenched my fist towards Mum and the public gallery then turned and looked towards Lord Lane. He looked stern. Come on, look me in the eyes, see how they burn with the anger of the terrible wrongdoing of it all. He'd done this a thousand times before, so he didn't need to be glared at as the messenger. He'd delivered what he'd been asked to do; it wasn't his job to bring fairness into the justice system, only administer it. I had been in custody since March 1986, now it was November 1989. On the Richter Scale of miscarriages of justice, I was non-league compared to the Premier League cases which this court had dealt with over the years. In terms of mistakes, I had got off lightly. In my cell I had remembered how MPs sit and pontificate about the death sentence. That is fine as long as people remember that nobody gets a replay when they are in their coffin. I had missed hundreds of Chelsea matches, relegation, promotion, and lost my girlfriend.

The police shook their heads. Wankers, I mouthed at them.

Lett looked finished, completely gutted. Go on, you bastard, look me in the eye. I could have been out earlier. Terry just sat there, a tear in his eye. I hugged him. 'Leave it out, Steve, we don't want the press to write that we're Bedhunters.' Vince was slapping his thigh. 'Come on, Chelsea. All together. Keep it tight, Chelsea,' chanting it like a mantra.

But it wasn't all over. Not just yet. Lord Lane said the time was getting late so he would come to Dougie the next day, and only three of us left the court. I didn't want to celebrate until Dougie was with us. Fresh London air, diesel fumes as well – magic. Seeing the Royal Courts of Justice from the outside as a free man made me feel very humble. I admired the architecture, something I'd never done before. I'd travelled all over Europe watching England and all I had ever seen was trains, train stations, the inside of a bar and a lager glass.

The next day it was Dougie's turn to milk the cheers of the public gallery as his conviction got changed from six years to four years, so with time served he was now a free man. After Dougie had spent a night listening to the radio about our release, his hearing took five minutes. He and his friends walked across the road together and into the pub. After our trial costing £5.5 million, and four further trials featuring other fans, plans for further prosecutions were dropped. Eventually a total of 120 men walked free from conspiracy charges featuring West Ham, Millwall, Crystal Palace, Arsenal and two Chelsea firms. Now, finally, everybody was free.

The *Daily Mirror* were outside. They asked Dougie what he thought about Ken Bates' comment that he didn't want the Chelsea Four back at the club and that they were banned from Stamford Bridge and he would go to court to enforce the banning order. 'He can say what he wants to, but I will be going back to Stamford Bridge. Now I know how the Guildford Four feel.' The *Mirror* gave him £20 for his comments. He took it and marched into the pub.

'I'm a born again boozer! Four pints of lager, peanuts, crisps, pork scratchings, the full works, darlin'. Dougie's back in town and ready to rock and roll.'

The barmaid had a tight white blouse on. She looked stunning. It was all Dougie could do not to stare at her. Sod it, he did stare at her until she noticed and became embarrassed.

After a few pints, Dougie got loud, the beer taking effect very quickly. The legal people on their lunch breaks from the Appeal Court opposite looked over at us and gave those nervous smiles that people give when they are not sure what is happening but see that it is good natured. A small group looked over as if they knew what these feelings were. As if? They didn't have a bloody clue. Dougie started singing. His friends joined in.

> We love you Chelsea, we do
> We love you Chelsea, we do
> We love you Chelsea, we do
> Oh Chelsea, we love you

AFTERMATH

Scotland Yard stated it had introduced 23 new rules to make sure there would be no repeat of what had occurred. The internal police report was never published. As far as I know, no police officer was ever disciplined or convicted over the prosecution of the Chelsea Nine or the other trials which collapsed.

Just before the three-year statute for issuing libel writs expired, the Police Federation, on behalf of three named officers, issued a libel writ against the *Daily Telegraph* for its reporting of the Headhunters trial outcome, but the case never came to court.

Stephen Hickmott, Terry Last and Vincent Drake sought compensation for a miscarriage of justice. On 18 May 1993, the Home Secretary offered a substantial sum of compensation without admission of liability. Only a handful of the 120 fans affected applied for compensation. Most just drifted back to their lives and tried to pick up the pieces. Some of the ICF fought for and obtained substantial compensation. Stephen Hickmott's papers were used by a number of solicitors in legal actions to obtain compensation and in the *Daily Telegraph*'s fight against the Police Federation libel action.

The property market crashed, which enabled Chelsea FC to secure their future with the freehold purchase of Stamford Bridge. Ken Bates had fought and won his legal battle. He then found a wealthy Chelsea fan called Matthew Harding to help inject the cash Chelsea needed for Bates' vision to come true. Despite Harding's tragic death in a helicopter accident, Ken finally got the stadium complex he wanted. As at December 1999, he was still fighting Hammersmith Council over the last jigsaw piece in his stadium plans.

In May 1997, Chelsea reached the FA Cup final. Hickey, Ginger

Terry, Vince, Dougie, Toomsy and others walked together along Olympic Way at Wembley to the match against Middlesbrough, which Chelsea won 2–0. In October 1997 England played the Italian national team in Rome. A picture of Stephen Hickmott and his friends observing the Italian police attacking innocent England fans was shown in the *Daily Mail*. The newspaper forgot its leader comment of nine years previously and under the headline 'General of Terror' blamed people like them for the trouble inside the ground. In January 1988, the *Daily Mirror* named Stephen Hickmott as one of 20 thugs out to wreck the World Cup, calling him 'The General'.

Following continual police harassment in numerous countries at passport control, including being dubbed the World's Worst Hooligan in a Swedish newspaper, *Aftonbladet*, in 1993, Hickey now lives in the Far East where he has business interests, occasionally returning to England on business.

Ginger Terry went back to work for a little while but now lives off the interest from his compensation award and travels around the world studying rare species of birds. He still attends Chelsea matches when he can, as well as England away matches.

Vince has gone back to decorating. He wasn't spotted at Chelsea for some time but started going once again when Chelsea got a half-decent team.

Dougie walked out of the court and he smiled at the thought of issuing proceedings for malicious prosecution and got on with his life with that trademark smile. He is now married with two children and is a sous-chef at an exclusive Sussex restaurant.

Shaun is married with a family and still follows Chelsea.

Willie is a head chef at a large London hotel and attends Chelsea regularly.

Toomsy is still a beer monster and number one Chelsea fan. He has reduced his pre-match intake to 10 pints but makes up for it after the match.

Young Peter still goes home and away with Chelsea.

Dale didn't bother to appeal and doesn't go to football anymore as he has a family and a mortgage, but he will be back one day.

Chubby Chris now resides in Thailand, where he owns a Chelsea sports bar. The annual reunions continue to astound the local population.

Kevin Whitton had his life sentence reduced to three years and his 10 years to seven. He is now out after serving seven years and eight months. As at December 1999 he has been spotted at Chelsea matches.

Walshy is currently living in south London after serving a long sentence for possession with intent to supply class-A drugs.

Jeff lives in Sydney, where he owns an upmarket bar restaurant.

Bill Gardner keeps his rheumatism at bay with his landscape gardening business in Surrey. Swallow owns a successful record label and lives in a rambling Essex country mansion. Many of the other West Ham faces are involved in security and club work. One named his house ICF Towers.

One West Ham lad used his compensation money to purchase a bar in Spain. Their annual reunions continue to depress the local population.

Some of the Gooners are working as bodyguards. Miller is now seeing the *Sun* page three stunner Kathy Lloyd.

Paul Scarrott died, aged 40, in 1996 from alcoholic poisoning after a massive drinking binge.

The Millwall lads are still singing 'No One Likes Us, We Don't Care' and continue to fight all and sundry at irregular intervals.

All the Chelsea lads deemed to be the Headhunters attended the 1998 World Cup in France, yet were involved in none of the trouble which occurred involving England fans.

As at December 1999, Winston Silcott is still in prison on a separate charge despite having had his murder conviction concerning PC Blakelock quashed, and received in excess of £50,000 compensation.

The police continue to maintain that gangs such as the Headhunters and ICF are still in existence, have never really gone away and are lying low waiting until the police drop their guard. The truth, as all football fans know, is completely different. In the autumn of 1999, a Private Member's Bill which gave the police further powers to be able to arrest and hold unconvicted alleged football hooligans slipped quietly on to the statute book.